God Will Say, We Will Say:

The Interpersonal Act
of Salvation

God Will Say, We Will Say:

The Interpersonal Act
of Salvation

Robert E. Joyce

LifeCom

Published by *LifeCom*
St. Cloud, Minnesota, USA

© 2010   Robert E. Joyce

ISBN 978-0-578-07906-6

For information, address *LifeCom*, Box 1832, St. Cloud, MN 56302

Contents

Preface

This book is the third in a trilogy entitled, *When God Said Be, We Said Maybe*. The three books highlight our creation *out of nothing*.

Theist culture has not heard enough about this unique, absolute act of creation. The whole of Christian culture in particular has been set on the details of redemption and salvation. Yet everything about our being in this world of space and time must have been caused or conditioned by how we received *or failed in receiving* our being *out of nothing*. From lack of adequate attention, we get the impression that we did not have the opportunity to receive freely our being, but that we were socked with it in our mother's body.

God Will Say, We Will Say: The Interpersonal Act of Salvation is based on our final and complete response to the reality of who we are and what we *will* to be *forever*. We could have "said it all" at the *non*-durational, 'eternal moment' of being gifted with our being *out of nothing*. But we must have said less than *fully yes* at that moment. So, here we are: 'all spaced out, doing time.'

The new vision for theists, and particularly for Christians, that is sketched out in the trilogy might be alarming to many. We might say that even Lucifer ought to be "jealous" about it. His once-perceived *primacy* for causing evil within our lives, found in the old view, is rejected. Under the new analysis, his responsibility is real, ugly, but secondary to our own.

Within the trilogy, we find that the meaning of our sin not only begins with Adam and Eve at some point in space and time, but also *originates with us individually*—independent of any spatiotemporal conditions. The messages of the three books trump Satan's role as the main source of evil. Satan could not have effectively tempted our first parents, if they had not already made themselves vulnerable —a perspective that seems to be missing in traditional theology.

When the serpent tempted Eve, she *and we* had already sinned and weakened ourselves, making the access by the tempter quite easy. Satan was a shoo-in for conquering the self-unaware couple in the

Garden of Eden. God knew it and told Adam: "The day you eat of it (the forbidden fruit), thou shalt die the death" (*Genesis* 3:17).

This third volume, as with the others in the series, attempts to get underneath the assumptions that theists have been making about our origins and our sin. Nothing said, however, is contrary to the faith of Christians. I am committed for life to the Catholic faith. And I am likewise determined to see and to assert things that are more deeply known—even if now, for the most part—only unconsciously.

The challenge is not to Revelation or to the custodians of it, but to sluggishness in the work of theology through the ages. God has been presented, it seems, as unfair or unjust, and as letting us be clunked by an original act of evil, "Adam's sin." Twisted rationalizations on the part of theologians over the ages have attempted to get God 'off the hook' for presiding over this obvious affront to personal human freedom and dignity that has befallen us, the progeny.

Failure in theology has been caused by thinkers being blinded both to mystery and to ontology. Recent theology can be criticized for its rather exclusive attention to historical conditions and objectification that would effectively place the thinkers about God higher than God. That placement may be unconscious. Nevertheless it is real.

Pope Benedict XVI has said that, to be scientific, theology must argue in a rational way, but that it must always be in accord with ecclesial faith. Theology must be centered on God, rooted in prayer, and in unity with ecclesial authority. And he remarks brilliantly how theology must *always* be nourished by dialog with our Creator and Redeemer.

The series, *God Said, We Said, God Says, We Say,* and *God Will Say, We Will Say* evokes this deepest, unconscious need and original privilege. We are seen as graceful dialogic partners with God from the start. Thanks to God.

Christian theology, moreover, is centered on the Cross of Christ. Although written with the three traditions of monotheism uppermost in mind, this trilogy likewise attempts to draw upon the Cross of paradox that takes Christ's salvific action to ever deeper levels. The Savior died to save us from our "maybe" to God that we asserted freely and immediately upon creation.

The creation of our *being* has been conflated with the creation of *becoming*. Our first moment *ex nihilo* (out of *nothing*) has been confused with the story of *Genesis* that is all about divine action *ex aliquo* (out of *something*). We have been fixated within a kind of Ptolemaic view of God's Being and of grace.

In addition, the whole of perennial theology within the three theist traditions has been beset by grandiose reductionism. Scholars have frequently noted that contemporary atheism and humanism have fallen into *scientism*: the reduction of all meaning to empirically verifiable, quantifiable, and measureable truths. But nothing similar has been witnessed about how theology traditionally has tended strongly toward what might be called *theologism*: the reduction of the meaning of creation and sin to the particular content in the pages of Scripture, especially in *Genesis*. Such "fundamentalism" endures, but without warrant in a comprehensive philosophy of being.

The *new ontology* is the specific *study of being as being, including the whole* of reality, *the natural and supernatural*. Revelations of nature and of reason are assessed together with the truths that are divinely inspired within the Scriptural traditions. The ranges of meaning, both of the scientific disciplines and of theology itself, are themselves bound to their respective, understandable biases. And reductionism seems to haunt them as an 'occupational hazard.' An open philosophy of being that is *both* pro-theology *and* pro-science would seem to serve better as the wisdom of the ages. Pope John Paul II seemed to be asking for such in his remarkably astute call for philosophers of being to "fly" with the two wings of faith and reason in his work, *Fides et Ratio* (1998).

The whole series, entitled *When God Said Be, We Said Maybe*, is an inside story of the creation, the crash, and the recovery of being. The idea of *truth* is hereby shifted beyond the clash between the traditional meaning as 'the conformity of the knower's mind with the known independent of it' and the modern meaning sparked by Descartes, where truth is 'a condition of clarity in the knower's own mind.' The new perspective regards truth mainly as a '*unity with* the known,' a "being-*with*" that for us, as we begin our noetic journeys, is largely unconscious. Truth is acknowledged as *interpersonal and as* something more than the simple *conformity* of one's mind, or the mere conditions of one's mind, or even the conditions of some kind of inter-subjectivity. Truth is being-*with* the mind and heart of God.

This "God Said, We Said" vision means that knowing someone or something involves 'coming to know what you already know *as being*.' And it is not simply a 'coming to know what you never had a clue about.' This difference in meaning can be gleaned by reading the Glossary at the end of each book. In further books and articles, my plan is to expand upon the meaning of truth and knowledge. The power of preconscious knowing can serve the future of all areas of intelligence, scientific and the religious, and can serve to reveal their complementary oneness.

The potential for exploration of the unconscious ought not to be the prerogative of the psychological and psychoanalytic. Philosophy and theology dearly need a common base of 'self-awareness' about the spiritual unconscious. Such insight could provide leverage for doing critical thinking in common about creation *out of nothing* and the origin of evil.

Readers are invited to use the Glossary as affording regular points of reference and as a text for assimilating the new theistic worldview in greater detail. Also, please note that Chapter 16, "A Call to the Three Traditions," is a repeat from volume 2, on the interpersonal act of Redemption.

The book's anecdotes and examples have varying characteristics. All are based on real happenings. Some are fictionalized, at least partly, either to protect the parties involved or to bring some points to a finer pitch. Some serve more as parables than as reports.

For review and helpful comments on certain aspects of Jewish and Islamic teaching, I am grateful to Professor Seth Ward, currently teaching at the University of Wyoming. At the time, he was Director of the Institute for Islamic-Judaic Studies, located at the University of Denver. His review occurred in the early stages of writing and he cannot be faulted for any inadequacies in the final rendition.

Thanks to all those who read the manuscript in various stages of development. Readers of the whole book include three people who deserve particular mention.

James T. Joyce, my brother, is a writer who afforded immediate encouragement and suggested developments for the overall work.

The late Dorothy T. Samuel, friend and author with penetrating faith, gave valuable suggestions on the presentation.

Mary Rosera Joyce, my best friend, beloved spouse, and fellow philosopher, has been involved with every phase of this work. She and I have discussed all of the major points and so many secondary ones that she could have written the book herself. In such case, she would have provided her own distinctive angles with a very similar message.

Thanks are due to Mary particularly for ideas and phrases such as passive-reactive energy, the need to anchor the beginning of the book in *Genesis*, the idea of renewal in the roots, and the concept of humans being rational persons—and *not* animals in anything but a figurative sense.

Mary and I have been married in life and in thought since 1961. I deeply cherish her loving work with this book and the others I have published.

The ideas for the present endeavor have been gestating since 1964. The key insight came to me suddenly in the midst of an informal discussion with a small group of University faculty members who were concerned with creation and evolution.

Along with the other two in the series, this book initiates a basic development and a deepening of the meaning of creation *ex nihilo*, the origin of sin, and implications for salvation. I welcome readers' questions, suggestions, comments, and critique.

Robert E. Joyce, Ph.D.
Professor Emeritus
St. John's University
Collegeville, Minnesota
December, 2010
LifeCom
Box 1832
St. Cloud, MN 56302
Email: robertjoyce@charter.net   Website: www.lifemeaning.com

Introduction

When you die, what will God say to you, immediately and forever? "Depart from me, you cursed…" (or) "Come to me, you blessed…"? If, "Depart," you will be sure to hate God forever. If, "Come," you will be sure to love God fully forever.

But neither event would be *God's* doing. The decision is entirely up to *you*. You are living now in the process of deciding whether to love God with your *whole* heart and mind or to hate God with your *whole* heart and mind. Heaven will countenance not the slightest *maybe*. Nor will hell tolerate even the most trivial *yes*.

This question is more than mega-momentous. What God will say is determined by three "factors." By your response at the moment you were originally gifted with being, by your big decisions through the fleeting moments of life in this world, and especially by your final 'attitude of choice' at death.

When God said, "Be," we said, "Maybe." We did not say *no*; but we did not say *yes*. We balked at saying a *full yes*, as we were called to do. And so our hesitance to be—and to be as God gifted us—seems to have required that we be afforded space and time as part of redemption. We needed a breath of 'fresh consciousness' in order to resolve our *decisive indecision* at the originative moment of *being*. We were given a "time out" and a "space" to determine what we really and everlastingly meant by the way we had initially received *being*.

The present book completes a trilogy on creation, redemption, and salvation. Volume one is *God Said, We Said: The Interpersonal Act of Creation*. Volume two is *God Says, We Say: The Interpersonal Act of Redemption*. Volume three, *God Will Say, We Will Say*, emphasizes that Salvation is not the same as Redemption, and that both hearken directly to Creation. The gifts of our redemption and salvation are seen as flowing from the way we received the gift of creation. There is nothing in the graces of redemption and salvation that was lacking in the grace of creation out of nothing.

In the first two volumes, there is an insistence that God's first act of creating (out of nothing) (*ex nihilo*) was *infinitely perfect*. All of its immediate effects had to be perfect (finite) beings—perfect persons, whether angelic or human. Any imperfection that existed or now exists *comes not from God*, but from *our originative response* to the gift of being. We committed an originative sin and are now experiencing the results of that imperfect act that is deeply repressed in the depths of our being.

We are now suffering from our own originative sins, as well as from the sin of Adam and Eve, our first parents in the process of our recovery and regeneration. We inherited our own originative sin *in and through* the original sin of Adam and Eve that was committed at the beginning of this recuperative world of redemption.

The gift of being had been partly rejected by us—by our saying "Maybe," even as God said, "Be." Here in the present world we are gifted with the opportunity to be-*come*: to come back to our perfect, gifted be-ing. We have been redeemed and prepped for personal salvation, on condition that we are truly willing to unite wholly and purely with God forever. The interpersonal act of *salvation* can only transpire if, at death, we respond with sufficient good will.

Creation and Redemption are acts of God alone. Salvation is also an interpersonal act of God, but it calls for our *willingness* to repent *sincerely* and to say fully and freely *yes* to the gift of Redemption.

All of life and of being is *gift*. But we have spoiled our gifts to a greater or lesser extent. We need the grace of God. Of course, we are grateful for the gifts of divine Revelation and supernatural vision. Nonetheless, how deeply are we *willing* to *receive* them?

Deepening Our Meaning

We know how readily Revelation can be distorted by not being received well. In fact, between the three major traditions of theism disagreements about important matters abound.

The Jewish tradition continues to look for the promised Messiah, while the Christian tradition claims he has come, and worships Jesus as God and Savior, even as the Islamic tradition says Jesus was superseded by Mohammed as the primary prophet of God. Mightily different ways of seeing.

Yet, we are mindful that all three configurations of belief and culture are rooted in the revelation of the God of Abraham, the God of infinite power and intimacy—the one and only God who saves. Jewish, Christian, and Islamic people turn their hearts to the same Being and to the incomparable promise of everlasting life. Mightily common ways of seeing.

When we consider how salvation is to be interpreted, however, we must *deepen our willingness to receive*, to be transformed, and to be renewed.

Theists believe that God is the one and only supreme Being, who created with infinite power and perfection. Still, there would seem to be an enormous problem about the way the three traditions counsel us. They tell us to live a life of revelation, but they never really give us sufficient reason to stop blaming God in our hearts for the way the original creation turned out.

How do we explain the suffering of those who, for one reason or another, are functionally incapable of sinning in the world of space and time? We ought to be confronted seriously by the lives of tiny children—before and after birth—and even by those adults whose lifelong mental impairments make them unable to commit even the slightest sin.

Millions of human beings have lived who were never functionally able to commit themselves, in this world, freely to the will of God. In light of this mega-reality, the traditional claims about the gravity and universality of our sinful condition in this empirical, space-time world would seem to lack sufficient credibility.

Although they participate together in this credibility gap on the origin and meaning of evil, the three traditions of theism do share profoundly the belief that God is the infinitely good Being and that all on earth are sinful. Despite various incompatible teachings on the "details," large and small, wherein there are sharp conflicts about what is true and false, all believe that only the one personal God can save us.

So, the fundamentals of the doctrines—at least those concerning the creation of the world and the origin of evil—are not necessarily matters of false teaching. What seems eminently desirable is that all of theistic belief be called to deeper accounting. The traditions may be required to take leaps of development in the basic meaning of the doctrines concerning our origin. The teachings themselves call for a more comprehensive way for us to believe what they are revealing. Revealed truth needs better theology.

A Shift in the Theist Worldview

A new theist worldview would change the perspective on evil and suffering. There would be a revision in our understanding of how God could allow torture and devastation to afflict innocent children and others.

The perennial mystery of evil would shift from an attitude of "how could God condone such a thing" to the question of "how could we 'innocent children' have done anything to deserve such treatment."

The trilogy, *When God Said Be, We Said Maybe*, of which this book is the conclusion, is not proposing a "new Faith." But it does intend to offer further deepening of traditional Faith and wisdom. The suppositions might be considered simply as tentative theories: that God's prime creation is interpersonal and that we responded immediately by freely failing to adore our loving Creator.

Even if taken only as hypotheses, such claims could prompt theists to examine the abiding paradigms or models of understanding that have been shared over many centuries, and by which they have been taught and are leading their lives.

The traditional paradigms were once themselves hypotheses and theories that interpret the main data of divine Revelation. They can be revised, even while foundational truths cannot.

The revelations that God is infinitely good, loving, and powerful and that we are sinful people—along with other claims—are neither hypotheses nor theories. These are truths.

But the manner in which these truths are conceived in relation to one another is open to grand supposition and revision. It is also the potential subject for authoritative religious teaching.

In any case, the age-old frame of thought for most theists includes, at least, the following two general versions.

One segment of believers tends to think that, for the coming into being of human persons, God creates passive matter out of which gradually higher and more complex forms arise, until the combined workings of God and nature yield the glory of physical creation: humankind. God creates each individual person by infusing the spiritual soul. This train of thought might be called evolutional theism.

Another segment of believers tends to assume that God creates primary creatures of every type—especially animate ones—directly all at once or immediately at various points of time. Each species is created all at once. God then allows these natures—including the human—to propagate offspring of their own species or kind. The species may develop, but only within themselves. This kind of thinking today is known as creationism.

In regard to sin, there is presupposed a kind of general archetype. The usual interpretative pattern states that the origin of human evil occurs only after Adam was created from the earth and after he and Eve were placed in the Garden of Eden. There they disobeyed God's explicit command and originated human evil.

This perspective implies that God can and does create creatures, even human ones, in an imperfect state, including Adam from the dust of the earth. But, even more critically, it says, in effect, that God does not *allow* self-reflective human creatures, other than perhaps Adam and Eve, to exercise full, perfect, decisive freedom from the beginning of their being. We descendants are forced to come into the created world under submission to the sin of our sole prime progenitors and/or to its consequences.

These traditional paradigms or patterns for understanding serve the special revelation about our created, sinful condition and help us to receive it and believe it. But they are hardly the fullest expression of the miraculous content of the beliefs themselves concerning the creation of humans and the origin of human evil. There is much room—yet within significant doctrinal limits—to re-conceive and reinterpret what is really being believed.

The supposition of the present book offers another perspective. It requires a major shift in our consciousness of creation and of sin. Its sharp contrast with the traditional views allows us to wonder which of these different, yet continuous, ways of integrating vision seems more plausible.

Which viewpoint, in other words, is less inadequate to the mystery of being? The new perspectives of this book or the old perspectives of evolutional and creationist theism? No interpretation explains everything. But which elucidation affords us deeper, more heartfelt participation in the process of understanding what is true?

The Power of a Paradigm

Participation depends on our paradigms. A paradigm is an over-arching model or pattern of conditions and assumptions by which we judge everything else. A working principle, akin to a worldview, determines how all the activities and natures studied are necessarily viewed, in order to present a coherent, intelligible whole.

When we change paradigms, we do *not* change endeavors. We simply adjust the set of postulates and assumptions under which we study; and we evaluate everything else in that *newer light.*

For instance, when scientists changed, in great part, from the Newtonian world of physics to the Einsteinian world of relativity, science did not cease to exist. Nor did scientific speculation become less important. Just the opposite occurred.

Scientific endeavor and its "natural revelations" received a grand charge of voltage in efforts to explain more phenomena. The new paradigm explained phenomena more coherently than the preceding one, the Newtonian set of assumptions.

Similarly, suppose theists relinquish the perspective of an older view wherein "God is assumed to be creating *ex nihilo* multitudes of imperfect creatures, only some of whom are perfectly free." And they begin to entertain a newer one where "God creates perfectly *ex nihilo* every person, having the perfect freedom to determine his or her destiny immediately." With such a sharp shift of viewpoint then, theology, philosophy, and all religion would be either set back or advanced from within.

But, while theistic paradigms are quite similar to scientific ones, they are also different.

On the one hand, scientific paradigms are apt to come and go. No matter how effective older ones might have been, the newer ones replace the older—though not entirely. While Einstein performs, Newton leaves the stage—or plays a bit of background music.

On the other hand, theological and philosophical paradigms do not tend to replace one another. Rather, the newer ones deepen and enrich the older—not by substituting for them, but by throwing more light on the same subjects.

In the case at hand, the common basic teachings are there. God, who is infinitely good and infinitely powerful, created us. And we are fallen creatures, totally in need of God as our Savior. Our sinful condition in this world would bring us to damnation without the saving power of God being granted and being received.

This is the way we know the Revelation to be. But the Creator's activity of creating should be more deeply received by our minds as well as by our hearts, the better to penetrate both hearts and actions. And the truth of our own perfect finite freedom ought to be more deeply received, despite how personally painful that reception might have to be.

Obviously, our once-gifted perfect freedom has been profoundly diminished. We can recognize this easily as we go about our lives in space and time. The prophets and the whole tradition explicitly call us to face the depth of our sinfulness and slavery to sin. But in addition to the consciously proclaimed revelation, there is perhaps an unconscious revelation about this sinfulness and its origin. The *unconscious* revelation is similar to the largest part of an island hidden below the line of ordinary vision. The Judeo-Christian covenants implicitly, gently—not explicitly, harshly—induce us to get in touch with our own receptive participation in creation "out of nothing" and in the origin of human evil. While so much more could be said, this book is attempting to indicate the grounds for receiving more deeply, in our common hearts, what has always been revealed, at least implicitly, in theistic Scripture and tradition.

Chapter 1

Creation and the Crash

A family comes home from a happy vacation. But they are shocked to see their farmhouse and several other buildings burning to the ground. The firefighters on hand had arrived too late and are vainly facing the overwhelming challenge.

The next day, the parents and children pick over the scorched effects looking for personal treasures. At times, there is a scream of delight to find a special belonging virtually undamaged. But silent sadness prevails.

Eventually they gather together, grateful that they are alive. Yet the massive extent of their loss is only beginning to sink into their awareness.

We should be quite sympathetic. In a manner somewhat similar to this nuclear family, all members of humankind exist on earth.

We are responsible for "taking a vacation," as it were, right at the moment that our being was gifted to us by God out of nothing. We balked at the maximum brilliance of our being, as it was gifted to us originatively and interpersonally. Actually, we did not vacate that brilliance; we *did not enter* the fullness, even though it was offered.

Now, as we are conceived and grow within this world we begin to "come home" to ourselves and to others. We might even recognize a condition similar to the charred farmhouse. At least, when we think about our circumstances in the cosmos, we know there is something wrong, lost, and incomplete.

Our time here is short; our existence, precarious. Nonetheless, we experience remarkable beauty and pleasure. As long as we live, we go through both genuine and escapist kinds of happiness. But we do not *really appreciate* what had originally occurred.

We could be quite positive, learning to appreciate the cosmos as a significant means for the recovery from our self-crashed condition. Instead, most folks seem to take the world for granted as being the best that God decided to do. They rightly look at our world now and say how good God is to give us all this beauty and sustenance. But they do not recognize how numbed they themselves and their world really are and how different must have been God's originating will for us and for our first parents.

The physical world is indeed good and beautiful. It would not even be amiss to speculate that the angels of God have been at work. But the void with which the world began, mentioned in the second line of the Bible, *could not have come from* the angels or God, nor even from Satan alone. That chaos, that void, had to have come from *us*, from our immediately free response to the gift of *being*.

Moreover, we fail to acknowledge the destruction we did to that original gift. Underlying the physical void, mentioned in the initial words of *Genesis*, is our self-wrought, spiritual poverty that caused it all and that everyone seems to have repressed.

We do not recognize the pure and perfect goodness in which all of us were created directly out of nothing. Much less do we affirm it. Nor are we now "seeing God," who brought us to be by this truly immaculate creation. We neglected immediately to receive perfectly the gift of our being. So, we crashed and are now in recovery, hardly able to realize our first act of *be*-ing and what we have done with it.

A "big bang" has occurred. Massive recuperation is in progress. Yet many seem to take the genuine delights of this world as though they were the "heights of heaven." They fail to realize that such are rather tiny peeks of pleasure that promise a glorious life to come, *if* we cooperate in our massive healing.

Multitudes have come to believe that we must have been destined for a supremely better condition of being. But, even people who are the most orthodox fail to acknowledge that we ourselves *caused* the need for the primitive conditions, known as space and time, within which we were conceived. In effect, they *unconsciously blame God* for creating us with a wounded, benumbed kind of freedom. And they neglect to envision Adam and Eve in the Garden as already *imperfectly* free—as they faced temptation by the serpent.

Progress Is Never Perfect

Despite our self-inflicted imperfection that caused the crash, God works to bring good out of the *yes*-part of our damaged selves. God does not bring good out of evil as evil—out of our *no* as *no*—but brings good out of good—out of the goodness remaining through the *yes*-side of us, who became self-maimed creatures. Perfection comes from an imperfect entity, only inasmuch as it is partly good and can grow; perfection cannot come from the imperfect as such.

Besides, process—from imperfect to perfect—necessarily signifies a precedent event. There had to be an original activity by which the perfect initially became imperfect.

How did the imperfect get there in the first place? Not at all by the activity of God. There must have been a super-cataclysmic crash of being—of my being and your being, and of the being of all persons who have become cosmic and live *in process.*

God had to reclaim us from within us. God never does anything simply "from the outside." Our redemption is being accomplished from within our wretchedness. As a result, Christians can affirm with Paul, missionary to the Gentiles, "Him, who knew no sin, he hath made sin for us, that we might be made the justice of God in him" (2 *Corinthians*. 5:21).

Paradoxically, we had a *perfect* beginning. The Quran states our origin simply. Allah is glorified and He is acknowledged to declare things to *be* and thereby they are, simply and fully (19:35).

Whatever qualifications one might make concerning its context, this Islamic claim about God's creating activity carries crucial truth concerning divine activity.

God wills someone to be, and that person *fully is*. No process is necessary. Nor is it possible from "God's side" of the gift. At best, process involves what is imperfect moving toward perfection—what might be called progress. How could an infinitely perfect Creator confer being on creatures who have even the slightest of originative imperfection, most notably an imperfect freedom?

The three major theistic religions—Judaism, Christianity, and Islam—celebrate the divine Being's absolute fidelity. When Moses asked God who, he should tell the people, was sending him, God replied with a striking phrase of divine identity: "I Am Who Am"

(*Exodus* 3:14). God *is* Eternal Being, who covenants with creatures by the very act of gifting them with their own perfect being and freedom, uniquely in the divine likeness.

Some contemporary theologians, however, have tried to translate the text as "I will be who I will be." They have made an apparent effort to instigate "process thought" into the proclamation. But, whatever problems of translation might arise, profound believers in the theistic religions know that the infinite Being does not change. There is nothing lacking for *infinite* perfection to change *to*.

God does not "become" something that was not *infinitely* there in the divine Self. And God's activity is infinite, without any limit. There is *no* process in God. There is unlimitedly perfect activity.

Process necessarily involves a beginning and an ending, although neither one may be apparent. Unlimited Being, however, is eternal, having neither a beginning nor an ending.

All process starts in the indefinite receiving activity of the created persons, through their efforts to respond to being-created. Their originative *maybe*-response to God necessarily begot *process itself.*

Looking around us, we see unstable beings—wounded, paralyzed, growing, processing, and struggling. We see a whole universe that is coming and going. We ourselves cannot escape yesterday, today, and tomorrow. We are in process, at least from conception to death.

Conflict prevails, especially in our thinking process that itself is wounded, paralyzed, growing, and struggling. At first, we think God created the stars exactly as we see them. Yet, stars blow up. All things in the cosmos are engaged in a process. Everything is going somewhere else. Nothing gives full tribute to the infinitely perfect Creator creating flawlessly.

Amidst our wobbles of reason, however, we can come into an immense realization: we have basically two alternatives. We can accept that this world exists just as God originally intended; then, obviously, God is quite an imperfect Creator. Or else we can affirm that God is an infinitely perfect Creator; that the world, including the stars and galaxies, does not *be* or *exist* as originally intended.

We can admit, nonetheless, that the present world exists, as God *now* intends, for rebellious created persons, who are being called to recovery. That we are quite imperfect, yet apt for reclamation, is an eminently reasonable claim. We can recognize it if we have a mind open to the inevitable mystery of opposites, the paradox, inherent in all profound truths. The present world *both* is *and* is not the way God intended it to *be*.

God's Will

The paradox or apparent contradiction is rooted in absolute truth. God originatively creates perfect persons with perfect ability to exercise their freedom *immaculately*. But if they do not, God intends absolutely that the consequences of the subversion of their perfect freedom take hold. Justice is integral to love.

God is willing the world of self-wounded, struggling creation that we so well know and experience. God wills—without specifically causing—the entropy and gravity that condition every move in the cosmos. God infinitely receives and responds to the sin—the big bang of *being*. That "bang" initiated the processes of both explosion and potential recovery.

God is willing every bit of every moment of struggle, success, and failure of every cosmic creature. God's will does not "control" things, but gives infinitely loving sustenance to all persons. As they directly and indirectly exercise the gift of human freedom and its consequences, God receives them without supporting even the least ill will.

So, God wills the world of process as essential to our need. We are called to struggle into an eventually full and completely voluntary affirmation of God and of God's will. This affirmation has to come from the depths of our hearts, not from the tops of our heads.

The consummation of process can come into being through the once-fallen person's free and positive response to be-ing. Only the more-than-originative divine power, an infinitely redeeming love, could ensure this potential outcome.

But such imperfect being could not have been God's originative will for any created person. The very being of process signifies an inherently imperfect response on the part of the creation.

By an infinitely perfect act of freedom, God gave being to the finitely perfect acts of freedom that created persons *are*. Every such person's be-ing is a *do*-ing that is free—originatively and perfectly.

If *no* perfectly free creature had sinned by saying *maybe* (*yes* and *no*)—and none had said fully *no*—there would be *no* process of coming to full freedom. There would be—simply, magnificently, and freely—perfect love in the heart of all creatures for the infinite Lover, and for one another. There would be immediate, pure, created *yes*-sayers forever. The immaculate creation would have been given an immaculate reception.

But we are blocked by traditional philosophic short sights. We think of God creating the world basically as the way it now appears. This absurdity comes from the rationalistic philosophers who have failed, by and large, to see a clear distinction between the receptive and the passive.

Once we see, however, that to be truly receptive is to be active—not at all passive—our entire view of creation changes. We realize that the fully active receiver of being would be able to respond immediately and freely with a *yes*, *maybe*, or *no*. The fully active receiver would paradoxically receive as he or she *wills*: whether in accord with the will of God fully, partly, or not at all.

The perfectly-constituted, free, created person receives his or her being. But he or she does the receiving both necessarily and freely —and does it well or not so well. In effect, an absolute *yes* fulfills receptivity itself. An absolute *no* demolishes the receptivity itself. A *maybe* reduces receptivity to a degree of passivity—partly collapsed receptivity. Such makes any further full, free, and independent *yes* impossible, without divine redemption and salvation.

This *maybe*-response would render the gifted respondent supinely dependent on the Giver. The dependency is a determinate condition that makes us unable to "save ourselves" by a free and independent action.

Those who said fully *yes*, confirming themselves as being forever receptive to God and to the divine Will, would be fully independent beings. Independent *with* God—*not* independent *from* God.

Yes-sayers would *be* sheer gratefulness for *be*-ing. Without God, of course, they would not be; so in that sense they are "dependent." However, the word "dependent" would not suggest passivity-in-being, as it has when applied to us who are *maybe*-sayers, and who have partially denied and damaged our own receptivity. We are dependent passively. In order to appreciate the effects of the partial collapse of the receptivity in our own *may-be*-ings, we might reflect upon what a "crash in be-ing" really means.

Our reflection can draw, at least partly, from our experience with relationships in our earthly lives. We could think about all kinds of failures, both interpersonal and impersonal. Interpersonal failures in our present lives would be "closer" to the "real thing": our partial denial of a full relationship with the Person (or Persons) of God from the moment we were created.

But since our prime denial has relevance even to non-personal creatures found in the world of inanimate matter and motion, we will begin our reflections by using, just as an example, one simple physical crash.

Chapter 2

Like Shattered Glass

When we first admire the beauty and variety of nature—the lakes and mountains, flowers and birds, people and personalities—we do not see much beyond what greets our eyes. So, we often assume we know what this world is all about, but then are surprised to find that we are wrong.

One reason that we settle on a comfortable confusion is that our self and its seeing power are themselves part of the shattered scene. What is looked at and the lookers are similarly fractured. The world we see and we the seers are broken together.

Looking at the cosmic world, including ourselves, is like seeing colorful glass shattered on a concrete surface.

Suppose I come upon particles of glass finely spread on a cement sidewalk. I admire the beauty and color of the glass and comment to my companion about its radiance in the sunlight. She agrees, and we think we have found a treasure.

Somewhat jokingly, I say, "Let's submit it to a contemporary art show." I then fantasize how to do it, saying that I would collect the pieces on a fiberboard. Then I would arrange them as closely as imaginable to the pattern formed by the "original" on the sidewalk.

The glass is so fine, however, that I cannot possibly do this. So I give up the idea. We continue our walk, wondering whether others who pass by will appreciate the "artwork" as the two of us have done. Not once did it occur to us that the glass might have been a precious vase that had crashed because of the carelessness of the one carrying it.

Let us suppose that a man's dying mother had gifted him with such a treasured vessel. Out of frustration with himself on seeing the breakage, he had taken a rock and smashed the pieces to obliterate any semblance of the original artistic vase.

The man had dropped his treasure and it crashed. Then, out of his immediately resulting shame and self-hatred he had demolished any particular recognition of his failure. The immediately destructive, repressive behavior produced fragments so small that we could not suspect the cause of the accident or of the original shape of the beautiful glassware. We simply failed to think about it.

If, however, some large pieces had remained, then we might more readily have surmised that this beauty on the sidewalk was hardly "original." We would have known that there was something that broke—a vase or plate perhaps—to cause the "accidental" array.

When looking at, and attempting to assess, "the real world," then, we constantly misread what is occurring because of our flattened kind of knowing activity. For many centuries, people thought that the earth is flat, because it looks flat when we are on the surface. They also thought the sun rose, moved across the sky, and went down below the horizon, because it looks that way. They could not see the totality of what they were looking at. So, it took a revolution in their awareness before they could realize that they were actually seeing the earth that they were standing upon turn, as the sun appeared to move.

Similarly, seeing a whole vase within those tiny pieces of glass is somewhat like trying to see God's original world within our crashed world, the cosmos. But that is something we cannot do, without a breakthrough in our awareness.

Pondering the difference between an original vase and its fallen, smashed condition might help us to see the origin of creation behind its crashed cosmic condition. We hardly suspect the human origin of the *physical cosmos* coming from the causality of the spiritual crash.

This analogy limps, of course, because it tries to understand the natural by comparison to the artifactual. It tries to understand any physical being of nature by comparing it with the products (a vase, a plate) of human reason and artisanship.

Despite this significant qualification, we might still use examples of artifacts that would help us appreciate the difference between the redemptive creation of becoming and the originative creation of being. We might see how creation, as we are first coming to know it now, is so different from the immediate results of the originative act of God that by infinitely loving intent, gifts us with *being*, even as we, immediately and partly, thwarted the act by weakly receiving it.

In the example, the original vase—that was representing a unique individual human being—was both beautiful and functional. It was not only exquisitely formed and colorful, but it could hold flowers: representing a perfect, finite, human person, who could freely and fully respond to the gift of *be*-ing on his or her own. The vase was both good to behold and good to "act with."

But when the vase impacted on the pavement its originality was lost in both beauty and function. Some beauty remained in the colors and shapes forming the spread of pieces on the cement. This crashed beauty was, however, no longer the attractiveness of the vase; it was a residual beauty in broken qualities.

Similarly, by our originative sin—whereby we freely *self*-ized or passivized our receptivity—we lost touch with our original identity. But the infinite power of God's creative love responded immediately to our broken condition of being. Divine love interfacing with our *yes-no* state of being began to effect a redemptive process.

To our *maybe*, God responded. And unconsciously our very being reacted against our self-wrought passivity. From its beginning, the redemptive process was co-creative between God and fallen human persons. It was *not* an originative creation (*ex nihilo*), but a co-creation *ex aliquo*—drawn out of the mess of degenerative freedom, coming from the *maybe*-sayers. The dynamics of interactivity might be understood as something like this.

On the one hand, God's activity was a redemptive response of love to redeemable creatures. On the other hand, the ontological activity of our deprived being was a violent reaction by the *yes* in our *maybe* against the *no* in our *maybe*. The interactivity between the divine response and the human reaction effectively co-generated a mega-explosion of redemptive energy.

Two inexorable initiatives—God's and ours—would have created the radiation of what might be called cosmic energy. The first effort would have been the activity of divine love toward the multitude of crashed persons. The second, but immediate, effort would have been the communal reactive surge of the passive-reactive condition in the beings of those fallen persons. This meeting of the infinite activity and the finite reactivity with each other in the depths of being could possibly explain the explosion (the so-called "big bang") with which the cosmic part of the redemptive creation began.

God's infinitely merciful power began working with our energy. That energy, the power-to-do-work, is part of our capacity to receive actual redemption and potential salvation.

The originatvely-gifted receptivity of our essence (pure matter) was self-smashed by our originative sin. We decimated our own capacity to receive who and what we are. But from within this self-smashed condition of our ontological matter, this fragmentating energy radiantly emerged, forming the spectacular "particles" of what we have called physical (opaque, dull) matter, namely, the elements of the cosmic world.

In our analogy, the basic elements of this world are symbolized by the particles on the concrete pavement. Eventually, in the process of temporal existence—whether vast or brief—these elements were shaped by God, and by the dynamics of fallen human nature, into the energies of plant and animal life. This cosmic process served as preparation for the broken and paralyzed humanity's entry into this world of potential recovery.

Moreover, in the case of the demolished vase, the original function was destroyed. Lost was the capacity for holding flowers or even weeds. Similarly, at the instant of originative creation, the creature's indifferent, self-directed response eliminated any ability for this resultant being, on its own, to determine decisively its everlasting happiness.

"Re-creation" or a kind of remedial, supplemental creation was the only hope. Such rehabilitation can be thought, by Christians at least, to be a part of redemption—or the preparatory development for the specifically redemptive acts of God incarnate.

The Crash Within

At the moment of creation, we betrayed our freedom—freedom for full union with God. Thereby, we came crashing to the ground, as it were, with an implosive-explosive "big bang." The very act of our utterly free will collided with itself; it collided with God's gift and thereby produced the "ground" and the "void" into which we fell: a self-made chasm.

We did not so much hit the ground of cosmic dust. We reduced, in effect, some of God's gifted power, the power to be ourselves, into a "dust"-producing energy. Eventually, and emphatically when we were conceived, we "nested" within this reactive passivity that we originatively occasioned. Within this passivized condition the grace of God works redemptively.

Of the glorious universality of creation that included all persons, angelic and human, the matter of our human essence "shattered into pieces," so to say. Both time and space then were started by the redemptive power of God. Time "began" and space "extended."

We can likewise speculate reasonably about particles from self-traumatized receptivity, specifically particles now known as atomic matter, beginning to shoot outward, forming whirling bodies of beautiful, but spiritually functionless, fallen physicalized matter.

Like a shattered vase, the crashed world exploded into zillions of zillions of particles. And this primordial, passive-reactive matter constituted a negative-positive process, shepherded by the very life of God.

Eventually, a second phase of passive-reactive energy—organic energy, latent in the original energy—was activated by virtue of God working with our fallen-away freedom; and thereupon tiny bits of organic matter appeared in the waters of the earth. Living things developed until the first humans came on the scene.

Humans were conceived, given birth, lived, and died by the millions and billions. Each one struggled to survive for a little while. Many did. But all of them were non-functional in terms of returning to the freedom and purpose they crashed and lost "before" time began.

Of themselves, they could not return. By their *maybe* to the gift of *being*, they created—from within themselves—the need for cosmic confines of time and space, of duration and extension. Moreover, despite their inherent struggle for further life, all fallen persons were on their entropic way to the everlasting garbage dump, except for one thing. Within divine grace their originative Creator redeems them and calls them to be saved.

Insofar as they have the opportunity in this world, they are called to be faithful in the little things that they may be able to unite with the magnificent reality for which they were originatively destined. Jesus, for instance, said that one who is faithful in the little things will be faithful in the great; and one who is unfaithful in little things will be unfaithful in the great (*Luke* 16:9-11 and *Luke* 19:16-19).

In any case, theists and non-theists alike believe that ours is a fallen universe. Hindus will call the material world *maya*, illusion. Buddhists say, "Existence is sad," and seek enlightenment. Paul, the great Christian evangelist, said, "For we know that every creature groaneth, and travaileth in pain, even till now. And not only it, but ourselves also, who have the first fruits of the Spirit, even we ourselves groan within ourselves, waiting for the adoption of the sons of God, the redemption of our body" (*Romans* 8:22-23).

According to the new perspective, God personally gave us the gift of *being*. But we personally dropped it and it smashed, forming within the covenant of grace a scattered actuality (fractuality) that we call energy.

God did not drop the gift; we did. But this originative stumble was not accidental, like the fall of the vase to the cement walkway.

Our dropping the gift of being was the inevitable result of the perfectly free partial unwillingness to receive it. It was not like dropping something "too hot to handle," but like refraining from a beautiful relationship that we freely neglect or reject.

God created each of us as fully capable of receiving—with pure gratitude—the perfect, finite being we were gifted to be. We were not frightened of, nor overwhelmed by, God's flawlessly given gift of being. We willed immediately to be at least partly *self*-centered, rather than fully *God*-centered. We looked freely somewhat to the gift, rather than wholly to the Giver.

We must have said, with perfect freedom, uncoerced by God and untempted by anyone, "What's in it for me?" rather than simply, "I thank You and praise You for creating me!" We must have been something like a man named Peter, called by his Master to get out of a boat and walk on water toward him. When the enthusiastic disciple suddenly became *self*-conscious about the whole thing, he started to sink (*Matthew* 14:30).

As a result of our diffident response to the gift—self-conscious, self-crashing, self-crushing—we are scattered in God's sight, fallen as we are within cosmic ground. We ourselves, however, together with billions of other persons, actually *caused* the cosmic, inherently passive-reactive condition itself. We caused the necessity for the cosmic ground into which we fell.

On our gifted-by-God side, we will ever be perfect in being and freedom. But, on our recepted (received) side, we retain only a kind of broken beauty—like shattered glass.

Our condition can be, at least, a dim reminder of our infinitely glorious Creator and of the totally radiant creatures we were gifted to be. We are like our original self only vaguely. So, we can say, we are not like the beautiful, functional vase in the example: holding flowers "of adoration and thanksgiving worthy of God." We are largely collapsed; and praises of the Creator can often be relatively hollow.

Left to ourselves, we are simply disabled. "Out of the depths I have cried to thee, O Lord: Lord, hear my voice. Let thy ears be attentive to the voice of my supplication" (*Psalms* 129:1-2).

From our own fixation in the fallen world, we respond to creation dully. With our self-constricted view, we think it could have been possible that we were immature children from the very beginning of our being. We think it is perfectly natural for God's human creatures to grow gradually to maturity.

We assume that we absolutely began to be in a world of trial and error. We think that, from the start, we were called to learn how things are and how to live fruitfully in this world, and then to be "rewarded" in the next.

In the case of the example of a dropped vase, the usual theistic worldview sees nothing wrong about our needing time to develop our sight and our insight. We are inclined to think that a learning process would be necessary in order to come into the meaning of the shattered glass: as originally a precious and beautiful vase. Would we not require a process of trial and error in order to learn and come to maturity and judgment about the glass and its origin?

Similarly, what is wrong with knowing and relating in this way to "the real world"? Must we not learn through experience? Good and loving children, for instance, simply cannot appreciate all their parents give them until they are deprived by loss of their parents' lives or by their own experience in moving toward independence. It would seem, then, that God created us originally to be immature children in order that we could come to appreciate the gift of being.

Be-ing and Experience

Such thoughts are understandable, but they overlook something. Could we not have appreciated fully the gift of being, received at the first moment of our perfect, God-gifted freedom? *Yes*, the meaning of "perfect, God-gifted freedom" is the ability to be freely *like* God, without qualification—not to mention, without quantification.

Instead, we are the family of spoiled freedom. By the originative depression of our freedom, we made ourselves to be that kind of offspring—critically dependent on others and on "experience" of good and evil, beauty and ugliness, for attaining true judgment.

We now suffer gravely from "experience-itis," the insistence on knowing everything by experience—even that of which experience is unworthy. And our Faith suffers.

Fixation on experience constitutes a major symptom of our passive condition. One could say we have consumed the fruit of the tree of the *experience* of good and evil. We insist on experiencing both good and evil.

Had we said freely and fully *yes* to God originatively, we would not have had parents, nor become children, nor married and had our own children. Such are valid ways to attempt our cooperation with *redemption* and to make recompense for the lost covenant with God, that we effected by our defective response to the perfect creation.

If we had said an unqualified *yes*, we would have been espoused of God, intimately and ecstatically in rapturous friendship forever. We would be engaged in one complete knowing and loving, beyond mere *experience*. (Heavenly glory will only be realized beyond the consummate heights of even spiritual *experience*.)

As it is now, however, we relish complacently the egocentricity and passivity of experience. "Ex-perience," like "ex-istence" (*ex-sistere*, to stand outside), is a form of "cast out" activity: a form of being that is *necessary for redemptive processing*, but not for our originative vocation.

Even when we gain some realization of our upside-downness, we can miss the essence of our *being*. Wayne Dyer, a contemporary guru, likes to say that we are not human beings having a spiritual experience, but spiritual beings having a human experience. The idea contains important truth. But to say that we are spiritual beings is not quite the point. Nor is mere experience, even if spiritual.

In essence, we are human persons—person-beings—who are now undergoing *ex*-perience, both material and spiritual. Such was not originatively created, but is part of our being self-cast out into the modes of being we call "ex-istence and ex-perience." Both modes are essentially self-fixated. We *ex-ist*, we "stand outside of" our own be-ing.

Existence and experience are intrinsic parts of our *derivative* beginning, but not of our prime beginning. *In and through these conditional dimensions of our being we can come to insight about our prime beginning. But, if we really want to see, we must be willing to go in, through, and beyond our existence and experience into being and contemplative creativity.*

Chapter 3

The Matter of Two Beginnings

The first day of school is an important beginning for a child. Still, we can suppose that some children, on their very first day in school, encounter two different beginnings.

The first beginning is, of course, the schooling itself. They have never experienced being in the school, with its particular kind of personal rights and responsibilities. It is, as it were, a new way of being for them. And if they happen to misbehave that first day, they might have another beginning: the punishment of detention, with its partial deprivation of personal rights and of a certain freedom of action.

"Staying after school" would represent a second beginning. These children have never had the experience of detainment in relation to school. They are thereby deprived of the freedom to go home at the appointed time. They are prevented from sharing immediately with their new companions the events of the first day and the joy of after-school play.

This little scenario might be taken as an allegory for our absolute origins.

In reality itself, we have had two beginnings. These beginnings happened at the same non-durational moment—at the moment of creation out of nothing.

Of course, the two beginnings at creation are not like those of these schoolchildren. Theirs was a temporal sequence common to both their first experience in school and their unique experience of freedom-restriction that had separated them from their well-behaved classmates. Besides, the children actually entered the "joys of new experience" found in the classroom.

At creation, however, we *maybe*-sayers did not enter absolute joy. We did not receive any beatitude. But we did receive the *power* to enter beatific life *immediately*. Tragically, we freely failed to act well with this perfect power.

Like the detained children, we "misbehaved." Therefore, we find ourselves now immersed in our second beginning. We are paying for what we did in failing to receive the magnificent opportunity of the first beginning: immediate, blissful union with God forever.

Carefully, then, we might reflect on how it must have been for us at our beginning to *be*. We can, however, say much more about what that instantaneous moment was *not* than what it was. But we can be sure it did not "turn out perfectly." We came out of it "less than whole." Actually, we came out of it as severely wounded wholes.

When the misbehaving schoolchildren remember later, they know they were quite conscious of both the first and second beginnings and they can easily recall them. In contrast, we fail to know much, if anything, about what we originatively dismissed and treated badly. We botched our *protoconscious* beginning, thus rendering ourselves profoundly unconscious. We made ourselves functionally incapable of responding to the *immediately* second beginning—the onset of redemptive action. Only now, upon being conceived in space and time, are we capable of coming to realize *something* of what really happened in our origins.

We can recognize that God must have created two beginnings: one for our being-at-all and, in view of our immediate response, one for saving us from ourselves. God's activity in bringing us to be is both originative and restorative.

So, now we must recover. The "beginning" we first come to know about consciously, then, is our second beginning—the cosmic world of space and time—the *restorative* creation. This world is observed and experienced through our senses, as well as through intellect. Its origins are described in *Genesis*. The Bible starts with the words, "In the beginning...."

Even though it represents considerable symbolism of the spiritual, we have to say that the Biblical beginning serves mainly to refer to the physical, imperfect world in the process of restoration. There are many "gap theories" of creation that speak of process and stages of creation. But they hardly touch upon the *immaculate* creation out of nothing and our response to it that caused the spiritual and material "big bangs."

The spiritual world includes many kinds of angelic persons. They also had a beginning. In the Christian tradition, the first words of the Gospel according to John are, "In the beginning...." That beginning is closer to the whole picture. It includes the worlds of both spirit and matter. "In the beginning was the Word, and the Word was with God, and the Word was God. The same was in the beginning with God. All things were made by him: and without him was made nothing that was made" (*John* 1:1-3).

In the ancient Testament, we find Wisdom being celebrated as an emanated Creator.

> "The Lord possessed me in the beginning of his ways, before he made anything from the beginning. I was set up from eternity, and of old before the earth was made....
>
> I was with him forming all things: and was delighted every day, playing before him at all times;
>
> Playing in the world: and my delights were to be with the children of men" (*Proverbs* 8:22-23, 30-31).

These texts, with others that are Christian and Hebrew, suggest figuratively—not literally—the life of the Creator at play and at work. They provide at least the setting for understanding the basic beginnings: both the beginning of our being and the beginning of our becoming.

The Order of Creation

Which beginning, then, is the real opener? The answer must be: God creating perfect, finite persons—both angelic and human—"out of nothing." Scriptural assertions, like those of *John* and *Proverbs*, challenge us to relate, more consciously, to the roots of our being.

God could not be *God* by creating beings that were immediately and simply *perfectible*. Perfectibility means that imperfection is essentially involved. Perfectibility, which is our present condition, comes from our response to being created perfect by God. It is the result of our response, that was neither fully *yes* nor fully *no*. By saying *maybe* to being, the perfectly-free creature caused himself or herself to be less than perfect—less than perfect in freedom and in everything else.

Because of the *no* in our *maybe* we could not simply *be*. We had to *exist*, as well as *be*. We caused ourselves into ex-istence: a condition of "being outside of" ourselves. We were self-exiled. Our manner of be-ing was not joyful union with God, ourselves, and others. Rather we had to *ex*-perience things—to "have" consciousness of realities. We could not basically know and love everyone and everything unpossessively, purely actively, and in nowise passively.

Our powers to know and love are now, however, largely passive. They are known as *passive potencies of the spiritual life*. Every passive potency is *an ability to be done to*, and *not* simply *an ability to be-with*. So, when we know something or someone in this world, our intellect is first stimulated by objects or things that are "outside ourselves." When we love someone, our will responds somewhat passively to the stimulation by the beloved.

But it was not intended originatively that these spiritual powers be passive-reactive at all. We were created pristinely with gifts like the pure ability to know and love, without *any* passivity involved. They were gifts to know and love everyone by pure acts of knowing and loving: within-to-within. No exteriority whatsoever.

Now, however, in our most spiritual activities, we are creatures of the cosmos. We are attached to the natures of passively material beings—as well as to the depths of the spiritual and the beingful.

Both accounts of origins in *Genesis* speak of the physical world as perfectible, with God masterminding and effecting the shaping of the whole. The void, the stars, the waters of the sea, the plants, and the animals are not perfect realities, but perfectible; and each leads to the onset of higher forms of existence, culminating in the human. All are creations of God, but in the perfectible, not the perfect, sense.

Addressing us as adults in grave need of awareness, the Quran speaks graphically. It indicates our perfectibility, responding to the absolute power of Allah. It speaks of him who has created each person from dust, then from a sperm-drop, then from a leech-like clot. Next, Allah is said to get each one out (into the light) as a child, and then to let the individual grow and come to the age of full strength. The text also recognizes that, while some die beforehand, many reach old age and come to a "Term appointed." All this development is afforded people in order that they may learn wisdom (40:67).

The accounts found in *Genesis* and in the Quran do not directly or necessarily speak of the originative creation of perfect persons. Such an originative creation had to have been the supreme creation, in the wake of which all of the realities spoken of in *Genesis* are developed for the sake of salvation.

Untold numbers of human persons gave their Creator a measure of originative indifference. This response to being-created did actually produce the passive-reactivity we know now as passive matter and energy. Out of this passively active kind of being, with its supreme fractuality, the perfectible realities, written about in *Genesis* and in the Quran, are fashioned by divine fiat.

Primal passivity, however, has only one origin; and it is not God. Nothing passive comes from, or by, infinitely pure Act initially. Only finite, but self-determining (free) persons could have been responsible for passivity.

Trees could not. Birds could not. The *inherent freedom* of persons and their receptivity, through being exercised badly, must have *de-structured itself* into a relatively passive, unreceptive condition.

Our prime receptivity (*the ability to receive being fully*) both imploded and exploded into passivity, by virtue of our first and failing act. We fragmented ourselves. Consequently, and from out of the resultant void of structure, God would form cosmic creatures, including all forms of subhuman existence, by working against our communal, personal, unconscious *resistance*.

Christian theists point to the struggles of Jesus in the process of redeeming the fallen. His brutal passion and death might be seen as expressing dramatically his encounter with the massive ill-effects of originative opposition to the primal, *interpersonal* creation.

The essentially cosmic beginning, delineated in *Genesis*, flows from originative sin, as well as from God's creativity. Perfectly free human persons had exercised a faltering form of response to God's creative Love. And *Genesis* deals with an important part of their incipient reclamation.

Moreover, God must have created originatively within every human person—the only kind of person able to say *maybe*—the structures necessary for possible recovery. In that way, anyone who might fail to say fully *yes* to the gift and to the Giver—and did *not* say fully *no*—could participate in his or her own salvation by receiving redemption lovingly.

At least billions of human beings actually failed originatively. So, together with their inherent conditions for recovery, God *began* the creation of the physical world as we know it. Cosmogenesis (the basic development of the cosmos) flowed from the free faltering of creatures in their ontogenesis (their beginning to be). Be-coming (being coming back)—if it is needed—follows back along the way of be-ing and is led by the Way of God.

Creation is both primary and secondary. The primary dimension—done solely by God—is the creation of perfect *beings*. Not "spirits," but full beings. The secondary dimension—within the sustaining and directive power of God—comes as a direct result of what these perfect finite beings freely "create" by their first, unholistic acts of reception.

The primary creation, as only partly received by us who thereby crash, in effect, "co-generates" with God the secondary creation. The "creation of being" thus served freely as a power-base for, and empowerment of, the "creation of becoming"—the creation effected for the sake of redeeming those who, at first, wavered.

At the level of primary creation, the good angels, immediately and freely, "co-created" with God their heavenly condition. The bad angels freely "created" (i.e., "anti-created") their everlasting hell. Moreover, any human person who responded in full gratitude and affirmation of the Creator, and of the gift of his or her being, freely "co-created" his or her everlasting heavenly condition, with no call for redemption. Any human person who fully rejected the gift of be-ing actually caused everlasting self-frustration.

Also, at least billions of human persons responded positively, yet poorly: partially refusing the Creator and hesitantly receiving the gift of being at the moment of primary creation. In so doing, they triggered, from within themselves, the activating conditions for potential recovery.

Whether these fallen or plunged human persons cooperate with those conditions—conditions of passive matter, space and time, motion and process—is a most crucial question. Their awakening willingness or unwillingness to repent by working with love under these conditions of trial will critically determine their final destiny.

Chapter 4

What's the Matter with Matter?

When you receive a gift, say, a package of treats from a friend, are you more grateful for the gift than for the gifter? Does the one giving the gift matter more to you than what the gift is, its contents and their value?

You would be quite a clutz, would you not, were you to value the gift more than the gifter? After all, the gifter delights in your being and is sharing something of the happiness that you bring him or her. Persons always trump things. The gifter is greater than gifts, no matter how many or how magnificent.

What about the gift of *being*? The gift of our being from God calls for incomparable gratitude. But are we more grateful for the gift, our very self, than for the Gifter, the unlimitedly loving God? We the gifts and God the Gifter are persons. Both are good. Yet the Gifter is infinitely good, while all the gifts are finitely good, taken singly or together.

Gratitude to God supersedes all other thanksgiving. But our being in this defectively limited world reveals, for those with hearts to see, our defective gratitude to God for creation. We might be grateful to God for the gifts of redemption and of potential salvation. But how thankful are we simply for *being* and for being *who* we are? How grateful are we for the gift of creation?

We need to confront our failure to receive God instantly and fully upon being created. We were not entirely God-centered with perfect praise. We were somewhat self-centered. We might well have been thankful both for our being and for our Creator, but we failed to be *Gifter*-centered, rather than *gift*-centered. We received ourselves more than we received God.

When God Said Be

God said, "Be." Thereby the created person was perfectly gifted with a unique act of *be*-ing: an act of *be*-ing for that person to *do*. Each created person's response to this absolute beginning *is* that act of *be*-ing. Every person *does* the act of *be*-ing that was gifted to that person.

Be-ing this being is a gift, not a grant. Each angel and human does, by personal be-ing, an originative response—whether the response is good or bad. By the very gift, the created person, who *is* the finite gift, *does* the *be*-ing of it. (God *cannot* do the being of a created person.)

Our first response was immediate, essential. The angels' responses were immediately and simply essential. But the responses of human persons were immediately and complexly essential. These persons were both spiritual and material. Human, matter-form persons are material as well as spiritual. To them 'matter really matters.'

Since God creates only complete being, originatively the matter of the human person was complete and perfect, having *no* passivity or imperfection. Matter and form were on a *par* as dimensions of the being of human personhood. Neither was superior to the other. A created person's matter (or power to receive) is just as essential as the form (or power to give).

At the moment of creation "out of nothing," form is not skewed to dominate and control matter. The human essence is two correlative sides: the giving and receiving structures. Form is the "givity" side of essence, even as matter is the "receivity" or receptivity side.

Form does not "operate on" its co-principle, matter. They "co-operate" in constituting what the person is called into being to *be*. In the dynamic act of being that each human person is, form and matter co-structure each other. Form as a receivingly giving principle of personhood reciprocally relates with matter as a givingly receiving principle.

Matter is meant to be "mater" or "mother" within us, fully active and *radiant* matter. Each person's matter is created as a special way, or "beingful womb," for receiving wholly our own being and for co-creating with God a blissful, permanent union. Its counterpart, form, is created as a cooperative "father" or principle of firmness and of beingful generativity in the essence, guiding every activity flowing from the being.

Together matter and form are co-structured to "give birth to" the human person's every act—especially the supreme, signature, first act of *be*-ing.

Matter, in its perfect purity, can be understood as an unadulterated *receptivity*. Originative matter is not at all a passivity, as it is in our present existence and experience.

Matter, as we know it in space and time, however, relates rather to the secondary creation—the redemptive matter that is articulated in *Genesis*. This matter is passive. It is opaque, so to speak. And this passivity can be regarded as quite a dysfunctional, yet recovering receptivity.

Receptivity involves the ability to receive someone or something affirmingly without self-reference—without "making something of it." When this ability is wounded, it becomes recessive, passive, reactive, and relatively ineffective. In short, matter becomes *self*-conscious.

We notice the change, for example, when a child's pristine trust in someone is broken. He or she is no longer as receptive or trusting with that someone and with others as well. Openness is withdrawn into a pattern of defensiveness.

Receptivity is, as it were, passive-ized. Cosmic matter, especially that of our own person—our visible bodies—might be regarded as levels of *defensive* receptivity.

Cataclysmic passivization or self-centralization is what we must have done to the whole of our own being. By our self-wounding hesitation to receive the gift of being and the love of the Gifter, we were passivized.

That free—even if partial—rejection of goodness was something we *did to ourselves*. It occurred with the subordinate "support" of billions of other dis-be-lievers in God's infinite love for us.

We passivized our whole being—including our matter and form. Our activities are now emanating from powers of the soul that are passive-reactive. These are basically passive potencies, rather than simply active potencies. We were created originatively with only active (agent) powers to know and love. But, by our instantaneous, free, faltering response, we added "passivity" to our intellect and will—to our knowing and loving. We became *not only* perfect, *but also* imperfect, persons.

As it is now, in the very activity of *do*-ing, our powers are abilities to be done *to*—as well as to *do*. We have passive as well as active intellects and wills. And our whole being is now largely obscure to ourselves and to others. We see neither the whole of what is looked at nor the whole of the one doing the looking. We suffer severely from ontological "cataracts," as it were, caused by the effects of the crash.

By responding only partially to the gift of being, the free human creature receives reluctantly who he or she is. Active receptivity then falls largely into passive receptivity or passivity. Active matter or prime receptivity is caused to be passive matter, to one degree or another.

This passive matter represents the free creature's unwillingness, and thereby inability, to receive the gift of being without reserve. We creatures in space and time are hardened instances of resistance. The living opaqueness and sheer functionality of our bodies testifies emphatically to *passivized* human personhood, as does our dullness of mind and heart.

Our first, purely free act has desensitized us to both our matter and our form. Only God's infinite love, working with this being-unto-death, can bring about a functional resurrection of our purely active potencies to give and to receive. These originative gifts of our being are at present only partially functional, heavily weighted by the passivity involved in empirically conditioned knowing and loving.

We exercised our purely active (gifted) receptivity and caused it to become depressed. The main evil is our *attitude of reservation*. The *matter itself*—the interior *mater* or mother—*remains totally good*.

Passive matter as matter is not at all evil. But, as passivity, it is the inherent result of a badly activated *immaculate* freedom-*power*. And *that* is evil. Evil has been done *to*—not simply *with*—matter, and the resultant passivity is an alteration in our matter—in the receptivity for, and of, our essence.

An example might serve to suggest the relationship. When we visit in a hospital someone whose limbs are all broken and bandaged, we do not think, "This body is bad." We know that the body is good, even in its contorted condition. The broken legs and weak body are not themselves bad, but their broken condition is the result of the bad. So, we can truly think of it as "good body, good structure, bad condition."

Similarly, we ought not to blame passive matter for our cosmic imprisonment, as is done in so many philosophies, East and West. *We* caused the condition, the cosmic congestion. We were really self-victimizing and self-incarcerating.

Of course, we might be trying desperately to hide the primal deed from ourselves by believing that our present state of impairment is fate or "God's will." We would prefer to assume that it could not possibly be originally our own doing. After all, who would want to think of having injured himself or herself on such a massive scale?

We are like the man who dropped the vase and then attempted to obliterate the vestiges of its form, so that no one would know what was actually done. But, by our signature act of freedom, we have smashed our own power to "recall" or to see what we have done to our own being. In some respects, spiritual repression is our way of life.

We even try to escape the primal blame by thinking that God made all the wondrous beauty of the starry sky above simply for divine glory and to edify the human creatures on the planet earth. Similarly, the man left the beautiful particles of glass on the sidewalk, but in a non-identifiable condition, such that casual passers-by would want to "credit it" to Nature or "nature's God." We remain incredibly egocentric in our worldviews, especially concerning "our role" and "God's role" in our lives.

In contemplating all the restrictive laws of matter, we are ready, if necessary, to blame them on matter itself. And, obviously, we would rather think of the matter of the universe and of our very own bodies as something about which we could not possibly have had anything to do. What could *I* possibly have to do with, say, *gravity*?

The ways of blaming matter, if not God, for our predicament are various. Traditionally, some Gnostic and Manichean thinkers have either insinuated or claimed that matter is evil. There are Hindus who do seem to indicate as much. In their respective ways, however, many recognize the truth that there is something bad about the passivity of this world's matter.

Yet we should be careful about what we mean. Passive matter may be the result of evil (originative sin), but itself *not* be evil. *Passive matter* may be the basis of the world of both good and evil because it is the basic condition to which much of human creation fell when it crashed by badly exercising its prime freedom. But it is *not* evil.

Matter is solely a gift of God, and with it, even in its malformed condition, God can work to bring restorative goodness.

We fallen human persons can ever move toward recovery. We are required to do so even within the passivity of matter. We can begin our receiving of redemption directly within our decidedly enfeebled condition.

We start by exercising our originative capacity to receive—from within—the gift of ourselves and the gift of others. All persons are essentially sheer gifts to themselves and to others.

Reactive matter continues as conditionally good. But this spoiled matter could have been unconditionally good and purely active—not at all passive. Free human persons could have chosen to be and to receive themselves fully as God intended.

Philosophers fail, for the most part, to distinguish passive, opaque matter from active, "transparent" matter. They often also neglect to distinguish the kinds of goodness in matter. Many simply reduce the lesser goodness (low level kinds of matter) to evil. This particular metaphysical tendency in the Western world has its counterpart in much of Hindu thought. The mind finds it difficult to see how matter and spirit are one—though not the same—in the human person. As a result, we often fall into a dualism of matter and spirit. Matter in various forms unfairly takes the brunt of our disparagement, while our spirit is fixatedly passive as well.

Theistic thinkers sometimes use phrases that indicate we humans, with our matter and spirit, are a "duality in unity." Such a thought tends, however, to suggest that the duality is the key and that the unity is what is striven for. It would be far better to call us a "unity in duality." Human persons are simply unitary beings, with dual dimensions—not dual "parts." Passive matter is good and plays an active function in both redemption and salvation. Judeo-Christian symbols, along with the Christian sacraments and sacramentals, carry the good news.

Matter really matters in our be-*coming*, in our coming back to originative being

Chapter 5

The Macho Grip of Spirit

Bullying seems to be one of our national obsessions. Boys on boys, girls on girls, siblings on siblings, political ads on rival politicians, and intimidations of all kinds abound in our social networks. But the bullying in the neighborhoods is not as overwhelming as is bullying in philosophical conceptualization.

Our inclination to intimidate, to browbeat, and to bully is all set out for us by traditional philosophers who think of the spiritual as having 'control over' the physical within human persons. The matter of the person is seen as totally dominated by the form or the spiritual soul. Bodily beings, including rocks and rills, as well as organisms, are said to be intelligible—that is, able to be known—only through the *form* of the thing. Matter takes a back seat in the explanation of why and how cosmic realities of space and time are constituted.

According to the tradition stemming from Aristotle, we only know something because we know its form. Form is taken to be the only "structurating" principle of physical things. Form is the dominant, "bully principle." The immense skewing of our receptive principle of essence (our matter) by our originative ill-reception of be-ing has rendered its own structure "invisible" to us. We are repressing the beautiful structure of receptivity, even as we view material being.

Tragically, even in the best traditions of ontological analysis, spirit and the spiritual are seen as "lording it over" matter. Form is 'top dog' over (passive) matter. The meaning of matter is taken from the dominance that spiritual form provides.

Because originative sin is not recognized, theological and religious thinkers are unable to know the inherent efficacy of our originative power to receive (receptivity)—our pristine matter. They do not see receiving as an act that we *do* and that receiving is *just as essential* as giving—both within the being of (Triune) God and in the being of created persons.

Philosophers have provided the passive "set up" for downgrading matter by defining prime matter as sheerly passive potency. But there is no such 'thing' as sheerly passive potency. Even Aristotle, from whom the term emphatically arose, thought of prime matter as an appetite for form. And Thomas Aquinas spoke of matter as being a *similitudo formae*, a likeness of form.

Without recognizing the reality of our act of receiving, done at the prime moment of being created out of nothing, most philosophers and theologians seem to think that the "being of passive matter, of prime matter" is gifted by God out of nothing. Since passive matter is defective matter, they are quite willing to acknowledge God as the Creator of defective creatures, who, then, must improve themselves on their passive base of being. Religious commentators are clueless about the decisive meaning of creation: that, simply out of nothing, everything created by God, who is both infinitely good and infinitely powerful is absolutely perfect, pure (finite) act.

Moreover, they have no basis for recognizing *agent* intellect as a *knowing* power; and they are mute about there *being* an agent *will*. So, they cannot see that God creates, directly out of nothing, only purely active intellects and purely active wills, with there being nothing passive at all about these powers of being and doing.

The huge gap between passive matter and an infinitely perfect Creator, as well as the gap between agent intellect and agent will, means that dualism is more than rampant in the tradition. Dualism almost inevitably creates a "duelism." The imbalance of perspective reveals itself in conflicting false assumptions.

People assume implicitly, and sometimes explicitly, that while matter is evil or a drag on the spirit, spirit is good. Life is then a duel between the bad matter and the good spirit. But the reciprocal relationship of good and evil, found in both matter and spirit, is then being overlooked.

Matter and spirit are utterly correlative. In beings who are self-damaged, spirit must be "proportionately" as distorted as matter. After all, the condition of the spirit is a critical internal source or cause of why matter is so incredibly mashed. At the core of our ontological repression, matter rebels against spirit because spirit has "done matter in." And spirit tries to dominate matter because matter is so unreliable, so "fickle."

The deep metaphysical tradition, stemming largely from Aristotle, holds that matter is the passive "receiver" of different forms, and has thereby a necessary part in the composition of all good things. But this tradition, on its own, seems to regard all matter—the whole physical world—as unfallen and as good without qualification.

In its own way, the Aristotelian tradition fails to see the difference between passive and active matter. There is no distinction between "opaque and transparent" matter. The matter of the world of space and time is recognized as basically passive to one degree or another. And, if there were any "transparent" matter, it would be "invisible." There seems to be nothing to "recognize" about that.

So, the Aristotelian viewpoint is unwittingly shielding itself from seeing how this world's human inhabitants are responsible for the passivity and opaqueness of what is called cosmic matter. Humans are basically viewed as essentially cradled in "mobile being" with their volition virtually confined by the parameters of passive matter and motion. Their volitional power with respect to *causing* passive matter is totally neglected. Such appears to be unthinkable because it is "unseeable."

The Matter of Supreme Creation

But, in the new perspective concerning creation and the crash, cosmic matter is recognized as the result of our originative failure. We are responsible for the passive condition of matter (receptivity) and of the cosmos in which we dwell.

We could have co-caused a perfect self, transparent to itself and to all other beings of fully good will. We could have co-caused with God this perfectly fulfilled self. We could have fully activated our capacity to receive our identity.

By being immediately faithful to our purely active prime matter (pure receptivity), we would have received fully the being given us by God in the unconditional act of creation. The matter of our supreme creation would have been purely effective in its receiving.

Instead, the matter of our originative creation was quite impurely effective. Freely, yet partly, we immediately distrusted the gift of our being. We caused thereby our receptivity to fall into passivity. This passivity came from the *no* within our *maybe*. Due to the *yes*, however, there was a positive reaction to this passivity, so that our being became passive-reactive, passive but in a recovery mode.

Yet we could not recover without God's response to the *yes* in our *maybe*. God's redemptive response causes (caused) our passive-reactive matter to generate the passive-reactive *energy* that became a source of the redemptive process, described in *Genesis* as the days of creation.

By this derivative, redemptive, non-originative creation, God is sustaining the spatiotemporal process. For Christians, the cosmic process can be taken as the preparation for God's determinatively redemptive act in the incarnation, death, and resurrection of Jesus, the divine Redeemer.

The plunge of our active receptivity into manifestive passivity left us profoundly comatose. But the immediately self-wounded matter of our being—together with God's redemptive response to our crash—co-generated the reactive "blast" of energy that would provide the primordial elements of the cosmos. From within these elements the infinitely benevolent divinity could begin fashioning the "second beginning," the redemptive creation, briefly described by the two accounts of creation in *Genesis*.

Matter and Sin

Due to our originative sin and the massive mess we have caused, we deny and repress. (One might wonder, "What else could we do; how else could we stand it.") We do not recognize the "truth of the matter": that matter, as we know it in its passive form, is the result of our own violation of constitutive freedom. We do not admit that God must have created us with the power of pure receptivity that we ourselves have spoiled and repressed.

The mistreatment of women and the feminine in both East and West, prophesied in *Genesis*, is, at least, one major symptom of our originative hesitation to *be* (*Genesis* 3:16). In both men and women, matter, or *mater*-within, is thoroughly smashed and reactive. We are consequently passive-aggressive in our being, knowing, and willing.

Insofar as this resultant matter is passive, it is not really knowable (intelligible) in itself. The ancients recognized this. All of our own bodies and the whole world around us are largely constituted by this primeval passivity. In order to know material realities we have to detect matter through its forms. Forms make matter knowable to us, even as they dominate it.

The form of a tree or the form of a squirrel reveals something of the nature of the primal passivity out of which this world is made. Form is "lording it over" matter everywhere (*Genesis* 3:16).

Indeed, space and time themselves are dimensions, co-created by God, that emerge from the results of the original crash. Neither of them nor any of their "contents" is radiant with the perfection of being. Space is our kind of fallen-flat, damped-down field of lost beatific vision. And time is our fallen-away, frustrating attempt to relate with eternity.

As a consequence of the primal fall, we are inclined to think that we were somehow created immediately and simply in space and in passive matter. But the greater truth is that we *caused* space to be—at least, we created the need for it.

We also tend to think that we had merely a beginning in time. But the foundational truth is that time had its beginning in us. The fallen-away potential vision of God and the fallen-away attempt to unite with eternity—known as space and time, respectively—are polar actualities of mega-fractuality on the collective part of all *maybe-sayers*.

None of the material things in our world is original matter. The stars, the galaxies, the flowers, the soaring birds, in consort with the radiance of the sun, are glories like shattered glass on a pavement. All involve forms of passive matter. We, too, are unfathomably passive, inert, and dense compared to our originally-gifted selves.

The "cast out" factor in all of our cosmically material creation also testifies to our radically passive and corruptible natures. Along with plants and animals, humans produce and eliminate waste in order to live. Excretion is a law of life. Death is the final excretion as we "cast out"—not the body, but—the passive bodily remains of our attachment to the world of space and time.

The waste and the material residue in both organic and inorganic processes throughout the cosmos testifies that this is not God's original creation. Everything here is part of a creation attempting to recover, and yet "exhausting" itself.

This inherent tendency in all passive matter toward renewal has been called telic or teleological—readily overlooked or denied by insensitive knowers. Every bit of matter holds an inbuilt tendency toward one or more forms. And all of the space-time universe, fractually and frustratingly, moves toward renewal in God's gifted redemption. In the midst of this divine gift, our "waiting, crashed human freedom" draws, within itself, physical energy ever so gently toward unity.

Matter and Our Fallen-ness

Traditionally, people are taught to think that ordinary, perceivable matter is created directly by God. But the new view attests that God creates directly only perfect (complete) realities that could be only persons: purely active beings—but not necessarily beings that will act purely. Upon first acting, many of these purely active beings impurified themselves.

As a result, God would be better regarded as primarily responsible only for the purely active receptivity (matter supreme) of these finite beings, as well as for their purely active "givity" (form supreme). For the origin of cosmic energy, God is secondarily responsible. We are the ones primarily responsible for it. We are the key reason for the existence of energy, for the "condensation" of cosmic energy into passive matter, and for all energy-based forms of action.

Somehow we are inclined to overlook entirely what the perfect creature would be like. And we do not realize that any imperfection, such as the passivity and density of matter—or the dynamics of energy—would have to have come specifically from a real crash in being. A fracture of reality itself.

Our thinking about the material world seems to be proportionately as dense as the visible world we think about. This incapacity is a consequence of the original crash of being. It is the consequence particularly of the results: our self-wrought opaqueness and self-skewed condition of soul.

In effect, even though we might claim that we are created by God who is infinitely perfect, we largely refuse to acknowledge personal responsibility for our inherently passive condition. And despite the realization through faith and reason that we were created by an infinitely powerful and infinitely good God, we see poorly what is implied.

We fail to see that every hurt, small or large—every disaster or calamity—is but a microcosm of the fallen human situation. All adversity comes to us ultimately and decisively by our own *doing*—not merely by all the actions done in this world by ourselves and others, but by virtue of our originative irresponsibility in doing imperfectly the initial receiving of our own being. We are each the *uncaused cause of evil* in our lives and of the need for redemption.

As a consummate result, within the world of space and time—the world of prostrated vision and neglected union with eternity—we hang. We are lodged between our *yes* and our *no*, longing to be saved from this predicament of alienation. Yet we are ready to deny that we could, in even the slightest way, be primarily, beginningly, and overwhelmingly responsible for our situation in the world of good-and-evil.

Chapter 6

Struggling to Be Actively Receptive

Everyone knows *unconsciously* that we ourselves are repressing the reason why we are in this world. If we had *not* sinned originatively, *ex nihilo*, we would not even *be* here. We would be fully with God, from the first and forever. Our very freedom to *be* would be full. There would be *no becoming*; only sheer *being*, free and joyful.

Few of us, however, are willing to admit that we are repressing our origins. We are not letting ourselves know that we know—actually, but implicitly—something momentous about ourselves and about the spatiotemporal world that is all around us and within us. We are repressing this knowledge about our *origins*.

We are forcing ourselves to "forget" our *doing* of a primal sin. And we are directly repressing the truth behind that sin: the truth that our being is perfect as *gifted* by God, and that we are even now perfect, while *also* being quite imperfect as *received* by ourselves.

Passively Receiving the Word of God

Because of our first sin and our repressing it, we inevitably receive the Word of God more passively than actively. We are instinctively disposed to treat dismissively the importance of actively receiving God's Revelation about ourselves and about our need for salvation.

Even holy persons can confuse being receptive with being passive. They do have a profound awareness of their own sinfulness, but they think it somehow started not with them, but with Adam and Eve. They are fixated in the convenient assumption that their *being*-in-this-world originates from Adam. They have not been taught, nor ever thought, how time and space started—for all of us—by causing ourselves to be-in-this-world.

Our partially failing response to our own being and to God, the Gifter, caused the need for matter and motion, space and time, to exist. The world of *passive matter* is part of *our* personhood that we caused the need for. God infinitely acted upon that need.

The whole world of passive matter was formed as the result of our immediate and free, clearly active, response to the gift of our being. Immediately, our *maybe*-attitude toward *being* caused the existence of conditions of passivity. God responded with infinite compassion.

This world, then, is not the "bright idea" of divinity. God did not make some kind of originative "decision" 'to fashion the world of matter and motion.' Such is a kind of 'fantasy theology' that keeps us in a state of repression about our personal origins. It seems to be in our "self-interest" that we repress the deeper dimensions of the truth contained in the story of 'original sin.'

We deceive ourselves so readily, so unconsciously. Our repressed originative sin carries into our thinking about everything that is critical to being human. We have many ways to think of ourselves that conceal the shameful side of our beginning to *be*. After they had sinned, Adam and Eve themselves might have had some shock of realization of how personally weak and imperfect they had been in the Garden, even before the temptation.

Upon realizing the ease with which they disobeyed their Creator, they covered their nakedness. And God even helped them, perhaps because they could not endure the truth of their pre-*Genesis* origins that caused them to become creatures of passive matter and motion. By being fashioned from dust and a rib, they had been 'drawn out of the well' of their sinful despondency. One can only wonder whether theistic believers today are ready for the root-truth of our origins on earth. Teaching about our ontological origins is hardly ever done.

Teaching about Prayer

Prayer is another prime area for self-deception. Notice how we are taught to pray. "Lord, have mercy on me." "Lord, make me love you and my neighbor." "Lord, have compassion on the starving people in Uganda." These pleadings are meaningful in themselves and are understandable within the context of redemption and salvation. But, almost inevitably, we are unconsciously implying that God amounts to being a kind of mega-creature. We instinctively insist on treating God as a kind of "precocious creature."

We go on and on, assuming God has to do something not yet done. In reality, we are the only ones needing to "do," "move," or be changed. God is immutable, infinite power and grace. Unchangeable love, by being unlimitedly loving. The gap, then, is totally ours, not God's.

We pray as if God is *all*-powerful. But we often do *not* prayerfully see God as *infinitely* powerful. The difference between "all" and infinite is, well, infinite. We think of God rather as a 'mighty agent' who is not dispensing all the power right now at his all-powerful disposal. We fail really to know that God is *infinitely* active, every single moment, in the life of everyone on earth. We treat God as having more to give than he is already presenting to us. We avoid recognizing our sin-blocked origin. And we are blinded by its effects that endure immensely at every moment, including this moment of prayer.

We keep replaying the blame game. We blame, consciously or unconsciously, Adam; Adam blames Eve; Eve blames the serpent; and the serpent blames God. The blame chain remains. We are all locked into it. And, at times, we wonder whether God listens to our prayers and really cares for our needs. It is another big way to deny that we sinned with Adam and Eve originatively, and it keeps us moving blindly onward toward everlasting judgment.

We ignore God's unlimited grace, ever-present to everyone. That grace is never limited by God, only by us in its effects. God has nothing to hold back, nothing to grant more than was already gifted in the originative causing us to be out of nothing. All is here, around and within our self-benumbed beings. But we are not at all receiving well. We are "stiffing God." By our dullness of mind and of heart—even within the midst of the sermons and homilies and counsels of perfection—we are being spiritually passive-reactive.

Unwittingly arrogant in our prayer, we include our usual prayers for God's mercy without much thought. It is more than phenomenal. It strongly suggests that we hardly mean what we say when we claim that God is infinitely good and powerful, infinitely loving and merciful. Do we really mean it? With our hearts and our lives?

We need to give *at least unconscious* recognition to originative sin, behind the original sin of Adam and Eve. Conscious realization is not, of course, required. Most, if not all, will die without it.

Contrition, however, for sins in this world comes with an attitude: about who we *are* and who we are *not*. The attitude by which we are sorry for sin speaks volumes about who we will to *be*. One person might be coming from an *unconscious affirmation* that there is an originative sin that explains his or her plight and the origin of all evil that might befall or be caused by this sinner. Another person might be coming from an *unconscious denial* of an originative sin.

One can, of course, deny that what is being claimed here is true. But then such a person would be called to surmise *why* it is *not* true. And they would be faced with this question: Are you not implying necessarily that God creates out of nothing imperfect persons who are forced to sin by virtue of the sin of their first parents? It would seem that deniers of sin that is personally originative are making the denial simply on the grounds of our spatiotemporal logic—a logic that begs the question of how space and time, and logic itself, came to *be*.

But *that* is the issue. How could space and time come to be the determination solely by an infinitely good and infinitely powerful God? Impossible. The need for our being-in-space-and-time and for its linear logic could only exist on account of the sin we are self-invested to deny.

Simply asserting, of course, the reality of an originative sin would likewise not necessarily mean that one is knowing it to be so. One might be misunderstanding.

Whether it is true or not, everyone is certainly required to continue the work of becoming *spiritually united with God* by participating in religious and spiritual activities of learning and of the works of mercy. Such practice is done, the better to receive the truth of what one is affirming, consciously and unconsciously.

The Teaching Gap

Religious theists suffer from a pastoral teaching gap. For instance, there seems to be little or no teaching about the need to pray for prebirth children to come back freely to their perfectly-gifted being. These little ones must have said *maybe* to God *ex nihilo*. If aborted, they are face to face with God at the moment of their death, perhaps more starkly than we will be. They need our prayers, at their death, to support them in affirming *fully yes* to their Redeemer, being-to-Being.

Zygotic and embryonic persons include little people we never knew about. Even members of our families. All of them have sinned with Adam and Eve and us by saying *maybe* at the moment of their creation. Thereby, they require the services of having their being come back (of living their be-*coming*) through this purgative world. They need our prayers, perhaps more than the rest of us born people do. Yet, who is doing the praying?

The lack of consciously-affirming prayer for our prebirth brothers and sisters echoes the common theological theory that this world of passive matter and motion was an "original choice" of *God*. To the contrary, this world is the result of all the self-deprivation that we caused by our own individual acts of self-abusing freedom at the moment of creation out of nothing. Every person conceived in this world must be reborn or recreated by the saving features of God's eternal Love, with which they are to act freely in consort.

Besides, many other infants and vigorously-growing children are not genuinely affirmed by their mothers and fathers. They might live their whole lives deprived of being affirmed as gifts of God. They are prisoners of their own self-deprivation.

As psychiatrist Conrad Baars delineates in his book, *Born Only Once: The Miracle of Affirmation,* human beings need an emotional birth that is beyond the physical. They cannot provide this psychic birth to themselves, any more than they can give themselves physical birth. They must await the gift from someone else, and be ready to receive it.

Beyond physical and emotional birth, the Christian faith teaches the need to be "born again" spiritually. By the affirming action of Baptism, God's love is "poured into" us as unique persons. This "third birth" yields the functional potential for everlasting union with God. Many Christians believe that one can be baptized also, if necessary, by dying a martyr's death or by the real, if implicit, desire to do the will of God. In any event, by the beliefs of all theists, no one is thought worthy or able to enter into everlasting glory without receiving forgiveness for *all* offenses, both those that are evident and those that are repressed.

Normally, the human *maybe*-sayer requires these three births. The physical birth given by mother is a major move toward becoming able to say fully *yes* to life and love. Then, the little one somehow during life—preferably early, by the smiles and tender care of the mother and father—will be given a kind of emotional birth sufficient to attain a healthy personality. Psychiatrists, such as Anna Terruwe and Conrad Baars, call this second birth the "gift of affirmation" (Baars)(Terruwe).

Besides these two natural births, every child needs a supernatural birth of divine grace that wakes up both soul and body—enlivening the whole being. Believers say that only God can give this spiritual birth, occurring normally through a sacred ministry established for that purpose.

In any case, if sufficient development does not happen within the course of our brief, temporal life, then this 'birth process' will occur abruptly upon our death—whether this mortal passing takes place within the mother's womb or serves as the conclusion to a long life. Sudden and unprovided death is tragic because our *maybe* condition requires every bit of *yes*-development that it can attain. Tragedies do not happen because of some fault within infinite love.

We need earthly *be*-coming in order to increase the quality of our recovery as it ministers to a final act of repentance at the moment of death. At that instant, on its non-temporal side, we will be again emphatically in the Presence of God. And we will either rise beyond our passivity or fall back into it forever. We will either adequately exercise or abandon completely our purely active ability to love God, ourselves, and all others.

This teaching gap in the theistic community means that the truth of creation is being massively short-changed. Creation is not a story of some mega-creaturely Artisan, who *wills* a passive material base to *be*, in order to fashion molecules of flora, fauna, and all manner of inorganic substance out of it. Creation is mainly the inside story of our freedom, its nature, and the consequences of its self-abortive activity.

God Will Say, We Will Say demands a deeper, self-aware reading of the *Genesis* story of creation. The challenge is to know our being and the awesome truth of gifted freedom. We can begin to realize gratefully that we are eternally affirmed, both in being created and in being rescued from our original response. The largely-untold story of our freedom profoundly encourages our saying *yes* to God and to the entire community of *being*.

Pastoral Practices of Passivity

But where are the pastoral urgencies? Many have been taught that we were created—we began to *be*—at the moment of conception in our mother. But if we think that our conception was really done out of nothing, then this assumption amounts to another casualty of our cosmolock.

We think that a particular point in space and time was our starting point to *be*. Rather, we need to understand that space and time themselves were initiated, from within us, by our unwillingness to be perfect, at the moment that we were being gifted. Space and time are archetypes of passivity.

Earlier ages of Christians, for instance, were taught to believe in limbo, a condition where those never baptized were to exist forever in peace and tranquility, but without the ecstatic vision of God. It was a kind of theological "stopgap" theory that well illustrates how, in theology, there exists the deprivation wherein we fail to recognize an originative sin that preceded—ontologically, not temporally—the original sin in the Garden. The latter sin was done by Adam and Eve, the first persons to undergo—in this world—redemption from their own originative sin and potential salvation.

At present, even the notion of limbo, in the Catholic community, seems to have vanished from the official Catechism, and people are being persuaded implicitly, and even explicitly, to believe that tiny, aborted persons—since they have not committed sin in this world—are exempt from a serious final judgment and are received into the heavenly kingdom by virtue of God's infinite mercy. It would seem then that they are either sinlessly conceived or are the privileged subjects of "divine whitewash."

Were they created as perfectly free persons who "happened" not to exercise their God-gifted freedom or were they not yet given the perfect freedom to determine their own destiny? Or, perhaps, God decided for them? None of these alternatives makes sense.

The theological practice of loose assessment can only be another 'stopgap,' until the people of God are completely confronted by the meaning of the (originative) moment at which they were gifted with their very being out of nothing. Every one of them was *gifted*—not merely given, delivered, endowed, and the like—with uniquely perfect (finite) goodness, truth, beauty, oneness, and power to be-*with* God and all other persons. Their perfect freedom was a finite freedom to be-*with*.

At that moment, every *maybe*-saying human person must have responded with a unique interpersonal response to the Person(s) of God. At present, that response seems almost totally repressed. And it cannot strictly be remembered, since *that interface transpired before time began*—before there existed any duration at all and need for memory. This pristine response can be known, however, by heartfelt reasoning about Faith and in moments of intense prayer.

Everyone who is functionally rational can come to know the prime conditions for creation. But one has to *want* to know or be *willing* to know.

In any event, all theists can agree that, after due purgation in this world, everyone will meet God again: at the moment of either being saved or condemned by his or her own lived response to the loving redemption of God.

Chapter 7

Sincerity and Salvation

The issue of an *originative* sin—whether or not there is one—could hardly be more serious. Theists must begin to deal more earnestly with the famous crying and praying of David. "For behold I was conceived in iniquities; and in sins did my mother conceive me (*Psalms* 51:5)." God even proclaimed to Jeremiah, "Before I formed thee in the bowels of thy mother, I knew thee: and before thou camest forth out of the womb, I sanctified thee, and made thee a prophet unto the nations" (*Jeremiah* 1:5).

David was conceived in some kind of original sin that preceded anything done to Uriah and to Bathseba. Where did *that* sin as sin come from, if not from David himself, such that he was prone to much moral chaos, long before his infamous sin as King? Jeremiah was known by God even before he was conceived, if being formed in his mother included his being conceived. One must seriously take this testimony of the prophet himself. Surely, his being sanctified, while in the womb, for a special role would imply that his personal identity was clear prenatally.

The cases of David and of Jeremiah, along with others, as well as the testimony of sound philosophic reasoning, can lead to only one grand conclusion: to be a human zygote is to be a person; and to be a person is to be much more than to be an organism. The "natural capacity to sin" found at conception and in the womb bespeaks an actual sin, a functional sin, independent of temporal constraints, that made that "natural capacity" possible. Before we were 'scheduled' to inherit the sin of Adam and Eve, we had a disposition for being their heirs. We sinned with them at the moment God said, "Be."

How Sincere Are We?

God's gifting of freedom is infinitely perfect. It results only in our natural and functional *ability to say fully yes* to God at the moment of creation, and thereby never to sin, nor ever to cause any kind of "natural capacity to sin." Religious thinkers have confused the chief *ontological* responses that we gave to God at creation with the *moral* responses of early earth-dwellers. Thereby, even traditional theology has been crippled for many hundreds of years.

Believers, for instance, who think that if we do *not* sin within this world we go straight to God are sadly miss-taking the message. If Scriptural Revelation is taken as a whole, the inheritance of original sin from Adam and Eve does not have to mean that the sin of these first parents is capable of being inflicted *ex nihilo* upon each of the progeny.

Ezekiel, for instance, would seem to be speaking by the authority of God when he stipulates that "The soul that sinneth, the same shall die: the son shall not bear the iniquity of the father, and the father shall not bear the iniquity of the son: the justice of the just shall be upon him, and the wickedness of the wicked shall be upon him" (*Ezekiel* 18:20).

While this text may refer to individual episodes of sin committed in this world and does not really specify some kind of generational affliction from Adam, it does remind us that we were not forced to inherit Adam's sin. No one can be forced to sin—especially not by God.

Does God *cooperate* with each one's original *sin* by creating the soul at the moment of conception? Traditional theology has played our 'sin of origin' into an interpretation wherein God passively lets innocent creatures be bombed by their first parents.

There is a reason why each one of us has inherited Adam's sin. We are sinful persons. We have inherited original sin secondarily, even as that sin conveys to us primarily the "inheritance" of our own sin: our originative sin, an ontological sin, far from being merely a moral one. We are conceived as we are: as sinful from the moment of being-at-all by virtue of our *response to being*. We inherit the original (historical) sin of Adam through the course of being made generationally present to our (ontological) sin.

We are the being that we *are*. We cannot excuse ourselves in matters of being any more than we can give ourselves a pass on moral matters—matters of judgment in the spatiotemporal world.

Not everyone, for instance, who says, "Lord, Lord," will enter the kingdom of heaven. But likewise not everyone who says and thinks, "I'm saved, I'm saved," will arrive. How sincere has been that person's proclamation of accepting the saving graces encountered in temporal existence? *Feeling* sincere is not meaning sincere.

Many Christians, for instance, act as though they know they are sincere because it feels like it. They seem to think that God will save them no matter what they do, as long as they claim Jesus as their Savior at some point in time.

But it is difficult to believe that they *mean* it. They must fully face various Scriptural indications regarding the critical importance of sincerity, where it seems that sincerity must be 'proved.' Not that they do the saving of themselves. But that sincerity in accepting God their Savior must be lived out *all the way to the end.* Else sufficient sincerity is not there.

Sincerity would seem to be crucial to divine acceptance. God once said to Abimelech, "...I know that thou didst it with a sincere heart: and therefore I withheld thee from sinning against me, and I suffered thee not to touch her" (*Genesis* 20:6). The Psalmist sings of "Those who lead blameless lives and do what is right, speaking the truth from sincere hearts" (*Psalms* 15:2). And the evangelist, Paul, writes to his followers, "But I am afraid that just as Eve was deceived by the serpent's cunning, your minds may somehow be led astray from your sincere and pure devotion to Christ" (2 *Corinthians* 11:3). The Scriptural Revelation is definite in many places like these, as well as when it is taken as a whole.

If people who practice "sincere and pure devotion to Christ" can be really led astray, as Eve was led into alienation from God, then who of us can say our sincerely-believed 'sincerity' itself cannot be taken away and that we have need of being reformed, even time after time? Reformed from 'insincere sincerity.' Could not Eve have said, "I sincerely thought the serpent knew the truth of what he was saying."

How sincere we are at any moment, or in our lives as a whole, is a judgment *only God* can make. We need to work and pray constantly that we be purified of our deeply instinctive inclinations away from true sincerity.

Urgency

When will we admit consciously that God is, with infinite love and goodness, right now gifting us and all other persons? When will we stop treating God as a mega-creature, thinking that God might not be knowing about poverty or homelessness or sincerity, here and there, so that the divine love needs to be alerted by us to at least some of it through our imprecations? Or perhaps we are thinking that God is "deliberately" unwilling to "give to the poor and the homeless" because we are lacking in our prayers for them? Is God measly?

Can we not realize that God's healing power and mercy are ever-present to everyone? That all we have to do is acknowledge and live this decisive truth about infinite Being and Love? And, then, will we not be grateful for God's Providence, no matter how "things turn out" for us and for others in space and time? If we do know and live the Providence, we will have 'prayed our heart out' for others, as well as for ourselves, in thought, word, and deed.

Jesus was heard to declare, at times, "Your faith has made you whole." Operant faith does not come from God; it comes from us or it does not come at all. Faith is not ours on a loan from God. Faith is an absolute gift of God to everyone. But many have not received it well, neither its foundation all at once in creation nor its reality here and now as a somewhat gradual knowledge of the unseen.

The gift of Faith is *ours*. Faith is not part of God's Being or Power or Glory, but the gift of being able to know. It is given to us at the moment of creation out of nothing. It is gifted not as a dole or a donation, but as a knowing-power that is fully and freely ours. Our originative, immediate imperfect-response wreaked havoc with this pristine gift. (Jesus even wondered whether there would be any faith left on earth by the time he returned.)

It is not that prebirth people have no opportunity to receive the gift of Faith in this life. The infinitely powerful grace of God is ever-present. The gift is fully given at their creation out of nothing and is there at the moment of conception onward. But this ability to know has been only partially received by each one of us.

All persons, including prenatal children, are present to the heart of God. The 'circumstances of this world' that prevent the conscious recognition of God and of salvation are myriad and manifold. But they come ultimately from each one's originative sin at the moment of being gifted to *be*.

Because of the crash caused by our primordial sin, we have to be recreated *ex aliquo*—out of the something that is our fragmented freedom. And then we need to be awakened through experiences and activity in this world. Yet, basically, we have to rouse *ourselves*: to wake up and receive, in an unqualified way, the mercy of God.

God cannot receive the act of salvation *for* us. Although Christians believe that God does, in Jesus, receive the grace of redemption for us within his divine Person, they cannot believe that we can save ourselves.

God is the only executive agent of salvation. But we are necessary to God in order for the divine act to be effective. We cannot be saved without us. It should be obvious: our salvation is impossible without God. But it should be equally obvious that we cannot be received into "everlasting dwellings" without our wholehearted affirmation and totally free consent. Only we ourselves can do that co-operating activity. No one can do it for us. They can help. But we do or do not *receive* their help.

God's interpersonal acts of creation and redemption are effected without our co-operative acts, though not without God's will (intent) that we co-operate. We can readily 'go to hell' on our own. But the interpersonal act of *salvation* cannot be done within us without our personal reception. If we do not co-operate with that intent of God, we are lost forever.

The interpersonal character of salvation cannot be denied, even though many think of it as "God's act only"—a bailout from God.

It might be wondered why we have not also recognized creation and redemption as *interpersonal*. But that might be because the kind of "interpersonal" involved is different. In these latter kinds, God is the only agent, we are sheer receivers of being and of redemption (for better or worse); but in the *interpersonal act of salvation*, we are, in our own finite way, "just as active as" God.

The redemptive or re-creative creation is part of "God's Way," articulated by two renditions in *Genesis*. This redeeming kind of creation is cosmic and *ex aliquo*. Redemptive creation includes the cosmic processing, but is much more of a spiritual renewal from within us. This inner, life-of-the-spirit "source dynamic" is largely repressed. But how we are interactively living our innermost life of grace is causing what happens manifestly in the world of space and time. By our fruits we are known.

From Passive to Active Receptivity

How do we convert emphatically, from being passively receptive to being actively receptive? How can we shift our emphasis?

We can do so first by one great shift of *meaning*. We must realize that everything passive is the derivative, subjunctive form of being and could not possibly have originated with God *ex nihilo*. God cannot create anything passive nor "passivity itself" and still be God, infinitely actual and perfect. The effect of an infinitely perfect Creator who is the sole agent can only be perfect as caused.

This shift from the passive to active reception of the Word comes through realizing that everything passive comes out of ill-received being on the part of human persons, and nowhere else. God *cannot* create *ex nihilo* snowflakes, apples, horses, and the rest. Only persons—angelic and human—with their total freedom. God simply creates the beings of the cosmos or of the earth, *ex aliquo*, out of the chaos we self-disruptive persons have originally made of ourselves. We created this mess originatively by partially defying God and partially negating ourselves in giving our *maybe*-response to *be*-ing.

God's *power* (not "energy") works with the *yes*-potential of the energy that emanates from the original crash. God forms, for our sake, a "platform" for ontological rehabilitation, for coming out of our resultant comatose-like condition of being. We are massively resisting God, knowingly or unknowingly. Resistance on the part of the freely self-wounded creatures, fighting unconsciously to deny their plight, explains totally why cosmic recovery takes so long and will be insufficient for many.

Freedom First

Every created person—whether angelic or human—was gifted to be out of nothing and was *a sheer ability (freedom) to be and to be self (what and who one is uniquely)*. Our whole nature was freedom from the beginning. There could have been nothing of *unfreedom* about any created person at the moment of absolute creation.

At that moment, however, we *caused*, by our *maybe*, our own set of conditions of unfreedom, that are now being manifested socially, culturally, and spiritually. We *constituted* our own unfreedom. Our freedom-nature was ontologically damaged—not as gifted, but as received. We imploded ourselves upon ourselves. But we likewise exploded ourselves—that is, cast ourselves—out of ourselves.

The imploded part of freedom was, then, no longer freedom, but an impediment to fully functioning freedom that had been so gifted and intended by God. It was, we might say, a "stuffed freedom"—a semblance of real freedom. It was energy that remained with us and was the base on which God created (redemptively, eventually) our bodies, with all their functional parts.

Instead of being functionally free in the midst of our being; we were made (by us) functionally unfree. We were left with a kind of "look alike" freedom that seems to be there bodily in blood flow, breathing, and molecular motion of whatever kind. And spiritually we find ourselves to be persons without the freedom to exercise, anywhere nearly perfectly, our knowing and loving powers. We are passively constituted, despite the latent residual teleology in every cell, whereby we strive for unity within each cell and the unity of cell-to-cell, organ-to-organ.

We likewise exploded our freedom. Part of our fully free being fragmented and started to be formed into "the passive universe." Along with the exploded, fragmented freedom from multitudes of all other *maybe*-saying persons, our own exploded personal freedom actually went into making up the cosmos.

Scientists and others do not seem to understand that when they study things in the cosmos—whatever the form of energy: electrical, gravitational, organic, and the rest—they are dealing with human freedom, albeit dysfunctional and fragmented as such. This freedom has been passivized by our free, immediate, partial kind of willing, done at the moment of creation *ex nihilo* and is now what we call the physical world of space and time.

When we study the cosmos, we are studying fallen freedom with its present "antics" and dispositions. This crushed, barely-operative intimation of freedom is "unhinged" from its very own agency: a human person or persons who said *maybe* to their very be-ing. Moreover, every subpersonal substance, from the brute physical to the organic—from molecule to monkey—is created by God not from nothing, but from the energy emanating out of the freedom-crash of the multitudes of human *maybe*-sayers.

All matter that we normally encounter is passivized receptivity. It is passivized originally in one of two major ways: internally (by the implosive acts of genuinely-free human persons) or externally (by the explosive acts of these same genuinely-free persons). Unless and until we transcend this passive receptivity in our mindsets and in our worldview, we will attribute passivity, and hence imperfection, to the interpersonal acts of God and will not be actively receptive of the interpersonal meaning of salvation. We will lumber along in our repressive, self-defeating perspectives, instead of breaking through the virtually universal, cosmolocked kind of thinking and knowing into prospects for ever deeper growth, reconciliation, and renewal.

Chapter 8

Freedom in Forgiving

Astronauts in their spaceship returning from outer space face the ultimate challenge. The tiny capsule must enter the atmosphere at just the right angle. If it tilts too low, the craft will turn over and burn up. If it tilts too high, the astronauts will 'bounce off' the atmosphere, shooting into outer space, and will be lost forever. What is crucial is the "attitude" or angle of the craft's speedy entry.

Every person can identify with these outer-space travelers. We are, after all, heading at break-neck speed toward home in God's eternal heart. At death, our *deepest attitude will determine us* as saved or lost forever. This "inner space" adventure will be finalized by our own will. Not by God's will. And not by what we *want* to be so, nor by our *wishes*, but by what we are *willing* to do and be.

Eye Has Not Seen

Perhaps the Jewish giant to the Gentiles declared it best. "...Eye hath not seen, nor ear heard, neither hath it entered into the heart of man, what things God hath prepared for them that love him" (1 *Corinthians* 2:9). However empty our hearts might be, we are surely heading into the heart of God, who caused us to *be*.

What is our set attitude? Are we too bowed down in self-pity and small-mindedness, so that we will burn up on directly impacting divine love? Or are we too puffed up with our ego-centric concerns, so that we will be deflected away forever from the heart of God?

Parables and stories of inspiration are utilized frequently in the Judeo-Christian tradition, so that the deepest areas of our hearts do become sensitive to the transcendent meaning of the One who saves. Deeper than ordinary speech that is geared to practical concerns in space and time, dramatic figures of speech address what is acutely real. Jewish stories of practical wisdom abound. The parables of Jesus are made into channels of charity and wisdom. Vast Islamic Hadith can be seen to supplement the meaning of the Quran.

The Prodigal Son, the Good Samaritan, and the 'living parable' of the Woman at the Well, and many other paradigms are brought to our minds and hearts to continue the work of deeper meaning, as we make our awesome journey within inner-space. Our *attitude* about the meaning of their inspirational contents—the way we receive these messages—along with our willingness to live in accord with their meaning, determines our individual destiny.

We need the assistance of many people, as well as the guidance of religious authority, to discern, as best we can, the significance of parables and stories. If the prodigal son had not departed and gone off to waste his inheritance, there would have been no real story of the prodigiously loving and forgiving father who waited, and then rushed to take his son into his heart.

The teaching also seems to be that heaven rejoices more over the conversion of one sinner than over many who do not need God's mercy. But this meaning ought not to be taken literally. It is not an indication that we should go forth and sin, so that we can "repent," the better to receive God's mercy. The idea is that, relative to the spatiotemporal fixation we are all operating within, there is more rejoicing over extraordinary repentance than over stable fidelity. It does not refer to the infinite joy of God and the perfect finite joy of the good angels that is gifted to all who are good.

The great stories of conversion and of fidelity are told specifically about the redemptive creation and the becoming, the coming back, of fallen persons. These narrations only indirectly have reference to the story of creation itself *ex nihilo*—out of unqualified love. They are stories of creation *ex aliquo*—out of the redemptive side of God's loving heart. God's love for the saint and the sinner, for those who said fully *yes*, *maybe*, or fully *no* is the 'same' infinite love. God loves all being forever in its ontological goodness, created by God alone.

Right Prayer and Right Attitude

Our inner-space 'trajectory' is guided by right prayer. But prayer is guided by right attitude, or misguided by lack of such. No one can pray or do anything without an attitude that is more or less right or wrong. Yet, good attitudes come from good prayer, even as bad attitudes can be fostered by lack of any prayer or by doing bad prayer that is caused by badly formed attitudes.

In the mystery of human destiny, attitude is the emphatic result of a person's *agent* intellect, the purely active power by which being is known; and prayer is the emphatic result of a person's *agent* will, the purely active power by which being is loved.

Ordinary intellect and will are active, but not entirely so. They represent simply part of the dynamics of human being and doing. Their manner of acting is the result of the originative fall of be-ing. In the Western world, since the time of Aristotle, "agent will" has been unconsciously denied (repressed) by intellectuals, and agent intellect has been recognized only as the conditioning light for knowledge, but not as a knowing-power itself.

At the instant of creation out of nothing, however, God must have gifted every person with a purely active intellect and a purely active will. There was nothing passive. The defective response to being, given by us human persons who said *maybe*, would have caused or created within us the compensatory, redemption-oriented, passively reactive powers to know and to love with which we largely function in this fallen world.

From our self-created passive base, we human *maybe*-sayers have to be stimulated by other beings in order to act or to be active. Upon being gifted with being, we relinquished that gifted ability to be finitely and wholly like God. As a result, we could not be purely active, acting without any "stimulation" or "activation" by God or by anyone else. By our originative sin, we flattened our ability to act like God and like all full *yes*-sayers. We thereby needed stimulus. We passivized ourselves largely into our 'continually awakening and sleeping' condition of body, emotion, and spirit.

Consequently, we are inclined only to think and talk about the impoverished side of our perfectly-gifted intellects and wills—the side that requires our senses for support. We think that the basically *passive potencies* of intellect and will—that are really derivative, compensatory abilities—are 'the real thing' and that they are the only kind of acting intellect and will that is ours.

These powers of ordinary intellect and will, of mind and heart, are the spiritual parts of us that comprise only the wounded, passive part of our originative (agent) powers. These passively active capacities of intelligence and spirit result from the originative break with God our Creator, and from the disruption within our own being's ability to *be*—a break that involves the structure of agent intellect and agent will. Ordinary intellect and will are the self-damaged spin-offs of the agent intellect and agent will. We act spiritually thereby in shadow and darkness, relative to our calling into truth and goodness.

Yet even as the physical sun above the clouds shines brilliantly, similarly the 'spiritual suns' of agent intellect and of agent will are shining, while we users are claiming staunchly our identity only with the fallen part of these purely active powers. The intellective 'sun' is the ultimate source of any light and ability to know that we have; and the voluntative 'sun' is the ultimate source of any warmth and ability to love that is ours. We have abandoned our originative intellective and volitional powers, even as we partly broke with God and abandoned our originative relationship. 'My God, my God, why have I forsaken you?'

But traditional philosophers still regard intellect and will—along with the senses—as passive potencies, that have to be stimulated by their particular objects before they go into operation. The sense of hearing needs sound to cause it to respond. One cannot hear colors. The sense of seeing needs colors, not sounds. The memory needs past experiences. And even the intellect and will need things that are knowable and lovable in order to be activated: to 'go into' acts of knowing and loving.

The idea is that we cannot create the things we know and love; they must be given to us. They must, in some sense, "be done to us." There is little perception of our originative ability "to be with" what we know and to know it within that "with-ing" way, and without our "being done to" by it in any manner. Our ability 'to be done to' is assumed to be coordinate with our being created persons, rather than with our defectiveness as knowers and willers.

We think creatures have to "receive" their 'objects' of knowledge and love. That if they did not have to do so, they would be God. Only God, it is said, 'produces' the truth and goodness that God knows and loves. We do not, because we are not necessary beings. We need not exist, and our knowing and loving comply with this contingency. Just as our existence is donated to us in creation, so are our opportunities to know and love.

Traditional theists are conditioned into thinking that this reasoning is sound. But they seem to be dull to the meaning and character of a gift from God. They take the way *we* go about giving and receiving gifts in this finite world and apply it to the way *God* gives and receives gifts. They regard God's way of giving *being* and our receiving of it to be like our ways of giving and receiving in space and time. Instead, we need to brave a seismic shift in understanding.

God's Ways and Our Ways

God's ways are always infinite in manner and meaning. Our finite ways, including giving and receiving, are not *comparable* to God's. We must come to see that our ways of giving and receiving are a bit like God's; but God's are not like ours. The creature is a bit like the Creator, in that both are being-at-all; but the Creator's manner of being is unlimited and eternal. The creature's whole being is limited and, at best, everlasting.

When God created us who are persons, we were gifted with being by an infinitely giving act. God's act of creating us is infinitely powerful and able to give us be-ing that is fully ours and not at all dependent on God for its *be*-ing. Only our sluggish, rental-mental minds think that our being depends on God. Why? Because we force God into our field of interest, the cosmic world where every effect depends upon its cause.

But, in the activity of bringing beings to be out of nothing, there was no possibility of anything being dependent. There was not any dependency or passivity in the Creator to "pass on" to the effect, the created ones. The activity of creating passed nothing to the created person. All of the being of the creatures was gifted absolutely with a free relationship to their Creator and to one another.

People might think then, "Well, did we create ourselves; or did we co-create ourselves with God?" No. We need to stop treating God as another finite cause, unable to do gifting without depending on the effect or having the effect depend on the gifter. Of course, we ought to say thank you to God. But not in the spirit of "I owe you one, Lord."

We have conflated creation with redemption. So, we thereby fail to contrast our relationship with God in creation, as one of full inter-*independence* thanks to God, with our relationship in redemption, as one of full *dependence* upon God. For redemption and salvation, we owe God everything. For creation out of nothing we really *owe* God nothing. In gifting us with be-ing, God was not compensating us for anything. Before creation, we did not be. So, we could have *no* input into the meaning of God's creating act.

By avoiding the difference between our "needless," yet essential relationship to God in creation *ex nihilo* and our desperately needy relationship in redemptive creation and salvation, we can hide from ourselves. We do not have to *admit* our originatively perfect gift of being and our sin that abused it, causing all of the need for rescue and dependency.

If we were whole, our attitude toward God and being could simply be consummate gratitude, without even a slight tinge of dependency or passivity. That is the kind of attitude to be found in the holy ones who live in glory. Their gratitude for be-ing is not *self*-centered and passive, but *God*-centered and fully active.

The originative way to be was to be *with*-God, rather than being *for*-God, *toward*-God, or thankful to God because of a supposed act of divine condescension. God did not "condescend" to create us out of nothing; nor even condescend to redeem us from the mess of our "something." God is not a mega-creature, who acts like we would act if we were God.

Our acts of gifting or giving are ever finite. But they are also defectively so. We are living in an inherently substandard world and our every act falls short of what our acts would be were we living in finite glory.

Only to the extent that the person draws upon the 'sun above the clouds,' while taking into account the light that this same sun also provides 'under the clouds,' will effective understanding occur. We ought to be acting quite consciously from our agent intellect for knowing and from our agent will for loving. They are God-centered, most deeply within us, above the clouds of the *maybe*-saying world. Our passively active intellect and will, that cope with indecisive matters of myriad kinds, are not enough.

Christians speak of "the flesh" and "the mind" and their "deeds." From the flesh and the mind they distinguish "the spirit" that lives 'above the clouds' of worldly wisdom. Therein God has gifted us with peace, joy, courage, and vision. We have only to "access" it and to "really receive" it.

Forgiving Ourselves

According to many believers in God, we are gifted with the power to forgive ourselves. And that power is most critical for receiving the infinite Love of God within us. That love was fully gifted at the moment of creation out of nothing. So, even now in daily life, when we think we are forgiving others of their offenses against us, we are really doing so only to the extent that we are not holding a grudge against ourselves.

As we forgive ourselves, so we are able to forgive others. Our sin of origin—not saying fully *yes* to God at creation—has been literally blocking us. Our forgiveness of ourselves and of others for flawed behavior in this life is partial and effective relative to the degree to which we (albeit unconsciously) have really forgiven ourselves for originative sin. If we do not know it consciously, we still can and do know it unconsciously, and so are acting relative to this sin in a way that is more or less authentic.

The reality of our unconscious guilt for committing an originative sin that is now unacknowledged is buried in the deepest recesses of our spirit. It must be faced before we can be saved—before we can co-operate with God's infinite mercy.

If this encounter with our originative sin is *not* done here and now, then it will be done in the face of God at the moment of death. At the moment of creation, God had said *Be*, and we said *Maybe*. So, when God will say *Come*, we will say *Thank You*, but only on condition that we are not blocked by our conscious or unconscious resentment. After all, we cannot help being resentful—at least, unconsciously—about having been afflicted with Adam's sin, without our (conscious) consent. Why did God apparently 'subject us' to various ways of actual and potential suffering during our lifetime? Some Christians might even go about wondering, at least unconsciously, *why* we were not conceived immaculately, as was Jesus' mother.

In any event, if we are willing to prepare ourselves well for death and for this encounter of salvation, all we have to do is see what we are looking at. In this world of contingency, we are met with its joyful surprises that play amidst cruelty and eventual death. The energy of this mortal world, ultimately stemming from our own dramatic fault in creation, comes from the crash of our being. We can only say *fully yes* to God if we receive with whole hearts the dark side of the Gospel, as well as the Light. The Light of the world is lighting up the darkness within us and around us. We must open the e*yes* of our *hearts*. Without our opening, the Light is ineffective.

In our spirit, we know, consciously or unconsciously, that we need to forgive others for their offenses against us. And we need to know that we cannot even do it successfully without forgiving ourselves for being in such a world in the first place.

Some would even say that we need to forgive God. But they are overlooking their originative sin and blaming God for it.

We are self-poisoned with originative sin and its guilt. So, only we with God can release it. Forgiving ourselves consciously for saying *partly no* to God within our being is needed in order for us to be free.

"Forgive us our offenses, as we forgive those who offend us." That was the teaching of Jesus about our prayer. But the underlying requirement is forgiveness of ourselves. That endeavor can only be undertaken by us first admitting our primal sin and then forgiving ourselves. There is no question that God can and does forgive us—if we are *willing*. We are the only 'question-mark upon ourselves.'

We can choose now and forever to hold onto the hurt we did to ourselves at our creation or we can release our self-resentment and fully receive the divine mercy and the originative gift of everlasting life with God.

Chapter 9

The Heart of Compassion

A woman had just lost her baby through miscarriage. She was telling her young daughter what had happened. Seeing the pain in her mother's eyes, the girl expressed her affection by a big, warm hug and a kiss, saying, "I wish I could kiss your heart and make it all better."

A bit of compassion from the heart of a child for the heart of a mother reminds us of our power with God. Jesus loved little children and he reminded his followers to become like them in humility and simplicity. He even went so far as to say that this was the way to heaven.

He also compared himself to a hen that would gather her chicks together under her wing. Tragically, he found that his offspring were not of a mind and heart to nestle in his company. One might say that their lives were miscarriages of love. They were more often childish than childlike.

We human persons exist in space and time, but we are all wrapped up in ourselves. According to Christian tradition, we have brought about the suffering of God. Yet God is not deprived of our love and worship. Infinite Love cannot be diminished.

Our finite loving and worshipping are, after all, ultimately from us, the potential lovers and worshippers. These acts can only come forth from our hearts freely. We can readily deprive ourselves of many acts of the heart, including love and worship.

God originatively gave all created persons the complete power to engage freely in intimate communion with divine Love. Obviously, you and I miscarried.

We are now naturally confused about the "effect" on God. We would feel rejected and deprived by someone withholding their love from us. So, we might think that even God must feel likewise when created persons fail to love the Gifter of their *being*.

But we can come to clarification of our thought.

God is neither an owner nor a loaner. God infinitely gifts created persons with their own perfect finite being and power. There is no such thing as borrowed being.

On the one hand, those who fully responded to creation added nothing to God's infinite Love and Glory. Finitude cannot be added to infinity any more than time can be added to eternity.

On the other hand, we who have failed to love and worship took nothing away from God. God gave us our own power to love, and it was inherently a free power. It was not at all God's power; it was *our* power. And our own mis-exercise of it was essentially *self*-depriving.

But in the wake of our sin, the Hebrew prophets looked to a future of compassion that would transform sinful human nature. Ezekiel speaks with the voice of God saying, "And I will give you a new heart, and put a new spirit within you: and I will take away the stony heart out of your flesh, and will give you a heart of flesh" (*Ezekiel* 36:26).

In the Islamic tradition, Mercy and Compassion are highly notable among the many names and attributes of Allah. Faithful adherents implore the mercy of Allah who is most Beneficent and Merciful. The tradition highly regards mercy and compassion upon fellow human beings (Muslim and non-Muslim) and on animals. In the Quran, the true believer is the one who desires for others what is desirable for himself, including affection (Cf., e.g., *Surah* 2:143 and 207).

According to Christian tradition, God's compassion even includes suffering. God suffers in and through the human nature of the Word Person, Jesus Christ, who is fully human as well as fully divine.

This divine Person assumed, by an infinitely perfect act, a perfect human nature and then he allowed himself to be conceived in the imperfect world of space and time. For the practical purposes of completing the divine work of redemption, God incarnate thereby let himself be "imperfectized."

Jesus is therein capable of suffering deprivation within his human nature. All persons who are lost, or who stray along the way, afflict his compassionate heart. The Person of the Word of God does this suffering in his human nature, not in his divine Nature. Nonetheless, he suffers as a Person—not simply as a nature.

Theists know that, underlying every instance of good or evil, the infinite heart of God receives and affirms the saint and the sinner, without being passively affected by them in the divine nature. God wills infinitely to receive all and to forgive those who are willing to repent.

Repentance and Forgiveness

All theists say that repentance is necessary for recovery from sin. They believe that we are personally involved with good and evil, and that only God can effectively liberate us. If we do *not* believe, and especially if we are closed to our potential for believing, we cannot be saved. Repentance, therefore, is positive and life-giving.

Repentance involves, first, receiving ourselves. We are called to receive ourselves not only with our original perfection of forever-being-a-gift of God, but also with the encrustation of our sinfulness. And we are moved to receive ourselves even as we are: within our profoundly self-distorted, yet recovering, condition.

Through an authentic belief about repentance, we can become increasingly more personal. A merely functional repentance reveals itself as being impersonal. Beating one's breast is not the same as opening one's heart. A person-to-person relationship is always heart-with-heart. If we are going to say *yes* to the gift of being, we will necessarily say it to a Person—to God as personal, the person-all Being, *not* as to a superior Force.

Our originative creation was Person-to-person. Nothing could be more personal than one person receiving the gift of being-at-all from Another. In addition, what could be more impersonal than freely failing in many ways to receive this incomparable gift?

Moreover, we tend to rationalize our condition by thinking that we were originally given a less-than-perfect personal being. But that would be an impersonal act. God did not do such. We were the ones who have acted with our being so impersonally to begin with, and who continue to consolidate it by our attitudes and actions in this life. We are in grave need of forgiveness and repentance.

Without true knowledge of sin and a genuine sorrow, we cannot receive God's affirming love and forgiveness. We are simply self-blocked. A Creator, however, so loving and interpersonal as to give us an interpersonal being "out of nothing," will forgive immediately at the moment that the created person effectively repents from the heart.

Personal recovery, then, realistically begins with sorrow for sin (contrition), repentance, and forgiveness—repentance before God, and forgiveness of ourselves and of one another, in likeness to God forgiving us.

Repentance and Compassion

Steven, the reckless motorist cited in *God Said, We Said*, felt compassion for the victims of his alcoholic driving. He felt deeply for their families and friends, and for himself. But suppose he had merely said to himself and others: "I am sorry for my irresponsible use of alcohol that caused these deaths and injuries. Now, I must get on with my life. There is little that I can do about it further. I must be realistic."

His "repentance" would be perfunctory and impersonal. It would be largely verbal, and self-centered. "I'm sorry this happened to me; and, of course, I'm sorry this happened to the victims, too. But I have to be concerned first with myself. If I let their pain get me down, I will just sink or rot in failure. That's the way life is. We have to make the most of things like this. Just 'forgive and forget.'"

Steven's superficial "repentance" would then be reinforcing his passivity. He would be refusing to recognize the enormous grief he had caused in others. He would not be "walking in their moccasins" at all. His sorrow would not be coming from his heart, but from his self-motivated practicality. Such "sorrow" really betrays a sadness; it amounts to the deprivation of elation that is often confused with sorrow. He would not be responding interpersonally.

In the actual case, Steven had real compassion for the victims. His repentance was shown to be personal. Both the good of the victims and his own good moved his heart. He knew that the rest of his life would be interwoven with theirs. His single bad intention at a birthday party—to act for himself even for the moment—caused most of the grief he and they are now sharing. His contrition and compassion made the difference between his personal repentance from the heart and what could have been merely impersonal regret.

Our compassionate repentance for having offended others makes little sense, however, if we fail to show repentance and compassion toward the most offended one of all: our Creator. Every act of personal negation—from the root-act of saying *maybe* right down to everyday bad choices—denies God's being as "I am Who am." Nonetheless, can we really be compassionate toward One Who is infinitely perfect and infinitely powerful?

Yes, if we realize that this infinite power is not a "power over us," but an infinite power-*with* us.

God's power is not what we might unconsciously take it to be: the power of an often-benign tyrant. God's power infinitely enables the finite freedom of the creature to love, to forgive others, and to be compassionate. But this infinite power likewise infinitely respects our finite freedom, including the ability to remain unmoved.

Chapter 10

Compassion for God

People who think of God as a self-enclosed object high above them cannot feel compassion for God. They think the infinite Absolute requires no compassion because nothing hurts the invulnerable. To them, God is far less sensitive than a rock.

But Jews, Christians, and Muslims believe God is personal. The personhood of God is undoubtedly the sole ultimate foundation of all the perfection found in created persons. Our finite perfection reflects its infinite cause.

As a cause, however, God is not an origin from which our finite qualities "flow," as though "the infinite became somehow finite in us" while remaining infinite in God. God is the creator of our finite qualities inasmuch as God brings us finite being, truth, goodness, beauty, and all our other attributes perfectly "out of nothing." We do not flow "out of God" with being. We are gifted to be by—not "out of"—the infinite being, truth, goodness, and beauty of God.

Receiving Is the Key

Nevertheless, we can gain a glimmer of God's infinite goodness and beauty by dwelling on the finest qualities of human persons. Through our own experience, we know that persons not only give, but also receive. To be a person is to be a lover or a potential lover: to be able to receive the beloved and to give of self.

Yet we cannot relate well interpersonally with someone who does not receive us as we are. For instance, people who do something good for us, but who cannot receive the good we do for them, are blocked from being our friends. Friendship means mutual sharing. Moreover, mutual sharing means both giving and receiving.

How then can God, as infinite Love, be potentially our supreme Friend?

God gives us our being ("out of nothing"). This Giver not only gives, but also receives our free, creature-response. God receives *yes* with joy; receives *no* with sorrow; and receives *maybe* with both sorrow and compassion.

This infinite receiving is in no way passive or like our own. God's receiving—hence joy and sorrow over good and evil—is infinitely active love, not somewhat passively affected love. Neither our joy nor our sorrow can measure, or be the standard for, what God's infinite manner of joy and sorrow really is.

God is not sorrowful with respect to the Divine Selfhood, but is sorrowful in relation to—not in dependence on—the world of *nay*-sayers. We hesitate to think of God being sorrowful because we project our meaning for sorrow, which inevitably is contaminated with sadness, onto God. With infinitely active receptivity, God receives, the evil done by created persons.

Christians even believe that God became incarnate in Jesus to show sorrow and compassion through suffering and through his healing care for sufferers. As incarnate, God suffers in human nature somewhat as we do, though incredibly more so.

God, however, as infinite Being and source of infinitely healing mercy, cannot suffer passively in divine nature. God receives us with unlimited love, and without being passively affected.

If God could suffer in any way passively, as we do, there would be no assurance of our being able to be redeemed and saved from our self-wrought condition. God, too, would be deprived and in need of saving—even though much less so (Weinandy).

Unfortunately, many try to bring God "down to our size," even in respect to our suffering. This reflex downsizing constitutes another remarkable manner of denying or dodging the truth that we are the sole effective causes of our own predicament in this existence: our being-in-a-world that causes pain and suffering.

Ego-centric "Compassion"

When Jews and their fellow theists ask, "Where was God at Auschwitz?" they can begin to realize that God was right there. God was not suffering as we would do, but was infinitely receiving the suffering of those inmates and of their persecutors. God was not *experiencing* anything. Experiencing something always involves passivity. Receiving as such does *not*.

God's activity of receiving is difficult for us to understand, so sodden with passivity has our own receptivity become. With open minds and hearts, however, we can come to realize that divinity does not "experience" the violence and the suffering, but receives with infinite love reality itself, including the violence. God is infinitely free to be-*with* us in sorrow, despite how ignominious our condition might become.

Rabbi Harold Kushner tries to articulate the compassion of God, when he says, "I would like to think that the anguish I feel when I read of the sufferings of innocent people reflects God's anguish and God's compassion, even if His way of feeling pain is different from ours" (85). He likes to think that God is the source of his sympathy, as well as his outrage, and that God and he are on the same side in standing with victims of violence.

Observing from our typically egocentric point of view, Kushner tries to understand God on our terms rather than trying to know us in God's light. He hopes that his anguish over sufferings of "innocent people" reflects God's anguish and compassion. But he might do better to believe that God receives all of the suffering of *seemingly* innocent people with infinite freedom, justice, mercy, power, and love.

Rabbi Kushner recognizes that God's way of "feeling pain" is different from ours and he desires to think that God is the ultimate source of genuinely human sympathy and outrage. In these respects, he articulates important truths. But he assumes that we people are so good that we do not deserve severe adversities. He also assumes that we know a great deal about who is, and who is not, truly a victim of unjust aggression.

Kushner thinks we should not seek explanations for the suffering of the innocent, but rather make a caring response. He advises that we come to the point of forgiving the world and forgiving God for our condition of pain and anguish.

But, if we had a sound explanation for horrendous evils that afflict us, would we not be empowered to give a more truthful and loving response? Our unwillingness to face our own depths of sinfulness forces us to put explanation and response into separate categories.

Like so many Jewish and Christian theists, Kushner has moved far away from the notion of personal responsibility for the origin of evil. He has become distant even from the personal responsibility of Adam and Eve for their disobedience in Eden. He sees it as a step into maturity.

There is a latent demand that God be like us, or else God is not compassionate. Our likeness to God then seems to be less important than God's "likeness to us." By such an attitude, we continue to live out the actions in Eden and our originative infidelity that qualified us to become Adam's progeny.

Even beyond Kushner, what might be called the "shoah scandal" represents a dramatic move away from personal responsibility for the evil in our lives.

In "protest theology," people who follow Wiesel, Blumenthal, and others treat God as necessarily like us humans in space and time. So they protest. They positively accuse God of irresponsibility and of abuse toward his "innocent children." They blame God for letting his chosen ones be devastated by their enemies.

Such thinking seems to be calling God to account for divine freedom and responsibility. While there is an acknowledgment that we too are sinners, God is put on trial for violating his children.

The theology of protest is enveloped in the literalism of Scriptural rhetoric about God dealing with people. So, adherents seem to be incapable of imagining or conceiving how our originatively created freedom could have been badly exercised and repressed by us.

God becomes a captive to our history and to our spatiotemporal consciousness. On the one hand, Kushner has forsaken the idea of God being infinitely powerful. On the other hand, there are "protest theologians," who have forsaken the idea of God being infinitely good.

Many Christians make a similar mistake. They regard the story of fallen creation as the story of God. Jack Miles wrote a highly touted book called *God: A Biography.* It attempts to reveal the Bible as a literary work of art. Miles and other authors make God sound like one of us; whereas traditional belief holds that we are poorly, but sincerely, trying to be like God.

In this regard, further, we find little help from the brilliantly written treatise by Karen Armstrong called *The History of God*. The book delineates, among other things, the struggles of the three main traditions of theism in understanding the Creator and the workings of the divine in space and time.

But, of course, there is *no* such thing as either the biography or the history of God *as God*. The God of history has *no* history. The Creator of the cosmos is *not* cosmic. The God of space is spaceless. The God of time is timeless.

For Christian theists, the incarnate God is the Lord of history and, as incarnate, is at the mystical heart of history. But the Word of God became flesh by the free action of God *in* history, *not* as a *part* of history. God is *not a part* of history; but history is itself a part of the human endeavor of the redeeming Person of God, the Word made flesh.

In short, God should in no way be portrayed like one of us sinners. For Christians, even the incarnation is the story of God becoming one with us, except in sin. Jesus has suffered the effects of our sin without sinning at all.

Confusion rules when we fail to differentiate radically. God is the primary, but transcendent, subject *within* human history. God is fully *within* history, but not *of* it. God is fully within and fully other than space, time, and history.

Within highly-passivized ways of receiving divine Revelation, the people of God painfully wrestle with their own concepts of God. They fail to distinguish carefully their own identity from that of God, their redeemer and potential Savior.

God's omnipresence should not be obscured by the machinations of fallen creatures who attempt, consciously or unconsciously, to escape from admitting originative sin. Nor should these creatures' futile attempts to conceal this primal sin include their implicating God as subject to their own history.

Many look for God in the corners of the universe, as though God were a lost or hidden object. Such is the sad occupation of those who have lost faith in the God of immanence and transcendence. God is constantly "dragged down" to our passive level of being in order to cloak the nakedness of our passivity-creating sin.

In her book, *He and I,* Gabrielle Bossis exhibits profound personal faith in God's trans-historical presence. Representing the words of God, she has written, "There is no solitude anywhere since I am everywhere" (374).

Everywhere, God is love unconditional, both giving and receiving at once. God gives *infinitely* the divine Self *to* every victim of unjust aggression and *infinitely receives* this suffering person. God even gives to, and receives, the one who is doing violence to others—and who is thereby violating himself or herself most of all.

If God were able to confer being on creatures, but would not be capable of receiving their response to that gift, God simply would not *be* personal. Divine power for receiving (infinite receptivity), however, like divine power for giving (infinite "givity") is different from anything we *experience* in this crashed creation.

Even now our own finite receptivity is not something we can ever experience. But we know it by simple intuition. We may know the reality of receptivity and all other spiritual qualities *in* and *through* our experiences, but not *by* them. We do *not* "experience" true love, for instance. But *through* our experiences we can *know* someone really loves us.

God's infinite receptivity is the opposite of passivity and is not at all a divine experience. There is nothing in God to suffer passively. But that is why both good and evil are profoundly received by the divine Heart in an interpersonal, infinitely active way, and why, to God, the good is joyful and the evil is sorrowful.

Joy and sorrow are the infinitely abiding features of the divinely interpersonal love. As different as they are, "joy and sorrow" are features of paradox, not of opposition. Unfortunately, we readily confuse them with "elation and sadness," their psychic counterparts, found in the depths of our defective, experiential human natures.

Infinitely great is the divine joy over one sinner who repents. Just as great is the divine sorrow over one sinner who rebels. Infinite joy and infinite sorrow are the only kind of joy and sorrow that God as God can be.

Realizing this Godly sorrow, person to person, heart to heart, we can become wholly compassionate toward God. Compassion for the infinitely offended heart of God opens our hearts to true repentance and reveals the authenticity of our own sorrow for sin.

Our sin is finite; but the One whom we offend is infinite. Not "passively infinite," which would be impossible. God is infinitely actual and, insofar as our offense is real, God is infinitely offended and infinitely sorrowful. God cannot be merely finitely offended and finitely sorrowful.

'Infinite Feelings'

People might wonder how God can have feelings and still be infinite. But God does not have feelings like us so much as we have feelings—at least some of them—like God.

Our joy can be like the joy of God—over the return of a "lost sheep" or of a "prodigal child." And we can be sorrowful for the divine Being, who is "like a shepherd with many lost sheep" and like a "father with prodigal children."

Our compassion for God can be somewhat like God's infinite compassion for us. Divine joy and sorrow are spiritual "emotions" or conditions of be-ing. By our own such feelings, we can share in the life of God. Joy and sorrow are not the equivalent of elation and depression or "happiness and sadness." These are necessarily based on passivity. Joy and sorrow are based on active receptivity.

Part of the reason we might think that God is without feeling must be that we ourselves have so little feeling for God. We think of God as an abstract being, when God is not at all abstract or distant. We are. Our minds and hearts are so benumbed that often the only way we relate with God is mentally, and as an unconscious compensation for our own dullness. We are also hung up on psychic and emotional feelings that we have and that God as God does not. And we are largely self-blocked from spiritual feelings, like true joy, sorrow, and communion that are infinitely real in God.

But when our Faith becomes as much a matter of the heart as it is of the mind, and is accompanied by sufficient spiritual growth, we can "feel with" the One in whom we believe. We can even *be* our compassion. We can *do* our *be*-ing with active receptivity.

Compassion for God manifests the heart of a friend. We might be weak and dependent friends. But our compassion does not come from our weakness and dependence; it comes from exercising the *unconditional independence gifted to us with our creation.*

This independence-*with*—not independence-*from* or -*of*—is the source of our friendship with our Creator, and makes it possible for the divine Being and ourselves to share deep mutual compassion.

Within our weakness is our strength. Within our dependence on God is our independence-*with* God. The very grace of God, infinite receptivity, has taken on our passivity in order to redeem passive persons. By this redemptive grace, we can know ourselves and God in a whole new light.

Chapter 11

Compassion for Ourselves and Others

Suppose you learned of a man and woman in your neighborhood who were victims of a house fire. They were badly burned and were hospitalized in critical condition, with the prospect of death or, at least, severe disfigurement for the rest of their lives.

You would be moved to help them, if you could. You would feel compassion and a desire to do what might be reasonable to secure their recovery toward a stable, happy life.

But what if you then heard that they had started the fire? Not to burn themselves to death, but to make sure the fire got a ferocious start before they fled, with the prospect of insurance money in the future. A gas water heater had exploded right after the fire got going and they had become trapped by the unexpected blaze. Firefighters risked their own lives to pull them from the inferno.

Their plight was caused not by accident, but by acting upon their emotional and moral defects. Would your new knowledge change your willingness to help them in some way? Perhaps it would not.

Your compassion would probably be intact, but you would realize that these people need extraordinary help in order to recover. Their self-hatred had caused their predicament. Exposing and healing the hatred would require something well beyond what you could do for them. They would need not only helpers; they would need a Savior.

All of us are in this world of cosmic dust because of the disaster for which we are chiefly, though not solely, responsible. Adam and Eve did not start our fire. We did. They started their own.

We started ours originatively and personally. And, in refusing to admit it, we become further complicit with Adam and Eve. Are we even worthy of compassion?

Compassion for Ourselves

Yes. Rooted within the independence and potential for friendship that our Creator originally gave us is the power of compassion for ourselves. We are empowered to become aware of the gloriously perfect lover we were created to be, and of the cataclysmic loss of friendship that we freely willed, repressed, and now regret. We are called, finally, to acts of contrition and repentance. Then we can be compassionate toward our suffering selves.

We can feel true sorrow over how we offended our own being. Our originative personal choice not only offended the infinite heart of God; it ravaged our heart, too. Entering into our hurt, we can begin to feel sorrow more for who we *are* not, than for what we *have* not.

This deeper kind of compassion for oneself is not based on guilt and shame, but on a grieving sense of loss. "I could have been a perfect friend; now I am a desperately recovering friend. Why did I say *maybe* instead of freely, spontaneously, and gratefully *yes*?" "My God, my God, why have I forsaken you?"

True repentance, of course, includes guilt and shame. As a basis, however, these qualities are self-centered. Dwelling too much on them weakens the soul, rather than heals. Guilt and shame may open the door for genuine repentance, but compassion lets us enter.

False compassion is also quite possible. To the very degree that "compassion" is formed around the self it is false. Many people seem to use their feelings of sympathy, normally directed toward others, as a pretense for any behavior they themselves happen to choose. "God understands that you are 'only human.' So, don't be negative. Do whatever you decide is the best for you. Follow your conscience and all will be well with God."

With advice like that, compassion for self is impossible because it is based on the spirituality of self-service, not God-service. True compassion for self and true repentance yield no excuses. Good must be done and evil must be avoided.

Discovery precedes recovery. God's truth, not "our truth," must be discovered, assimilated, and lived. Or else, recovery is impossible. Based on a growing spirit of friendship with God and knowledge of self, true compassion for oneself heals and strengthens.

Compassion for Others

We were not created to be alone, but to be "all one." We were created together, as a community of *persons*. Not as a tribe or a hive of humans. Creation is social and personal, neither "public" nor private. Creation is the act of God infinitely alive, in whom there is no privacy, but simply infinite interpersonality.

Receiving our own being involves the being of others. To *be* is to be *related*. To *be* is to be-*with*. And as my repentance invites your forgiveness, your repentance summons my forgiveness. Compassion for myself involves compassion for you. We can sympathize with one another mainly because of what we have done to ourselves as persons, not merely because "we are all in the same boat."

Suppose that Steven, the college student who killed two people in the DWI accident, had awakened in the jail cell with several other inmates. In the other prisoners he might have experienced attitudes different from his. One inmate might adamantly deny personal responsibility for the murder that occasioned his lock up. Another might admit partial responsibility for raping someone, but still might be holding a grievance against all women. A third might be angrier at his fellow inmates just for being there than at the storeowner, who reported his disreputable deeds of lifting thousands of dollars worth of merchandise.

In this situation, Steven's compassion would be tested. Could he feel sympathy for his guilty fellow inmates as readily as he did for his innocent victims and their families? Not as readily—especially if the imprisoned companions showed little remorse and sorrow for their crimes.

If they were to come to repentance, however, they could evoke his compassion for them as other recovering self-victimizers. And even if they are not repentant at the moment, their capacity for eventual transformation remains a basis for some compassion.

The gift of sympathy for *maybe*-sayers like ourselves affirms the communion we could have had and lost—and the communion we still can have if we receive God's redeeming love.

Compassion for Persons in Hell?

Compassion for total *no*-sayers, however, may not be possible. Genuine compassion involves feelings, as well as love, for sufferers. And, in their total hate, *no*-sayers offer *no* basis for our feelings of compassion.

Even so, love for *no*-sayers is possible. Love for one's enemies goes beyond all feelings and experiences.

Total *no*-sayers are lovable, not on the basis of their ill will, but on the basis of be-ing. Their being—originally and forever a perfect gift of God—is not annihilated by their own hatred for God.

Nor is this initially-gifted structure (essence) of being or image of God damaged. This giftedly-perfect structure continues forever, behind the blockage in their nature and despite the weight of their hate that has driven them into hell.

Their receivedly ontological nature, however, is damaged forever. By their sin they destructured their participation in their own be-ing.

Though they do their best to tear themselves apart, they cannot *not be*. In their essence as gifted by God, they cannot *not* be the perfect finite being that God gave them to *be*. Despite their total rejection of this originative self, they are giftedly perfect forever. Their gifted essence stands right within their self, even as their nature has been corrupted by being horribly recepted or received.

God's everlasting call to "be who you are" goes unheeded, even as these persons—angelic and human—continue to hate. Saying *fully no* to God is necessarily an act of quintessential hatred, closing out the potential for any reciprocity with others, including God.

Such persons are still *giftedly* able to love perfectly. Nevertheless, the ultimate, total *no*-saying amounts to complete destruction of both the functional and the natural capacities to love and to share any mutuality of joy and sorrow.

Their destruction of the natural capacity to express themselves—to express their essence, as perfect gifts of God forever—prevents them from ever acting effectively at the core of their being, wherein contrition could begin.

Even though the hatred of the haters renders *them* completely incapable of loving, they are still lovable. Depending on one's particular theistic belief, one may or may not understand how God can love Lucifer, while Lucifer completely hates God.

But we know that this prince of demons was *fully free* to say *yes* at the moment of saying absolutely *no* to God. So, while God cannot be compassionate toward Lucifer and the others who freely and fully hate, God continues to love the self-condemned in themselves, in their essences.

God loves Lucifer: loving him as this person, Lucifer, but not as a hater—what the evil one made of himself. God's love brought into being—and cannot annihilate—Lucifer or any other created persons. Infinite goodness cannot withdraw the originative creation—an act of *infinite* wisdom.

"You are to be, for better or for worse. No matter what you freely choose to co-create, your being will always be good and loved by me." Evil-willers as gifted to be—whether angelic or human—are infinitely loved, even though they are incapable of reciprocating because of the ultimately perverse way in which they *received* their being.

God loves Lucifer and all haters-of-God in their essential potential as beings for loving. God loves them for their essences and for their (lost) natural potential. But God does not sorrow with them because of the loss, since that loss is willed—albeit destructively—through the perfect ability to will that God gave them—their agent will. God absolutely respects their will, even if not what or how they will.

Jesus counseled his followers, "...Love your enemies, do good to them that hate you" (*Luke* 6:27). He died to redeem those who hated him. Christians, then, believe that we fallen humans are all called to love our enemies as God loves them. We are enjoined to respect their freedom as God respects it, even while we work to counteract the bad effects of what they have willed.

Love for enemies is a condition for our own ultimate recovery. If we do not respect the God-gifted will-*power* of our enemies, we do not respect our own will-*power*.

In the case of Lucifer and other total *no*-sayers, any hope for recovery is in vain. There is no hope for "an ounce of love" from them. We can love them as we love our this-worldly enemies, in that they are gifts of God to themselves and to us. But we cannot love them in what they do, as enemies of God, to themselves and to others.

Those who absolutely reject the gift and the Giver know what they have freely spurned. They said absolutely *no* to God and to the gift of being. (We might find it difficult to understand how anyone could possibly say *fully no* to God, unless or until we realize how we are even *no*w "half-way" there.)

There is *no* question of these total *no*-sayers "not knowing what they do." Perhaps, more than anything else, it is because they do not *care* what they are doing that they have no hope of salvation.

Despite the divine offer of infinite love, they willfully retain no functional potential for receiving love from God or anyone—least of all from themselves. They are loved by God and by other creatures of good will. But, by their willed indifference, they have constituted themselves unable to receive even infinite love. Such is hell. God infinitely loves them, but cannot be compassionate toward them. God cannot "reach out" redemptively.

By their indifference to their own finite freedom, they have taken themselves "out of the range" of even infinite compassion. God cannot honor, in the least, their fully negative rejection of goodness. Unlike their very being, their whole *existence* is a "product" (or anti-creation) made out of their own defiance, of which there is nothing to affirm—not even the slightest *yes*. They have completely *willed not to receive*.

To receive or not to receive, that is our crucial decision. There really is an opportunity for decision that we all share, and in which we can be truly compassionate and supportive of one another. But this decision is a self-determination each of us finally makes alone: person-to-Person, heart-to-Heart, with God. Or else impersonally, heartlessly, against God.

Chapter 12

Receiving Pain and Suffering

We are now living within the recovering universe. Recuperating from a crash. In addition, as we grow, we are in constant danger of re-crashes that would be symptomatic of the original "big one." As children, we first awaken in a largely passive, lethargic condition concerning the meaning of life.

Our range of exposure to actual and possible pain and suffering begins to test our receptivity. We are receptivity-challenged.

Some of our experiences can be terrifying and even excruciatingly painful. We might lose consciousness and even our sanity. Will we receive them actively or passively? Will we actually affirm them or merely endure them?

If we receive actively the constant *maybe*—the realization that something bad *could* happen to us at any moment—we are accepting a basic condition for ultimate recovery from originative sin. But when we receive something bad that *actually* happens to us we are responding with the most healing receptivity of all. Within suffering, we can actually grow spiritually. Absent suffering, we can wither.

Experiencing pain and suffering with a receptive heart deepens our spirit and opens our eyes. But an unreceptive heart, with a "Why me?" attitude, closes us to the process of recovery.

Learning from others can help, especially from others who have dramatically faced the question, "Why me?"

Examples of "Why Me?"

Brian Sternberg, for instance, was a young athlete who must have felt he had good reason to say "Why me?"

In 1963, Brian was ranked as the number one pole-vaulter in the world, setting new records and giving every promise of becoming a gold medalist in the next Olympics. One tragic day, while routinely practicing on a trampoline, he broke his neck. Then there began his frustrating life of virtually total paralysis.

Joni Eareckson Tada also seemed to have plenty of reason to say "Why me?"

In the summer of 1967, this vigorously healthy young woman dove off a floating platform in Chesapeake Bay and hit her head on a rock in the water. That was the sudden, shocking beginning of her life as a quadriplegic.

Phillip Yancey, in his moving book, *Where Is God When It Hurts*, offers a Christian account of suffering, including an analysis of how these two athletes dealt with their life-smashing conditions.

Why Brian? Why Joni? What do such dreadful "re-crashes" mean?

In view of the free, if partial, refusal of fallen creatures to *be*—made at the moment of creation "out of nothing"—we might wonder about the ultimate meaning of personal suffering. Does extreme suffering here in space and time mean that this sufferer must have professed an especially *no*-sided *maybe*? In other words, do we get exactly what we deserve?

No one-to-one connection exists, at least not in earthly life. At the moment of creation "out of nothing," Joni's and Brian's responses could have been more *yes*-sided than that of many who seem to have a breezy trip through this life. The new perspective on originative freedom affects directly the meaning of the mystery of suffering only the root level.

Ours was an originative, *untempted* failure in affirming freely and fully the Being of God and our own *being*. But how this works out in the branches of spatiotemporal life would seem to be impossible to surmise, not to say calculate.

We would not even be in this crash-prone world if we were not suffering from the shock of our own *maybe*—a *maybe* charged with a particular quality and degree that cannot be known consciously by us here and now. Besides, tragic events, like those that happened to Brian and Joni, could easily happen to any one of us in the future. *Maybe* they will; *maybe* they will not.

At any rate, Brian and his parents continued to believe that God wants complete physical healing in this world, and that, with enough faith and prayers, the healing would come. (Fortunately, it can be reported decades after the tragedy that a special surgical operation did help to enhance his life somewhat.)

But recovery in this world is not necessarily bodily: not as long as death is this life's physical destiny. Matter—now so passive and opaque—becomes fully active and radiant only in the resurrected life.

Joni came to understand acutely this passive condition of earthly matter. She endured pain and suffering that cut her off from her wants and desires. Her experiences reduced her to the core level of her being. At that level, she wanted to die.

Then a Christian friend called Joni's attention to her Redeemer, himself unable to move or get relief from pain on a cross. By uniting her condition with his, she actually received her paralysis and began to *be* her being, positively.

After initial bitterness and violent questioning of God's personal love for her, Joni received her Redeemer and accepted her likely unchangeable physical condition. She became positive in attitude and exquisitely creative as an artist. She learned to use a pastel pencil held between her teeth. Moreover, she has become active in ministering to countless suffering people. Her international outreach to disabled people is made through an organization called *Joni & Friends* and in other venues.

Many of her temporal gifts had been stripped away. But, like the ancient character known as Job, Joni did an active receiving of the gift of her being, along with her receiving of the Gifter. In consort with many Jews, Christians, and Muslims throughout the ages, she began living under the inspiration of Job, a Biblical archetype of suffering.

Inspired by *The Book of Job*

The Book of Job challenges our meaning for suffering. Naked, full of sores, and sitting in filth, the formerly prosperous Job had little to call his own—not even his fatherhood. His wealth was gone and his children were dead. At some point, he protested his condition and questioned God.

The answer came in a flurry of powerful words, all saying one thing: I am *God*, who are you?

Was God trying to humiliate the pitiable Job? Or was God calling Job's attention to the wealth he still had in his poverty and misery: his naked be-ing? Rather than demeaning Job, God was affirming him by saying, in effect, "I am God, be who you are as I am Who I am"?

God does not give Job a direct answer to the question *why* a good person suffers. So, Job does not understand. Nevertheless, he says, "For I know that my Redeemer liveth, and in the last day I shall rise out of the earth" (*Job* 19:25). Job somehow knew that Faith goes beyond "understanding." He did not know, as the story has it, that Satan had prompted his suffering, and that God allowed it to test his fidelity.

Some think that Job's tests and sufferings are about the hardest thing to believe in the Hebrew Testament. It sounds as though God is making Job into a mere tool to get a point across. But it is more than a story of "manipulation."

Job, like Adam and Eve and the rest of us, had originatively sinned and was being tested as a way to bring him to awareness of who he is and who he is *not*. Like us, he was fixated within space-time awareness, out of which he evaluated his life before God. So, his trials were inherent ways to call him to who he is in his nakedness of *being*—deeper than space, time, and history.

The trials were part of the compassion of God on behalf of Job's becoming illuminated about his condition, right from within the heart of his being. And, as well, the story instructs all of us on the predicament into which *we have put ourselves*.

If God was allowing Job to be put on trial to see whether he would recover from his primordial *maybe*, Job seems to have passed the test.

He did show weakness and moral bitterness at God for seeming not to protect the helpless and the righteous, and for letting the wicked prosper. But when God exposed Job's ignorance over the ultimate workings of the divine, he readily conceded.

Job never doubted God's being, authority, and power. His trust in God proved to be unyielding. It appears that he turned out to be spiritually stronger than Adam and Eve at the origin of history. Eventually, even in this world, God "rewarded" his trust.

Stories like those of Job, Joni, and Brian show that pain and suffering constitute the test of all tests. Like nothing else, suffering can bring us to our roots, and it can reduce our *maybe* to a *yes* or a *no*.

How much some people suffer in comparison to others in this world is really not ours to evaluate. We can be sure, however, that all of our suffering is ultimately just, and it is done in the immediate presence of divine Love.

The sufferer is purged of selfishness. Each person is receiving the opportunity to share in God's action of redeeming and saving.

We should not be disturbed that God seems to spare many the extremity of suffering visited upon others. We simply need to be convinced that *no* sinner suffers beyond what is just—*ultimately*.

If the Creator lets many of us "off the hook," it is not necessarily because we are better, or less unworthy, than those with decimating conditions. It might even be that we are not as worthy to suffer as they *at this time*. And it might be that we are due to suffer extremely in purgative conditions after death, once our basic *yes* has been secured. We might have to show ourselves willing—not merely wanting—to receive our share in God's salvific activity and to live out our own reparative *yes*, from the depths of our being.

Even in this life, if I am being tortured, I cannot honestly say, "I don't deserve this—ultimately." But I can cry out in anguish and in a genuine urge to have the assailant stop. He or she does not have a right to do this and, by this act of violence, is only compounding the devastation to himself or herself, to me, and to others.

Such an act ultimately symbolizes the *originative violence we all did to ourselves*. The violent results of even the slightest originative demurrer before the *infinitely loving* God are simply beyond our powers of assessment.

We must do paradoxical thinking in our Faith-knowing. What we might regard as "chance acts" of benefit or of violence are really both chance and not chance.

The good and bad that happen to us in this life include what might be called incidental benefits and harms to our existence. But they are symptoms of the supreme act of freedom in our be-ing: the *yes* and the *no* of the *maybe* that now constitutes our relationship with God.

In any case, who can say what kind or degree of suffering is too much for any of us? Who are *we* to say?

We might have to accept simply that we once freely refused to receive fully the ineffable gift of being-at-all and of being ourselves. *And if we can admit that we did freely, if partly, refuse—and have so far denied it—then we will realize that we have freely failed to receive the most intimate act of Love: creation itself.*

And no matter how much we suffer, we can hardly "make up for" that still largely-repressed, originatively free, failure in loving at the moment we were created.

The Gift of Suffering

Empowered by our struggling *yes* and by God's infinitely receptive love, we can receive suffering as a gift. This receiving can purge us of the spiritual effects of sin. A willing endurance of our trials can help us to mature, and to value what really matters.

Suffering can be turned into a prayer for oneself and for others. Our willing *yes* to the suffering we encounter makes it a reparation for sins—our own and those of others.

As we come naturally near death, we will likely experience the pain and loss of bodily functions and of emotional and spiritual consolations. Such blessings afford an opportunity for dying to self and to self-centered satisfaction.

We can yield our whole being into the only Will by whom our hearts are immaculately created. We can enter the dark night of self-dying, making it actually possible for us to be embraced by the receiving, infinite Light—a light that is *receiving, not hiding.*

Our sin is great—*greater than we can imagine or conceive.* God's mercy is infinitely greater than our sin. But our recovering goodness of will can receive the gift of suffering and reveal itself through the peace of patience.

The Quran, for instance, presents Allah as mightily compassionate and merciful. We are not necessarily punished immediately upon sinning. But we are given a time for suffering.

This revered book enjoins believers to persevere in patience and constancy. People are to vie with one another in such perseverance and to strengthen one another, in the fear of Allah, that all might prosper (AL-E-IMRAN *Surah* 200).

In union with the Will of Allah, believers are encouraged to endure trials in profound humility. The immense difficulty in so doing is acknowledged, but people who persevere in prayer with a lowly spirit will succeed. (AL-BAQARA *Surah* 2)

In the same Surah, we read about the glad tidings that are to be given to people who patiently persevere and who pledge themselves to Allah, even if afflicted with grievous adversity (AL-BAQARA *Surah* 2). Like faithful Jews and Christians, devout Muslims are to be united with the most Merciful One and with those suffering well.

For authentic theists, the only way to recover from the originative crash—whether recognized as such or not—is through a positive receiving of the pain and suffering that comes our way against our liking and wanting. Receiving-with-God our suffering is necessary for salvation—for ultimate healing. Failing to receive suffering is rejecting God's gift of mercy—no matter how often we claim to be "saved."

We were not created originatively to want or to like suffering. We were created to will the good freely: to be and to be fully ourselves, resulting immediately in perfect bliss. Had we done so we would not have suffered at all—at least, not without our free consent. But we said *maybe* and crashed, deforming ourselves—becoming shattered beings of spoiled beauty and power. So, now we are called, not to want or to like suffering, but to receive it and to be willing to let it awaken our be-ing and our being-*with* God.

There is no way for God really to save us by smoothing over our primordial self-wrought condition. God is not a "cover-up artist." God is a Savior, not a *Salver*. God creates and recreates always from within. Our sin requires a "re"-creation by God, who among other things brings us into and through a struggling, space-time world and its accompanying spiritual, moral, mental, emotional, and physical afflictions.

Without our final *yes* to God, through acts of repentant reception of God's redeeming life—occasioned by every test that comes our way from within and without—we *cannot possibly* be restored to the potential glory of our beginning.

Upon our death, the full *yes*-power of gifted originative freedom will be engaged once again, for the final determination. And who is to say what will be the enormity of suffering and pain, at that moment, through which we must willingly pass?

In that final moment, we will be offered the critical opportunity of willing afresh our love for all. And, if we do will so, we will be received joyfully forever within the heart of God.

Chapter 13

The Final Choice

Who are we willing to be—forever? Not wishing. Not wanting. *Willing.*

By our final choice we will decide. The choice is *not* God's, but ours and only ours. Yours for you; mine for me.

Mother Teresa of Calcutta revealed something stark about the deepest of human choices. She was giving a talk at a National Prayer Breakfast for U.S. government officials (Feb. 3, 1994). She told how her Sisters had picked up a man from the streets. He was infested with worms. And after they had brought him under their care, he remarked how he had been living like an animal, but that he was now happy to die like an angel, loved and cared for. Once they had removed all the worms from his body, he smiled and said he was going home to God. With that, he died.

Mother Teresa then commented, "It was so wonderful to see the greatness of that man who could speak without blaming anybody. Like an angel—this is the greatness of people who are spiritually rich even when they are materially poor."

A simple human person, while being eaten by worms, can be on the verge of heaven. Experiencing the infestation does not feel good, but the final choice goes into and through the feeling-experience and beyond.

A greedy and complex person, while feasting daily on gourmet dinners and indulging in all manner of fleshly pleasures, can be on the verge of hell. Experiencing earthly delights can lead to peak pleasures. But one's underlying final choice goes right through felt experience into the character of the self and its commitments or lack of them.

Whenever I am feeling good, I might be thinking, "This is great! Of course, I am choosing to go to heaven." But if I were all alone, starving and shivering in one of earth's back alleys, then what?

I can feel bad, while willing the good. For instance, I can feel terror and still choose to endure the smoke, heat, and fiery risk of a burning building while trying to save a child's life. Or I can feel good, while willing the bad. I can even cheer the misfortune of an adversary, and wish him still worse kinds of trouble—and feel good about it.

So my deepest, truest choice right now does not depend ultimately on how I feel or experience.

My feelings, however, are extremely important. They are like my circumstances. My feelings are always with me and are always a challenge.

At times, they buoy me up and allow me to "put my heart into" my actions of doing good for others and enjoying the gifts of life. At other times, my feelings serve to manipulate, or even to tempt me to swerve off-center, and to wander away from my better self. Every emotional situation tests the character of my choosing to be either who I *am* or who I am *not*.

Every Moment

The will of God speaks in every moment. But so do the wills of all other persons—angelic and human. We are challenged at all times and everywhere by forces within and without. Yet, our fixation on time tends to block out eternity, and our preoccupation with space tends to lock out spiritual vision.

At every moment, we can say that we are confronted by God's will, but also by what is *not* God's will. Still, God always wills that we say *yes* to the being of good and evil—that we acknowledge the reality of what is, whether good or bad or both.

The present moment is utterly special. It "contains" every other moment in time and eternity. This moment relates intimately with all other moments. Yet it constitutes a unique "configuration" of these "momentous" influences. So, in the present moment, we are relating with eternity, but also, variously with the past, the present, and even the future.

What is so unique about this moment now?

Absolutely unique is the way that we are relating to everyone and everything that is. This moment is critical. We cannot relate at any moment in the past or the future the same way we relate now.

The twin features of every being as a *being*, whether created or uncreated, a□re necessarily influential. This present moment is, like *every being*, both unique and super-related to all else. Everything that *is* bears these two correlative attributes: uniqueness and super-relatedness. No sameness. No unrelatedness.

Each moment is overflowing with God's will. If we and others have mucked up our lives, then we will bring to ourselves and to all others this muddled condition of good and bad in so many facets. And that is part of God's will: that we *receive* the way we are at every moment. *God* does not *will* the super-congeries of conditions present at every moment. The cumulative planetary and supernatural forces of personal will did that willing. God's will is that each person receive this moment as it is, and launch from there in love.

Paradoxically, God's will necessarily includes the reality of our past validations and violations of God's will. God wills that both our good will and our ill will, along with their effects, be the true basis—the "launching pad," as it were—for effective loving now. God wills that, at all times and everywhere, we exercise our ability to love to the fullest extent we can. Anything less is not God's will.

The will of God does not involve us in assuming, at all times, postures of prayer. But it does mean to "pray always" with one's heart, no matter what may be the work we are doing.

The will of God demands a deepening *yes* to the being of what is. *Yes*, especially to our abilities to change our attitudes from unloving to loving. Our grace-filled potencies are real and are to be willed ever more fully.

Also, and most paradoxically, we are called to accept whatever is evil in its *reality*, without willing any more evil than already exists. We can attempt to acknowledge, without repression, whatever is evil—just as it is and *no more*. Whether conscious or unconscious, denial of what is—whatever it is—is another "bad start."

We are called to will simultaneously whatever is evil and whatever is good—including especially our potencies for good. We must become committed to willing the good to be ever more and the evil never to be or to be ever less.

Such is the meaning of love, solid and true. *Evil must be admitted by us to be in our lives as in others'*—and that means that we are willing for the evil (that already is) to *be*. If we are *not* willing for the evil to be and to be what it is—evil—we participate in our originative sin all the more, by denial.

Evil Really Is

After all, evil cannot be otherwise; since it already is the way it is or has been. But we need to refrain from repressing the way it is. In not repressing evil, we can be freer to be really good. So, it is, paradoxically, profoundly good to acknowledge—within us—all the evil, as well as all the good. True humility requires admission of *both* our originative sin *and* our creation as perfect persons.

We can act authentically by letting the good transform us, and by alleviating, at least, some of the effects of evil. But this can happen only on the condition of our receiving—accepting *willingly*, not *wanting*—the evil that we know and experience, along with the good. Denial only keeps evil festering.

Past ideas of evil in the theist tradition have been helpful, but also failing. In the Christian tradition, theologians have had a difficult time recognizing the *real being* of evil. They tend to follow Aquinas and many others who define evil as the undue absence of good, as the deprivation of what ought to be.

But is that deprivation itself *real*? Does it really exist or is it merely a kind of absence of being? Does deprivation or evil really *be*? If so, it would seem that God is its creator, since God is held to be the Creator of all that *is*.

God, however, is *not* the creator of *all* that *is*. Rather, God is the creator of all that *perfectly is*. Most of "our world" is, but is *not fully*. The beings around us are *part*-beings, not *whole*-beings. Only persons are whole beings—able to receive and welcome themselves and all others. Only persons are the result of God's direct creation out of nothing.

The traditional notion of being has lacked the realization of the *intrinsic receptivity* of every being that is created by God out of nothing. Nor has there been much appreciation of the intrinsic infinite receptivity in the Divine Being.

Receptivity is one of the transcendental characteristics of personal being. Even God receives evil as it *is* and as it is *really caused* by failing created persons. And so we can say, God creates beings (persons) who create themselves: by acts of good or evil and by acts of virtue or vice.

These features of good and bad, coming to *be* by the power of created freedom, are real. They are realities that were afforded by God's gift of created freedom in giving us the *power to make be*. Not to "make be" out of nothing, but out of their own perfectly gifted being. Here we could say that evil really exists, but does *not* fully *be*.

The origin of moral good and bad—including the primal moral act of disobedience in the Garden—is rooted in our primal act of truly personal, originative freedom at the very moment of creation out of nothing. This signature act is so real—and so repressed—that it is "miss taken" for being less than real and for "not existing." But the existence of this act—if unrepented—will last forever.

Does this personal, originative sin represent the deprivation of being? Deprivation of full being, *yes*. And it is quite real. The self-frustration of hell—as well as the self-fulfillment of heaven—is forever. There is real being in heaven, and in hell.

Our Deepest Choice

In this world, however, our whole human condition is a little bit like the sentiments expressed in an old love song. The crooner sang about the beloved's lips saying *no*, while the eyes were saying *yes*. Whether the "eyes have it" or whether the observer is just reading into the eyes what he wants to see, there can sometimes be a huge gulf between our outward deportment and our inmost decision-making.

Only God can fully know and heal the disparity. We ourselves can try, but we can gain only marginal success "on our own."

Like a steadily flowing stream beneath the surface of the ground, the deepest choice of my life underlies all the other (relatively surface) choices. At this underground level of my being, I cannot *not* choose. At this depth, to be is to decide about my being.

My will, however, is polluted and damaged by the contaminants of self-deception coming from my originative willing. Even so, it is still a free will capable of everlasting commitment.

Choosing to be the person God gave me to be is choosing to be a *gift* of God. This incomparable gift is, at present, self-diminished and recovering in God's grace. By choosing to be a gift of God and living it out as gift, I am trending toward confirming the *yes*, given in my originative *maybe*.

By choosing *not* to be the person God gave me to be—a perfectly free person, who is now self-defaced—I am choosing *not* to be a gift of God. I am choosing not to admit my radical faltering and need for recovery. By that neglectful manner of being and deciding I am trending toward confirming the *no* in my originative *maybe*.

My deepest choice is my decision to be or not to be who I am—to receive or not to receive my being as it is being given. This choice is not a determination to be what I want to be. My wants are not at issue here, only my will. Wanting and willing are different. Wanting is contingent. Willing is decisive.

My deepest willing—to be or not to be—is rarely, if ever, fully conscious. But it is no less real. And my conscious everyday wants and choices can reveal to me at least something of what I am actually deciding below the surface. Pondering the quality of my conscious choices, I can detect, perhaps with probability, my deeper direction.

Besides, willing or not willing to be who I am comes in degrees. At any given time, I can be more or less willing. But I can never escape the freedom and activity of making this choice.

Choosing to be who I am, with a pure and simple willing, is to confirm the *yes* in my originative *maybe*, at least to some significant degree. Being unwilling to choose to be who I am—insisting on what I might want to be—is to confirm the *no* in the *maybe*-creature that I am, at least to some degree.

How strange that I am here—somewhere between receiving the full goodness of being and *not* receiving the gift at all. I am now immersed in millions of tiny choices about everyday things. But the *attitude* I take toward even the minimal choices is *itself a choice* that

I make about who I *will* to be. My attitude is a "choice-atude"—an utterly free stance toward God and being.

Somewhere deep within me, I must be saying, "*Maybe* it is good to be, but *maybe* not." If I really stop and face myself with this *maybe*, what do I hear myself saying? How is the core of my being responding in the midst of all the feelings and events that test me?

These challenges give me an opportunity to move out of my self-inflicted, passive *maybe* and to grow toward an active, grateful *yes*. But if I do not get into the habit of saying *yes*, I am trekking along the road of *no* in my heart.

Maybe—the attitude of my crash in be-ing—is moving toward either one of its poles: toward either simple, strong affirmation or simple hard negation. *Maybe* does *not* last longer than a lifetime.

The End of Maybe

Stranded between *yes* and *no*, I am now in the condition of saying, "*Maybe* I will and *maybe* I will *not*." I am stalling. My indecision is the wavering kind of *yes*-and-*no*.

But there is another kind of *yes* and *no* in our redemptive life. We ought always to adhere to this *yes* and *no*. We are called to say *yes* to doing the good as good and *no* to doing the bad as bad. This is both a *good yes* and a *good no*. Since we have sinned, it is a required remedy. *Yes*, there is no *maybe* about it.

At the same time that we are living in the *maybe* world, we are also living and judging from within the *non-maybe* world. In this thoroughly other, but not separate, world of ultimate meaning, "*yes* and *no*" is *not* the same as "maybe." From that world of ultimate decision comes our "take" on the world of *maybe*. (For Christians, the *yes* is to Jesus as Savior as in 2 *Corinthians* 1:19. For Jews the *yes* is to Yahweh. For Muslims, the *yes* is to Allah.)

I am not in the midst of *maybe* in order to remain indecisive. I am here to decide. Is the answer of my whole being *yes*? Or is it *no*?

Besides, *not* to decide is to decide *not* to decide. And that willed indecision—is a virtual *no*. A decisive indecision.

Death might come early or late in life and be something for which I am relatively prepared or not. But my state of willed decision or of willed indecision, flowing underneath life at the moment of death, will determine whether I am basically a *yes* or basically a *no*.

Being conceived in space and time gave me the opportunity of recovering from my prime indecision about who I am willing to be. Death ends my crucial options forever. Death will consummate my challenge. I will have to decide one way or the other.

Maybe death will come years from *now*. Maybe it will come tomorrow. Maybe it will come within a few minutes. Whenever it comes, that will be the end of *maybe*: my last occasion for a full *yes*.

Reincarnation?

Millions, however, depend on reincarnation—with its continuing round of conceptions, births, and deaths. But that is an imagined way of catering to my present indecision. Reincarnation gives too much credit to *maybe*. It tries to make God just as indecisive as I am.

Opting for reincarnation says, in effect, "I will finally serve God with my whole heart only if and when I am ready to do so." Such a condition, placed upon the absolutely decisive Love by whom I was created, stems from the *maybe*-attitude that I created originatively. The attitude of reincarnation reveals an overbearing commitment to a most subtle kind of selfishness.

This indefinite condition is mine, not God's. If I commit myself to having an indeterminate platform (*maybe*) for saying *yes* to God, so that I can decide if and when I will ever be ready, how can God *save* me at all? The idea of having an indefinite cycle of rewards and punishments (*karma*) from one life into another, right here in this world, keeps God waiting on me. If I thought that reincarnation were true, I would be asserting that God could *not* be *God* without me.

The karmic claim is that I am subject to reward and penalty for the endeavors of some previous life in this world. But the transcendent supremacy of God's commands could never be duly honored by this attitude. In fact, the mass of people who believe in reincarnation do not seem to be looking for, much less discerning, God as a *person*. Nor is God the one to whom they are totally subject.

Reincarnationists are saying, in effect, that with each reincarnation the "maybe" condition of the soul, found in the previous life, was not enough. They think that what is needed is further reward for just deeds and further punishment for unjust deeds.

But this "maybe condition" can, in principle, go on forever. There is no final choice on the horizon—neither final reward nor final punishment. There is *no* horizon. As in moral relativism, where truth is relative to the disposition of each ego, my self remains king in every decision—whether good or bad.

Then there are the process theologians and philosophers who say that God, too, is in process—not just creatures. These academics only strengthen thereby the subtle *maybe*, found in reincarnation. They say implicitly, "Keep this process going so I will not have to make that final choice. After all, I am not ready. As long as the process keeps on going and going, I do not have to decide finally."

By this way of seeing it, we can continue to think that we are being "dynamic," while our lives are being treated unconsciously as remarkable processes of "dynamic *passivity*."

In pantheism of whatever type, we find ourselves defining God by the image of humankind, rather than the reverse. In process thought, as in karmic reincarnations, God is not transcendent. God is simply "immanent"—an "immanence" that is not a true withinness. There is an identity of God and creature, either wholly or in part.

"Furthermore," believers in process seem to say, "A God who is radically other than I is not *with* me. A God who is not in process with me is really absent." They do not realize that the so-called absent God is really the absent creature. The creature is hiding—in many self-delusional ways—from the intimate presence of the One who is both infinitely-other and infinitely-within.

The "process God" constitutes a projection of preferred indecision; it conceals a static mentality trying to compensate for itself. Among other things, process thinkers overlook a simple pastoral principle: if you ever find yourself more distant from God, *know* that it was not *God* who moved. Moreover, according to the new perspective, any distance from God that we might find was made *possible* by *our* originative distortion of freedom.

The Crucial Now

In the presence of the living God, by faith and reason, I can know that every "now" is the moment of my final choice. Now is always crucial. Time and eternity are united especially within the present moment.

All my past choices, good and bad, repented or unrepented, are influencing how I am choosing *now*. All the decisions of my life are focused toward my final choice.

If I would die *now*, my self-determination before God will be as unending as my new, timeless life or existence. If I die in ten years, my choice at that time will be my everlasting destiny. Right at the moment of my death, am I more *yes* than *no*, or more *no* than *yes*?

This concern should turn me toward my roots. Therein I can foster deeper growth in union with God. But such depth-realization could be immensely uncomfortable. My preference—to relax and to enjoy the branches of living—might be caught up short. If I realize that my destiny is now, not later, I am pressed *now* to think about death, my roots, and my final choice.

Blandly living out my *maybe* is so much easier. "Maybe I will think about it tomorrow. Maybe next year. There is still time. There will ever be time."

But I am as much within eternity right now as I will ever be in this life. Time is totally within eternity. No injustice is done to me if I die in three minutes. This very instant, I am able fully to receive God's power and to say fully or mainly *yes* to being who I am with God. This present moment is all I really need or have.

The next hour and the next day will only test me again and again. If I keep implicitly saying *no*, not even God can *make* me say *yes*. God can only give me an opportunity to say *yes*, and thereby to receive the infinite assurance of unconditional love—granted that I actually *say* this *yes*. God would *not* be God without this infinite respect for my God-gifted finite freedom.

Making me say *yes* would be unjust and impossible for God. As C. S. Lewis remarked in *The Great Divorce*, "There are only two kinds of people in the end: those who say to God, 'Thy will be done,' and those to whom God says, in the end, 'Thy will be done'" (69).

Even from their setting in the Garden, well before the banishment from paradise, Adam and Eve were challenged by God not to confirm themselves in the attitude of *maybe*. "Of every tree of paradise thou shalt eat: but of the tree of knowledge of good and evil, thou shalt not eat. For in what day soever thou shalt eat of it, thou shalt die the death" (*Genesis* 2:16-17).

In other words, do *not* eat of the "Maybe Tree." But once they chose to unite *to their own substance* the fruit of the "Maybe Tree" by consuming it, Adam and Eve effectively banished themselves from the Garden.

God said, "Thy will be done," sending us all tracking into the *maybe* world of space and time that was caused by our originative failures in freedom.

Many are spending their lives here in joyful service that enables them to express their repentant commitment to the fullness of God's will. Others may only seize, at the moment of death, their final opportunity to say *yes*. In their heart of hearts, they could be making that commitment at levels deeper than are perceivable by those who stand around their bedside.

In any event, God vowed, "....Thou shalt die the death" (*Genesis* 2:17). The promise that God honored in the Garden by casting out Adam and Eve would be fulfilled. They would live in the *maybe* world itself that they helped to cause—the world that ends in death.

Chapter 14

The Purpose-Gifted Life

My final choice, then, is not simply one that comes at the end of a "horizontal" line of choices. It is not final in that way. *Finis* (the Latin root of "final") can refer to a linear, temporal kind of end, but it also means purpose. Purpose is immediately meaningful and, as it were, "vertical." My purpose—why I exist, living in this outcast world—is *now*. Not just in the future. Purpose is as deep and high as "Why am I?"

Am I here simply to do my own thing in my own way? For me, then, God would be essentially irrelevant, and at best a sparring partner. God would have to say to me "Thy will be done. Have it your way."

But without God I cannot honestly say, "I am." Not just for tomorrow, but vertically forever, as this created person, my true purpose is "*Thy* will be done." My final choice is a purpose choice. I am faced with it *right now*.

Whose will am I choosing: God's or my own? Even if my will is good, it is not simply good because it is mine, but because it is in accord with God's will. Am I recovering from *maybe*, or perhaps am I secretly nursing it?

Loving Is Saying *Yes* on the Way

Recovery from *maybe* can only come through my continuing attempts to say *yes* to the potential for doing good, and *no* to the possibilities of doing evil. Saying *yes* with all my heart at every moment is the reason I am here. God's will for me is that I be like God, who is Love. But what does it mean to be like God, to love?

We can form a central definition of love common to all persons: human, angelic, and divine. Love is *willing the truest and best for both self and all others, whatever the cost*. For divine persons, the willing of love is infinite, unlimited. For both angelic and human persons, willing is naturally limited—but not necessarily defective.

For fully *yes*-saying created persons, the willing is perfect. But for us *maybe*-saying humans, love is not perfect and comes only in degrees of willing: willing *more or less intensely* the truest and the best, as effectively as we can determine, with our wobbly minds and hearts.

This common definition of love applies diversely to the various directions of love, such as creature-Creator love, parent-child love, spousal love, friend-to-friend love, and so forth. Every genuinely loving relationship involves the willingness of the parties to act for the truest and the best, according to the particular relationship and despite the cost. To the extent that such willingness is lacking, so is the love.

In its roots, love establishes the dynamic condition of *being*: a disposition toward everyone, not just toward one or a few. I cannot will the truest and best for you and not will the same for everyone else.

I can and do love some people more *richly* than others, but not more *intensely*. My spouse and family members, as well as friends and relatives, mean more to me than people I have never met. I have more feeling for, and experiences common to, those who are closer to me.

But *willing* the truest and best is not a matter of feeling nor of merely durational valuing. The willing that is love is timeless and spaceless, no matter how much time and space it takes to develop it.

Willing the truest and best is mysteriously varied. Even in their smallest deeds, some people intensely will what is best for everyone. Others, in their most notable enterprises, might not even will the good for anyone at all, including themselves. They do only what feels good for themselves. For them, loving means little more than strongly *liking* someone or something.

At any given moment, each person can increase or decrease the *intensity of willing* the good. For example, I can increase my love for my best friend. At the same time, that increase will necessarily include a proportionate increase in my love for *all* others, including people I will never meet—even including my enemies. The light and warmth of my love then radiates more effectively out to the whole world.

This increase in *good will* toward one and all might be illustrated by the way a miner works.

Think of a miner's hat with a light on top. Suppose there were, in a room, many people wearing hats with floodlights on top that emitted light, not simply in one direction, but in all directions. And assume that the intensity of light from each person could be regulated by a rheostat type of switch at the waistline whereby each could, at will, gradually increase or decrease the intensity of his or her light.

If one person increases the intensity of individual light, it radiates in all directions equally, while adding to the light in the room for everyone. Of course, those who are, at the time, physically closer to that person receive more light than do those who are farther away. But the proportion is constant. If the one who is farthest away moves closer, the same intensity of light grows brighter for that person. At any given moment, there is just one degree of intensity of light coming from each person. All persons benefit in a proportionately equal way.

In everyday life, people often think that when they intensify their love for *someone* they do so by excluding—even hating—others who are seen as the loved one's enemies. But we are called to *love* our enemies, not to hate them. How can anyone really say, "I love my friends and hate my enemies," or "I love my friends and hate their enemies," without slipping into the emotion-driven meanings for love?

As beings trustfully resting in God, we must will the truest and best for our enemies, as well as for our friends. The truest and best for our enemies, and for our friends as well, might include, in God's Providence, some devastating things happening to them and to us. But, to the extent that we were really loving, the *wreckage* would be what we were *willing*, though not wanting, to occur.

By contemplating the good in *anyone*, I can dispose myself for increasing my love for everyone. The challenge is paradoxical.

On the one hand, whenever I increase my love for the one who is affectionately closest to me—*if* it is really love and not simply more affection—I increase my love proportionately for everyone.

On the other hand, whenever I increase my love for a stranger at my doorstep, I likewise increase my love for my best friend and everyone else. Even the one who is farthest away from me in being, space, and time is given a proportionate increase in love. Love of neighbor is both universal and proportionate.

Many confuse loving with liking. I like my best friend more than anyone else in the world. But I do not love my best friend more, proportionately. Friendship is really a matter of loving *plus liking*. In addition to loving, friendship is the desire to be with, share with, and enjoy the company of the other. But there is no genuine friendship without love at its core. Liking, alone, is not enough.

We can love people we do not like. We can love our enemies, while we *thoroughly dislike* them. We can even love, yet dislike intensely, a Hitler or a Stalin, even as we indeed hate what they did to themselves, as well as to others.

But we cannot be friends with someone we *do not like* and with whom we have no desire to share. We can love such a person, nonetheless, by willing the truest and best for him or her.

In order to give love the "acid" test, we might think of the person whom we dislike the most in this world. How well do we love him or her? That is the degree of *real* love we are doing for our closest friends—and for ourselves.

Loving our neighbor, even as we love ourselves, is not simply the question. It is a reality that we *cannot* love our neighbor any more than we love ourselves. nor can we love ourselves any more than we love our neighbor.

Christians believe that, with a couple of historical exceptions, we are sinners and somehow enemies of God. At the same time, we are striving for friendship with our divine Friend. The expenditure of redemption is borne in the wounds and suffering of Jesus. Christians affirm that the Savior's suffering was caused not only by our sins, but also by his love—loving us to the core of our being, even in our sins, and despite the cost to him.

Saying *yes* to our *being* involves the root kind of love. This love wills—at a given time, to some degree or other—only the truest and best for everyone at once. This manner of love does not deceive anyone. This love is not greedy or possessive, nor self-serving, nor unchaste. It is a wholesome *yes* to the goodness of every being.

We ought to keep in mind that saying *yes* or *no* attitudinally in daily life is not-at-all a matter of quantity. Our attitudes are not measurable in terms of the frequency of saying, *yes*, *no*, or *maybe*. Nor does the duration of these determinations of will necessarily signify anything about their quality.

So, it is possible to discern only vaguely the underlying abiding quality. And it is even possible that the quality of a given person's response to *being* might even seem to us dull perceivers like that of a *yes*, when it is more of a *no*. Or vice versa.

Saying *No* on the Way

Along the way of life, the attitude of saying *no* takes many forms.

When the baby cries for feeding or diapering at 2 AM, the parents or the caregiver might decide to be unsympathetic. They might even rationalize, "That child needs to be trained to wait."

The baby, however, ought not to be treated as if he or she were older. A baby needs to be babied while a baby, so that he or she will not need babying even as an adult.

We somehow know this to be true, but we can always deny what we know, and opt for cruel indifference: a way of saying *no*. That *no* is not only to the baby, but also to *everyone* else, despite perhaps a kindly facial expression.

If we deny service to any one person in need who is within our practical reach of responsibility, we deny it *somehow* to all. We say to anyone and everyone, "If you were that child at this time, I would be willing to ignore you as well." Whatever we do to the least of our brothers and sisters in the human community, so we do, by primary attitude and intention, to all and to God.

But saying both *yes* and *no* in the *branches* of life is not at all the same as saying either *yes* or *no* at the *roots*. For instance, one can be a gracious, positive, charming person in everyday life, and yet be indifferent to the truest and best for self and others. Or a person can have "rough edges" much of the time, not being good at expressing feelings and meanings. But that person can still care deeply.

Wishing people well is not necessarily a sign that the one doing the wishing is on the way to saying *yes*. Love is *willing* the good—not wishing nor even wanting it. Wishing is often superficial and frivolous. Many times it is "truly meant" as long as it does not *cost* anything in time and effort. People usually want others around them to feel good; otherwise they themselves will feel bad. So the wish for happiness given to others can be a way of saying, "Let's all *feel* good, without necessarily having to *be* good."

Genuine love—love that wills the truest and best—certainly wills *being* good, as well as *being open* to "feeling good." But wishing for another person the happiness of "feeling good" might not include real love. "Have a nice day," might mean merely that: politeness, pleasantness, and little more.

Wanting can also be rootless. I want a new automobile. I want you to win the lottery. I want peace on earth. On and on. Wanting, or desiring, is filled with intentions of self-acquisition, even when the "want" is to benefit someone else. I want because I want. But the crucial test of love is what I am *willing* to be and do for the true good of everyone.

Beneath the surface of my mind and heart there is always the "underground" stream of determinative willing ("choosing"). If in the depths I decide that I am here in this world mainly for the good feelings of "number one"—me—then I am on the path of saying *no*. I do not even love myself—much less God or anyone else. I do not really care about the purpose of my being, as a gift of the person of God.

To the extent that I am satisfied with wishing or wanting what is truest and best, rather than willing from my heart and my behavior, my will remains ill. I am not habitually saying *yes*, and am probably saying basically *no*.

If I am on the *yes* trail, I am depending on the infinite power of God to sustain my willing the good—not just wishing or wanting it. But, if I am on the *no* trail, I do not "need" the grace of God to wish others well or to want what is best for me. I can choose these things entirely on my own. Willful self-interest refuses to be dependent on the power and purpose of God.

If I do not *actually receive* God's will, I will be willing to say *no*, even while perhaps wishing or wanting to say *yes*. Only by being-*with* God can I actually will to say *yes*. I was originatively created to be independent-*with* God, but by my primal *maybe* I am now quite *dependent on* God. I need God's grace desperately. And it is mine for the willing of it.

In saying essentially *yes*—even if weakly—I am *independently* dependent on God. In saying essentially *no*—even if weakly—I am *independently* independent *from* God.

If I attempt to find out with complete certainty which underlying course I am taking, I am likely to be moving along the well-worn path of saying *no*. By trying to gain control of my life, I am losing it. Becoming overly concerned with "where I'm at" draws me into wishing and wanting to love, rather than willing it.

Of course, it is good to try to discern the "way of *yes*" and how to maintain it. But hanging on for my own sake and getting anxious about my basic choice diverts my will away from God's will.

At the conscious level, I need to keep faithful to willing a loving *yes*. Then my whole unconscious life—including especially the preconscious—will be sent a heartfelt message. By letting go of my ego-concerns and by receiving the grace of my being, within the grace of God's Personhood, I become empowered to say the *yes* of love—of willing fully the truest and best.

Will It Be *Yes* or *No*?

When we were born, we came forth from our mother's womb into the wider world. Of course, while we were in the womb, we were influenced by this larger world—without our knowing it. We were there already. We were participating in the extra-uterine world even before birth. Then, we were born and we saw our mother and others, face to face.

Similarly, each one of us is now headed, at death, to go forth from the womb of this world of *both* good *and* evil (both *yes* and *no*) into the everlasting world of *either* good *or* evil (either *yes* or *no*). The *maybe* that trapped us into this condition of *yes*-and-*no*, of good and evil, will end in either a final life of *yes* or a final existence of *no*.

Our opportunity for a decision will be finished. Our determination will have been made. We will be born from the womb of this world *either* alive *or* dead—either toward absolute wholeness in be-ing or toward its effective disengagement. The passive-reactive matter of our body—not the originative matter—will be shed as we are born decisively into everlasting being. The "separated" stuff (the corpse) will be buried as an afterbirth by our mourners.

Our present condition relative to eternity has been partly revealed already by analogy with our prebirth existence. In the mortal womb of matter and motion (life on earth), we are like a child in the womb of his or her mother. We are gestating within space and time, even while existing in the "wider world" of eternity.

But, unlike a pre-birth child, we are making perhaps millions of choices over a lifetime. Our whole bodily life in space and time is "placenta-like." Yet, in this larger "existence-serving life" we cannot possibly develop our physical and emotional capacities to the fullest.

The promises of God, however, gift us with hope. We can go into the next world maimed physically, emotionally, and spiritually while our hearts are saying mainly a *yes* to the gift of being and to the Giver.

If so, in this birth (at death) we will be delivered toward the good of heaven. In virtue of our sincere commitment, God will be able to remove our deficiencies and renew our original active potency for absolute love. The worms and maggots of our lifelong spiritual lethargy can be removed even as we repentantly express our love.

If, however, our hearts are saying mainly a *no* to the gift of being and to the Giver—despite the finest development of body and mind in this world—we will be self-destined for spiritual and ontological dysfunction at death—slipping willingly into the evil of hell. We will have allowed the ruler of that chaotic existence to deceive us by appearing perhaps as an angel of light.

Birth was the closure of our mother's pregnancy with us. Death, however, will be the end of our pregnancy with ourselves, and of our potential for recovery from sin. As the "umbilical" connection to this redemptive world is cut, we will leave our self-imprisonment in space and time by being either transformed or transfixed.

Many Christians believe that we could well be subject to purgation after death. According to this view, the same goodness of being that gave us the possibility to recover and to say *yes* provides us room to clear out the effects of saying *maybe*.

Likewise purged would be the results of saying some temporary *no*'s during our life in this world. This purgatory would seem to be like a detoxification process. The duration or intensity of the process would depend on the extent and acerbity of accumulated moral and spiritual toxins.

We all die with basically *yes* or *no* in our hearts. Even the newly conceived babies, who die before their conscious exercise of choice, do come to the 'birth' of their death with an emphasis on *yes* or *no*, *carried over from* their originative *maybe*.

We do not fully know what happens at death. But, as indicated earlier, there could be at that moment, for all of us, including those who died in their mothers' wombs, a fleeting, yet full, opportunity. In that flash of final freedom, we would be called to say: "I'm sorry. Let it be done to me according to Your will." Or we could say, "My will be done."

Whether we live here for eighty years or eighty seconds, this life is the result of our having said freely an originative *maybe*. That first response was uttered at the non-temporal moment we were created as perfect, finite persons by the interpersonally loving God. We did our receiving of being with particular degrees of emphasis on either the *yes* or the *no*. Some said *maybe* with a *yes*-emphasis, others with a *no*-emphasis.

That prime act of originative freedom, our pristine root choice, was full and free and ours. So, at that moment, we did have enough self-determination to make our final choice, even if we were not granted the mercy of living a long life in the good-and-evil cosmos.

But we had not fully determined ourselves. We were decisively indecisive. So, now we are barely able to entertain the suspicion that we have repressed our indeterminate reception of being. Nor do we, therefore, know the extent of that failure. Was it weakly a *no*, and mainly a *yes*? Or was it weakly a *yes*, and mainly a *no*?

In any event, the Supreme Being, who creates perfect beings "out of nothing," brings redemption to all those who require it. And God invites, with infinite love, our *receiving* of this redemption: our *salvation*.

But who of us will be willing to *receive adequately* and thereby to recover effectively? How *authentically* are we loving?

At the moment of death, we will be born into the "outer world" of eternity. We will enter committed, like the angels, either fully to good or fully to evil.

Any purgation at that point will be of those who, by their final *yes*, are fully destined for permanent union. The final purification of the *no* in their residual *maybe*-saying will be a most joyful, if awesome, suffering for the sake of attaining a total interpersonal readiness to enter everlasting life. There is *no* "halfway house" in the immediate presence and glory of God. We must become immaculately pure in order to enter. We must "come clean."

Persons whose final self-determination is more *no* than *yes* will enter hell. Their insufficient *yes* will be self-condemnatory. In the midst of his parables, Jesus might have been referring somewhat to this condition when he said, "For he that hath, to him shall be given: and he that hath not, that also which he hath shall be taken away from him" (*Mark* 4:25). The deficient willing done by the person's weak *yes*□-attainment shall vanish forever in the darkness of the *no*.

People's unwillingness to accept the reality of hell is instructive. Many rage against God for "creating hell." But their rage is part of the fuel of hell. It is misplaced and would require therapeutic help, both psychological and religious. We need to understand that God's wrath does not literally create hell; the created person's own self-hatred does. One can shut out oneself, as well as any and all others. "God's wrath" is not the source of everlasting frustration. One's own willingness to be deceived can "do the job." The person would decide to continue in self-deception, rather than receive truth and thereby repent of originative and subsequent sin.

Believing in hell is one of the big tests as to whether we really believe in the freedom of the created person. Being self-determining as persons, we must be independent with respect to God, so that we might receive our being effectively. Not even infinite love can do it for us. We receive or reject salvation *independently*.

Believing that hell is a reality likewise magnifies our sense of the goodness of heaven. We know *why* the redemptive covenant was made.

At any rate, good-and-evil terminates with death that is a new birth. Then *either* good *or* evil begins. No longer will there be any temptation to indulge in the tree of the knowledge of good and evil. And we will have made our final choice. We will *be* forever whom we determined ourselves to *be*.

Chapter 15

Light within the Mystery

God promises that light will come from out of the darkness. The prophet Isaiah announces:

> "Deal thy bread to the hungry, and bring the needy and the harbourless into thy house: when thou shalt see one naked, cover him, and despise not thy own flesh.
>
> Then shall thy light break forth as the morning, and thy health shall speedily arise, and thy justice shall go before thy face, and the glory of the Lord shall gather thee up....
>
> When thou shalt pour out thy soul to the hungry, and shalt satisfy the afflicted soul then shall thy light rise up in darkness, and thy darkness shall be as the noonday" (*Isaiah* 58:7-8,10).

In the Quran, the message of Allah is clear. Surah 14 begins by claiming that the holy book brings us forth from darkness into light as the way to God.

Light is the quintessential hope of all the children of Abraham: Hebrew, Christian, and Islamic peoples. Light can come forth from the darkness of our own making, if we reach out with love to the homeless, the hungry, the naked. Our love calls forth the light.

The light is religious and revelational. It is also philosophical, and deeply so. The light is beingful (ontological). All three theistic traditions can relate to Sacred Revelation through the natural light of reason, as well as through God's direct gift of Faith.

Even prime Greek philosophers, who were not theists of special revelation, celebrated the light. With the story about prisoners in a cave, Socrates and Plato portray the human condition by presenting a parable. They imagined how some lifelong captives were shackled in a row—unable to move their heads—watching shadows moving along the wall of their chamber. They naturally assumed that these images were the only ultimate realities. And they were locked into evaluating the passing formations. They kept trying to predict which shadow would appear next.

Then came the liberator. He set free a prisoner. After experiencing considerable difficulty, the liberated one was able to climb out of the cave's passageway into the sunlight.

After his eyes had adjusted to the brightness, he saw much greater realities, and went back into the cave to break the news to the others. He told them that they were fixed on observing and talking about mere shadows and that genuine reality was outside the cave in a world of brilliant sunshine.

Those in the cave did not like what they were hearing. They did not know what a cave was, much less that they were in one. And they refused to make the painful effort to wrench away from their chains and pastimes, to recognize their imprisoned status, and to come home to the light.

Instead, they ridiculed their informant. A prophet of wisdom was thoroughly rejected. Unenlightened, self-darkened individuals prefer comfort to truth any day of the week.

Even the modern scientific revolution shows what a difference a shaft of light can make. At one time, people thought that the sun circled the earth because it looks that way from within "the cave."

Then Copernicus and others "climbed out of the darkness into the light" and discovered that the earth rotates as it journeys around the sun. They went "back into the cave" to tell the others that the sun, *not* the earth, is the center of our visible system of things.

The populace did not like what they were hearing. In pointing to their Bibles and citing texts, they used their time-honored, standard ways of interpretation. Some theologians even ridiculed Kepler and

Galileo. And they refused to look through a telescope to see some of the evidence for a new vision.

Likewise, in matters of religion, leaders of synagogues, churches, and mosques are often averse to enlightenment, even though the theistic tradition celebrates light. They realize how various are the forms of *false* light.

Nevertheless, they are called to discern the true from the false. Light is the prerequisite of vision. Under all paradigms—all patterns of interpretation—light is a master symbol of meaning and truth.

In the Christian Testament, the Apostle John begins his account of salvation by referring to the Light. He says that the Word of God is God, who made all things that were made. "In him was life, and the life was the light of men. And the light shineth in darkness, and the darkness did not comprehend it" (*John* 1:4-5).

Salvation requires "the Light of the world." As we live and move and try to understand ourselves in our problematic plight, we cry out for light.

Light often illuminates what we do not expect and even what we do not *want* to see. Our poverty that we have caused by self-centered consciousness is so pitiful that we do not want it exposed even to ourselves, much less to others. Fig-leafs of righteousness dominate our everyday lives. We would prefer to be "in the right," rather than in the light. The mystery of our history, personal and communal, calls for needed, though often unwanted, illumination.

But if we can bring ourselves merely to suppose that *personally* we participated in the origin of our darkness, then we can release more light into the darkness concerning the origin of evil itself. An added flash of light, darting from out of our preconscious (spiritually unconscious) selves, can make a critical difference. And much light would follow if our repentant hearts were to prompt the deeds of mercy broadcast by Isaiah.

Renewal in the Roots

Existence is a mystery, not a black hole. A mystery is a supremely *knowable* reality. And there is ever more to know.

In our essential beginning, we freely turned from God's immediate gift of perfect light and we became dulled by the shock. We were not, however, "blinded by the light." We blinded ourselves *to* the light.

Our initial unwillingness to be fully who we were gifted to be is now causing us to be blind, even in the ever-present brilliance of eternal Light. Infinite light radiates around us, while we encave ourselves with self-entertainment by means of relative trivia. Even our modest efforts to learn history, culture, philosophy, theology, and religion are plagued with misunderstandings.

Originally, we brought "darkness out of the light." now we long for light to come out of the darkness—the darkness that we created by our denial and repression of original freedom and truth.

We all have a "dark side." That is a truism for depth psychology. But, through wise therapeutic practice, enlightenment can come forth from within emotional shadowlands.

Likewise, we know, at least unconsciously, how light can come right out of the spiritual darkness that only we ourselves could have caused. Not even our first parents alone could have afflicted us. We must have done our part as well.

In the search for more light, religious people have been talking about renewal for many years. But, in important ways, conditions seem to be getting more superficial as time passes—there is more blight than light.

Many have been losing the light of their Faith. They have been growing indifferent and cold. Faith in God, who is both eminently within us and yet entirely other, has been steadily losing its hold. Europe, for instance, has formed a "Union" that is a conglomeration of nations committed largely to religious darkness.

In the West, as in the East, substitutes for Faith include a broad array of hedonistic and pantheistic alternatives. These "new age" alternatives often seem to promise enlightenment. But they also readily serve as avenues of escape from the transcendent light of a Personal God to whom we are accountable for everything we *are*, *think*, and *do*.

We have lost our interest and ability to grow—to grow within the total meaning of the truths involved. We are complacent about our way of understanding traditional teachings.

Where is that spiritual burst of light that is followed by growth in the theistic worldview? We need such light—along with a constant conversion of heart—so that there can be progress in our Faith-knowledge of creation, redemption, personal responsibility, and final destiny.

Genuine renewal always requires the deepening of roots. Many seeking renewal have tried, as it were, to uproot and replant the tree of Faith in what appears to be richer ground.

What the tree really requires, however, is a deepening of roots in its own soil, resulting in new growth for the trunk, the branches, and the roots. The tree of Faith is too large, as it were, to be transplanted without dying. We ought to attend to our personal roots, as far as they have grown, but always to do so in the common climate of Faith and reason.

In recent decades, we have been witnessing a subtle transition of cultural attention from what we believe to what we feel. Feelings have trumped meanings in the hearts of many—of young and old alike.

One of the major reasons for this tragic shift is the lack of light shining on our Faith in God's creation and on our abortive response. We have failed to advance to new and more effective paradigms, windows of truth, on the meaning of our origins. The root-growth has been retarded for decades—even centuries—and the meaning for believing in God has stagnated.

All the while, some ardent people of Faith have been actively evangelizing and succeeding quite measurably, here and there. They proclaim our need for salvation. But they do not seem to offer a fuller vision, based on the truth of our *personal* responsibility for the *way* we *are*.

Nor do they speak of the really precipitous drop in our personal freedom that landed us here. They teach the profound truths of Faith through the usual avenues of interpretation concerning creation and the origin of evil. And that is good, as far as it goes.

The traditional viewpoint affords much light. But there remains an indefinitely long way to go.

In Christianity, at least, theism emphasizes that we were deprived of grace by the sin of Adam and Eve. Yet, in this particular matter of meaning, we seem to be treated more as "members of a species" than as individual *persons*.

The leaders of our "species" or community sinned and so, without any necessary and essential freedom or responsibility as individuals, we are afflicted, not only by the consequences of that sin, but also by its character. Billions of individual persons seem to be created as already submerged in the being and activity of two other individual persons, their first progenitors.

This semi-tribal concept of our origins necessarily conflicts with many potential religious insights, including people's deep yearning to find a lost freedom. Some of the stirring philosophical and literary themes of the 20th century concerning individual freedom reinforce the idea of determining one's destiny. The essential freedom of the individual person is an emerging truth, even though often tragically distorted by self-centric and atheistic assumptions.

Additionally, some theological minds have rightly re-emphasized that our basic relationship with God is one of free covenant. Initiated entirely by the Creator for our good, the covenant stands between God and us, individually as well as communally. Yet, the old mind-set, whereby we think of ourselves as being clunked by the "sin of Adam," continues to cloud the credibility of the theistic covenant.

The call of the Hebrew prophets, however, along with the Gospel of Christ and the demands of Allah, can give renewed testimony to the nations. We have only to admit new light on the meaning of freedom and love. Individuals committed to the divine Personhood of Yahweh, or to the Triune Persons of the God, or to the absolute person of Allah can relate to their Faith with further immanent light on its meanings.

Light on the Great Repression

If orginative sin is real, then it is the subject of massive spiritual *repression*. Such inevitable repression would help to explain why so many for so long have been unaware of it. But how can we know we are repressing something so momentous?

First of all, even in our present world, repression is common. Yet, it is not sufficiently recognized. We see its power only in unusual cases, hardly ever our own. We are quick to deny that we ourselves have ever repressed anything significant.

But our *ability* to repress, even in our everyday world, is immense. Accepting this reality would open our minds to more light on our condition. Ignoring it locks out immense possibilities for growth. We thereby consolidate our "dark side."

The human person is an integral unity. And the spiritual dimension is formative of the whole person, right down to the toenails. So, the common phenomenon of psychic repression must have a spiritual cause and counterpart.

Certainly, the roots of all repression are not in the physical. The very passive-reactive character of the physical could be an effect of repression, but not its cause.

All repression *begins* in the depths of *being*. The roots of our daily ability to repress must somehow include the deep burial of our personally chosen solidarity with Adam and Eve. If we could break forth into the awareness and admission that this solidarity must have been freely formed, we would be profoundly renewed.

This book attempts to uncover our cozy relationship with Adam and Eve, our first papa and mama. It suggests how we might be relying much too heavily on their spiritual mess-up, so that we cannot be blamed too much for our own most deeply personal plight here in the world of spatial, temporal, and spiritual inadequacies.

Besides, this relationship with our earliest parents is not simply a matter of repression. It is also a matter of suppression.

Suppression is done consciously, even if only for a micro-second: we know something, but do not *want* to know or attend to it now. Suppression is a daily, hourly activity. And it is predominantly a healthy and inevitable part of ordinary conscious life, protecting our ability to focus on one thing at a time. We must suppress many simultaneous incursions within our conscious life in order to live rationally and sensibly.

Repression, however, is done unconsciously: we know something, but do not *know* that we know it, because we do not *want* to know it. We do not *let* ourselves know it. Repression is inevitable in this life, but represents something unhealthy. It is a kind of *denial* of what *is* and of what is *known*.

Still, we must be clear. Originative sin (root sin) was committed in a uniquely immaculate kind of consciousness. It was not like the encumbered consciousness we experience now. This sin's premier occurrence would have to have been dramatically and immediately thrust under our pristine consciousness, becoming repressed once the crash was "completed." And this signature sin is now almost entirely a matter of repression.

Even *original* sin—the sin of Adam and Eve—might likewise be repressed, at least in many minds. And unfortunately it is a matter of suppression in the slick mentalities of many theistic believers today. Consciously, if quickly, they might decide to put it out of their attention in spiritual and moral concerns, saying, "Let's be positive." Many even deny, consciously, that such a sin exists.

Some are now calling Adam's "original sin" an error, a mistake, not a sin. There are those who even regard it as a big breakthrough, whereby individuals attain a level of necessary independence in the growth of human consciousness. Nevertheless, few would be so self-blinded as to claim that all is well with planetary humanity and the cosmos.

If we are to speak of an *originative* sin, we are claiming that it involved our freedom, along with Adam and Eve. That primordial involvement would be now a matter of repression, an unconscious denial that we made a wrongful act of will at the core of our *being*. Because of that act we helped to cause this world of *maybe*-ing and its dynamics, and we were destined to enter it.

Our task is immense and calls for a blazing light. Repressed things can be recovered and dealt with through insight and courage, but often only with the greatest difficulty.

If we are repressing an originative failure of will, it would be extremely difficult to realize, since that very will has the power to repress itself. Who even knows that he or she has been gifted with an *agent* will: a will that is immediately and completely a power to do or receive without being passive at all—without having any passive conditions for being-stimulated?

Living in this world, however, we intuitively know that something is profoundly wrong. Yet most of us write it off as a "mystery" and go on with our lives. We have no inclination to pick up clues about any personal, root-responsibility for everything that happens to us.

The main question, however, does not concern clues about why this or that happens to us, but about why we are being in this kind of a world—why we are being here for both good and evil to *happen to* us at all. Virtually everything we think about induces us to regard such a question as impossibly impractical and unimportant.

Yet, we are all disposed to think, at times, "Why me?" "Why is such a devastating thing happening to me?" "How could God let this happen?"

After Alan had unknowingly backed his car right over his own toddler son, crushing him to death, he asked himself those questions endlessly. Any of us can identify with Alan's anguished cries.

But we must face it. We "feel more comfortable" thinking that we are victims of the irresponsibility of someone else rather than of our own.

Who wants to admit that we are in this world of good and evil because of our own willful reluctance to receive fully the gift of our *being*? We do not want to face even the *possibility* of such being so. But, as we blame someone else and repress our own responsibility, we continue to victimize and to batter ourselves *unconsciously*.

I will never forget the comment of a colleague, over forty years ago, when I suggested the idea of personal responsibility for an originative sin. We were within a small group of faculty discussing evolution. He instinctively turned and said, "Oh *no!*" with shock and gusto.

At the time, I thought it sounded a bit like "protesting too much." In any case, overwrought disapproval would be the dynamic of some of our responses. We might intuitively know there is some substance to the idea, but we find it an instinctively repulsive consideration. The depth of change within our hearts that might be required—not simply to accept it, but actually to live it—staggers the intellect and "naturally" reveals our preferential option for the darkness.

We are like the young health-care worker at the hospital in my neighborhood who, more than thirty years ago, became pregnant without being married. Her co-workers started to comment on her size, and she kept saying she was just putting on some weight.

In the final months, she continued to say that she was having a dietary problem. Even after the baby was born, she denied ever being pregnant—she was so unwilling to face her repressed guilt for engaging in genital relations outside marriage.

Despite how her condition came about, this woman was expectant with a good and beautiful human person. Caring for the child herself or yielding to adoptive parents, who might love and care for the child even better than she could, might have become a redeeming feature of her life. If she had accepted her condition of gestating a child, she could have inspired her friends and helped herself to make strides in her own redemption.

Similarly, we are pregnant. We are pregnant with our very own existence in space and time, including all of our vitality, curiosity, challenges—all of our joys and sorrows. Moreover, this condition of existence—our being distended—is fraught with both potential and actual sickness, as well as with impending death. Despite how it got started, this pregnancy is important—life under cosmic conditions—but only if we carry it to its salvific term.

Space and time, matter and motion, even sickness and death, are good as God-given saving remedies for those who said *maybe*. Yet they are bad in being inherent indications of the necessity for any remedy at all. We could have said fully *yes*.

Tragically, we are quite inclined to deny, together and alone, that we carry space and time, sickness and death, as a consequence of our own irresponsible choice. We do not want to face our personal responsibility for the very origin of *this* pregnancy. We are super-sensitive to the whole suggestion. We are relieved that it is just the "unfounded hypothesis" of someone else. We prefer to think, as it were, "The devil got me into this." And we are amazingly reluctant to give all of it to God.

But we can read discerningly the prophet Ezekiel. He reports God telling us that it is our ways, not God's, that are unfair. God says that when a virtuous person turns away from virtue and commits sin, the iniquity is the cause of death (*Ezekiel* 18:25-28).

God also indicates a radically personal responsibility for sin. "The soul that sinneth, the same shall die: the son shall not bear the iniquity of the father, and the father shall not bear the iniquity of the son: the justice of the just shall be upon him, and the wickedness of the wicked shall be upon him" (*Ezekiel* 18:20).

We might attend to declarations like these that concern our deeds in this life and their effects upon our final destination. If we do, we could begin to wonder whether we are personally responsible for having been destined, first of all, to *live* in this world. Is this whole precarious life itself *not* the result of our own originative sin? Are we *not* pregnant out of "wedlock"—disrupted from the covenant of creation?

Chapter 16

A Call to the Three Traditions

Does it make any difference whether, as a member of the human community, I have a decisive part in determining the origins of good and evil? Does it matter whether I am really able to cooperate, or to refuse to cooperate, in the decision of the community's leaders, say, Adam and Eve? Does it make a difference whether I am personally involved with the very origin of evil or whether I am an innocent victim of it, passively bludgeoned by the sin of my first parents?

Obviously, there is a great difference. The difference is similar to that between active and passive predicaments. For instance, either being the president of a nation intensely negotiating with terrorists about the fate of the inhabitants who are under the threat of nuclear annihilation or being a fearful couch potato watching on television the negotiations and the fate of oneself and one's family.

But which is truer? Is it truer to say, as the new way of conceiving holds, that I with others, including Adam and Eve, am one of the originators of the evil in this world? Or is it truer to say, along with what the traditional interpretation seems to claim, that I got bombed by ill-choosing first parents whose original sin deprived me of my "creation right" and effectively forced me into joining the "sin brigade"?

At first, I don't like either alternative. I prefer to think I am a good person having little to do with sin and evil—and certainly nothing to do with the origins. It is better for me and everyone else that I be positive rather than negative. Is the idea of the original sin of our first parents not negative enough?

But being *totally* positive about the original condition of my being in this world is not being *real*. The obvious frustrations and painful tragedies of life are being excluded. If I assume that I am simply good, without personally active association with the *origin* of evil, I fail to respond adequately to the perennial human question, "Why me?" And why am I subject to the sin of Adam and Eve?

Alan was a motorist who unknowingly ran over and killed his own child. Under similar circumstances, however, such could have been done by any of us. More importantly, Alan stands as the vibrant symbol for how we could have "run over" our original freedom and thereby blocked our opening to a free, immediate, and ecstatic life forever. If we had accepted that originative opportunity to unite with God at the moment of being created out of nothing, we would have excluded the experience of pain and would have entered rapturous joy—then and forever.

Reality invites me to think ever more deeply about *why* I am here. I am essentially good, but immersed in considerable evil. The evil is environmental, social, and individual. To live is to suffer and to risk assault from the forces of physical nature and also from the moral misdeeds of strangers, friends, and family—not to mention threats from vastly superior forces of evil.

My body gets sick, my mind fumbles at times, my feelings are mixed, my spirit reveals some dispositions that are less than fully virtuous, and I am headed for the colossal destruction of death—at least, physical and emotional death. While I am basically good, I have inclinations toward evil. And, especially, evil has inclinations toward me. I become prey even when I pray.

Could this inherent connection with evil have come through the design of a Creator who is *infinitely* good and powerful? Could this connection with evil have come to me through the "permission," if not the design, of this Creator—without my freely-given permission, too? The major message of this book is that a "*yes*" to either or both of these questions is a great miss "take."

That we are basically victims of the transgression of Adam and Eve is a false "take" on the holiness of God and on the freedom of created persons. God is *infinitely* perfect Freedom, creating directly from nothing only finite freedom that is *perfect*.

God can and does create an imperfect world. But God does *that* creation out of *something*—out of spiritual and material remnants of an original crash. God "cannot" rightly create *out of nothing* an *even slightly* imperfect world, and still be "God."

So, I can no longer regard you and me as essentially victims of someone else, including God. As painful as it is to receive, the truth must be that you and I are *personally* involved with the roots of good and evil. This is the truth, unless, of course, you are some kind of most rare exception, having agreed freely and fully to live here as a finite redeeming co-operator with the infinite activity of God.

Holy Ones Lead toward the Light

If this new view is true, why have we not heard more about the idea throughout history? And where is the scholarly documentation? Why should I or anyone else take it seriously?

Souls have been saved without it. Great heroes and saints never thought they were personally responsible for an originative denial of *being*. What difference would such a consideration have made for them?

These thoughts are almost inevitable. They have to do, however, with the *conscious* acknowledgement of personal responsibility for the origin of human evil. But we can know and act on the truth of something without ever bringing it into consciousness.

Toddlers, for instance, know and act on the truth that they cannot walk sprightly as do others around them, but they do not bring it out as a proposition in their consciousness. Even when we are adults, our every practical learning endeavor is usually undertaken with the unstated, subconscious truth that the practical knowledge is sought from an instructor who knows more than the one being instructed.

So, there is a big difference between how people closest to God would become aware of personal responsibility for the origin of evil and how the rest of us might hesitate to do so. When confronted by this idea consciously, would not the holiest be some of the first to acknowledge it?

The saints' sense of sinfulness and of human alienation from God, through their own fault, is keenly developed already. They could hardly be surprised to be told—if done by duly recognized religious authority—that every human being in the cosmos (past, present, and future), with the rarest of exceptions, is a co-originator of the evil that afflicts us all.

Saints in the Christian Church, for instance, profoundly identify themselves with the incarnate God's sufferings on behalf of each one of us, including themselves. To be instructed further about the mystery of God's painful world would be much easier for them than for us. They have a developed capacity for receiving the things of God and of knowing how severely we deform our own human freedom by even the slightest offenses against the Beloved.

Because of their sensitivity to the heart of God, people ardently devoted to believing deeply, and to behaving faithfully, also have a more profound sense of causality than we do. They do not deal with things merely on a practical, yet superficial level.

Saints experience everything as being-within the heart of creation where everything is super-related to everything else. These holy ones feel close to the least little good thing or action. They are repulsed by the slightest offenses against God and fellow creatures.

They know that God offers them infinitely intimate love at every moment. They are pained as the infinite tenderness of God is being constantly rebuffed by their own hardness and ignorance—as well as by the heartless attitudes of others.

Intimate lovers of God realize that the sources of sin are entirely in the hearts of those who *do* the sinning. They are supremely sensitive to our free failure to love God with whole hearts and souls. So they are particularly positioned to see that the normal episodes of guilt that we tend to experience, for past or present sins in this life, could be considered as symptoms of a sin that is much deeper than "the Garden sin of Adam and Eve.

Our temporal spasms of guilt would seem to radiate from the core guilt for sin's origins—the chief causal sin—now largely repressed and denied. "Out of the depths I have cried to thee, O Lord: Lord, hear my voice. Let thy ears be attentive to the voice of my supplication. If thou, O Lord, wilt mark iniquities: Lord, who shall stand it" (*Psalms* 129:1-2).

There would seem to be no limit to the depth of the need we have for God to rescue us from our self-wrought predicament; and the saints are the first to recognize it. Some are known to seek out, or to ask for, increased occasions to suffer for the sake of their own and others' salvation: sheerly out of a burning love for God. The idea of an originative sin would be more than just an idea; it would be the holy ones' natural platform for acknowledging our total need for redemption and salvation.

People of demonstrably heroic virtue breathe intimately with the *causes* of their aspirations and actions. They do not merely teach or preach the way of profound justice; they practice it with uncommon courage. We who act in pale imitation of these holy ones might be inclined to teach and preach and behave, while living largely out of touch with the *sources* of the ultimate truths that we proclaim.

We are often locked into the pragmatic policies and practices that might serve today, but blow away tomorrow. Religious leaders and teachers—even those of exceptionally good will—can be clouded by their own practical responsibilities when exercising their ministries. They are trained in the standard patterns of interpretation that have served so well.

Nevertheless, deeper soundings on truth concerning creation and the origin of evil can develop only through contemplative hearts, and even then with difficulty. The vast theistic tradition of mystical theology and spirituality testifies to the dark night of the soul and to God as a truly inaccessible light.

We approach God only through the 'dark cloud of unknowing,' relinquishing all egocentric attention to consolations of the senses, of the mind, and of the spirit. For the mystics, the necessary way to see God is through self-abandoned, ego-less love.

As we move toward our own death and the wrenching away from our fixations on earthly concerns we are called to live in the dark light of knowing God's welcoming embrace. Could it be that this knowing is commensurate with the knowing to which we are also called: knowing our originative, self-blighted, missed union with God, out of which the whole of creation groans and is in travail for the daylight of salvation?

This book on the new viewpoint for creation and sin supports the notion that we *do* not and *cannot remember* an originative sin. But the claim is that we do *know* it, even when we do not *know* that we know it.

Such a view faults *no* one for overlooking the prospect of personal responsibility in the heart of creation—at least as far as our practical activities and insights from this world are concerned. Just as good physicians are inveterately inclined to treat symptoms and overlook the systemic causes of physical disease, religious leaders can, by their training, consistently overlook the common, universal cause of all particular guilt—an originatively repressed act of freedom.

Moreover, simply to make the painful acknowledgement that we are each *personally* the cause of our *own* plight in this world would not indicate sainthood. The only test of a saint is a life lived in true abandonment to God and to divine purposes at every moment. It would seem, however, that if presented with this new perspective, the saints—especially the deeply repentant ones—would be those most willing to give it serious consideration.

At any rate, the new viewpoint on personal responsibility—if it were to be accepted—would require a painful conversion in our self-concept. We would have to stop watching the world largely through the remoteness of mental television and begin to live-a-vision—a vision based on a deepened spiritual intuition and knowledge of the *heart*. We would have to become people who know who they *are*, and who they are *not*, basking darkly in the brilliant light of God's mystical marriage—offered to us, but self-deflected, at the moment of creation.

In the past, saints and others might not have been prepared to articulate rationally or conceptually what they knew. But perhaps they quietly attained something of the new understanding, far more vitally than we who might talk about it will ever imagine in this life. Holy people lead us to the light, not so much by their rationally objective knowledge as by the intuitions in their hearts and by the luminosity of their lives.

The Sole Origin of Evil

"We have met the enemy, and it is us." Whatever the context, that catch phrase from a Walt Kelly comic strip has a profound meaning. We do not have to be saints in order to appreciate it. Every sin, every effect of sin, and every inclination to sin within us—in all its reality—can be traced to...us, first as individuals, and second as a "community of disunity."

Sin is from within. The defects and sins of every imperfect human being originate *entirely* from within. The activity of Satan or the original sin of Adam and Eve are occasions for our sins and for self-destructive intentions and behaviors, but they cannot be called causes or agents of *our* sins.

Every human being in (finite) likeness to God is self-determining. Each one determines the kind of human person he or she will be—whether fully *yes*, fully *no*, or indecisively so for "a time."

All of our sins, as well as our virtues—our moral and spiritual activities—are matters of original freedom and not of necessity. They stem from the same capacity in each of us: our personal human will. We are originatively endowed with an *agent* will, a finitely pure act of volitional power to cooperate with the infinite presence (grace) of God.

There must be a supreme, ultimate willing activity of this perfect personal power, the agent will, that is protoconsciously the prime cause of every one of our acts—whether virtuous or not. All of our multitudinous acts of good and bad decision-making, specifically at the moral level, are mainly *symptoms* of this primary causal act: our supreme act of freedom at the level of be-ing.

The sole origin of our present personal destiny is *not* the will itself as a *power*. *We* are. We do the willing *by acts* of willing. By the primal willing activity, we received being with willful deficiency. The partial failure was of the *agent in* the act—not at all in the perfect power to will, gifted by God. We received our perfect power to will (agent intellect) and 'used it' to miss-direct ourselves. The power was perfect and remains so. But we, on the receiving side of this act of misdirection, are now quite imperfect. Our agent will *as gifted* remains perfect forever; *as received*, by acts of this power that are determined freely by us, it is imperfectly active.

God, moreover, does *not* determine our final personal destiny. *We* do. God affords us the gift of being, of perfect being: of being-at-all, of being who and what we are, and of being able to affirm the goodness of it all. But *only we* can determine whether ultimately we accept *willingly* these incomparable gifts.

We must consider our first, supreme, pristine activity of knowing and willing. Therein we can characterize ourselves now as really being the protoconscious and preconscious source of our conscious daily acts. These acts flow from the results of a whole concatenation of levels of conscious and unconscious life for which they are a kind of culmination.

We can infer as much. After all, so many of our daily acts are evidently wounded ones—especially those having some degree of freedom. And all the rest may be characterized as wounded, if less obviously so. Or maybe more obviously so.

This deepest (protoconscious) activity of our willing, the moment God said "Be," therefore, must be the sole cause of our *maybe* kind of being—including our existence in this passively material world. Nothing or *no* one caused this particular *act* of freedom to *be*, except the sinning person himself or herself. God is surely the cause of our freedom as a *power* to do and be, but cannot be the cause of any of our free acts—whether of virtue or vice—nor of our *maybe*-saying response to being.

Some might say that only God is the cause of our freedom. So, they would assert that only God can be the ultimate cause of the evil as well as the good that we will with that freedom.

However, that is to miss the *gift* of *being*, and of freedom as a gift, absolutely and infinitely given to us. We exercise our own freedom, *not* God's. We have dishonored, however, that power to be free by its first free *act*, of which *we* are the *sole* agent.

Our originative act of freedom is a singular cause in respect to its effecting personal good or evil. (We cannot "blame God" for this one.) If, through our *agent* (doer) *will* and its respective *agent intellect*, we had acted perfectly well in receiving be-ing *ex nihilo*, none of these lesser imperfect acts would *be*.

Our originative, supreme activity of willing is caused not by the gift of freedom itself, but by us, the *doers* of this perfect freedom. From the moment of actively receiving our creation, we were the *only* prime agents capable of the *yes*-and-*no*, resulting in the present ambivalent disposition of our soul. We said neither *yes* nor *no*, but *yes*-and-*no*.

This "unhappy fault" (*our* unhappy fault) within the purely free willing on our part is the ultimate reason why we are still yearning for life and love, but doing it often in such inept ways.

We are blaming much of our situation on others and making a supreme effort to conceal from ourselves this ultimate responsibility of how we are *be*-ing. If only we had a better way of conceiving this supremacy of a person's agent will, we could increase the occasions for our understanding and for our cooperating with God's purposes. Perhaps we could say that each one of us is an *agent be*-ing. From the moment we *are*, we *will* our own *be*-ing, for better or for worse.

The new paradigm of personal responsibility for our every activity and experience is another way of seeing this primal willingness. It can serve as another window through which to see the light of God's truth. The vision afforded might be cloudy at first, then increasingly translucent, eventually to become transparent for many.

In this world, each person, by reason of originative sin, is the primal—not the immediate or proximate—cause of all the evil he or she perpetrates or for which he or she bears willingly or unwillingly. This originative sin is the supreme cause of our structural defects of being. From this sin have come also all of the major and minor transgressions, weakness, dullness, and confusion in our present life.

Many of us acknowledge the massive role of Satan and other evil forces in the institution and protraction of Adam's original sin in space and time. Nonetheless, we are called reasonably to admit *also* the primacy of a supremely personal cause of *self*-affliction. Were we to do so, we would let the infinite immensity of God's grace and mercy radiate all the more in our lives. We would be allowing the light and warmth of this mercy to heal us.

Despite being critically self-wounded, we are essentially free. The infinite presence of God calls us to affirm God's infinite covenant of intimacy.

Chapter 17

Deepening the Theistic View

Find meaning and reasons for the Faith and Hope that are in you.

This perennial challenge to all believers resounds in the hearts of those who live their religious commitments. The Jewish, Christian, and Islamic traditions have cultivated the exploration of Faith by reason, theologically and philosophically. Reason should support Faith, and not undermine it.

Even by its challenging questions, reason can support religious belief. Suppose that I have not committed original sin with Adam and Eve in the Garden, nor in any other originating way. Then the inevitable question is, "Why me?" Why do I have such an incredible potential for suffering, even as an infant—and especially as an infant?

But, if I did sin originatively in the moment of sheer creation "out of nothing"—with perfect personal being and freedom—then the inevitable question is, "Why *not* me?" How could I *expect* to evade even the most dreadful torments found on earth? Perhaps I will not suffer such. But I cannot assume a complete escape from tragedy. My flawed exercise of the perfect, untempted freedom, with which I was gifted, resulted necessarily in my desperate condition.

In this life, painful episodes are sometimes repressed. Inevitably, the repressions cause pressures and instabilities of mind and heart. Repressive matters beg to be released through conscious admission. They can be brought to consciousness, given intellectual admission, and even re-felt emotionally, in order that they might be effectively discharged. So, when treating emotional trauma, therapists are well advised to allow the patient gradually to realize the causes of past incidences of repression, without being bogged down by the details.

Similarly, spiritual guides would do well to let people recognize gradually *why* they are loaded with massive vulnerabilities in this present life of cosmic confinement. Moreover, they can eventually and carefully point out that all of these burdens are inevitably the results of a spiritually repressed, self-afflicting first act of freedom. We committed that act, fully independent of space and time and of passivity of any kind. In addition, we are now gradually waking up in the midst of the results. Here we are: beings of *ex*-istence. We are existing in matter and motion, space and time.

We might someday find ourselves, with others, suffering horrible atrocities right here in this world. Knowing *why* could make our lives more deeply meaningful than ever.

In his classic book, *Man's Search for Meaning*, psychiatrist Viktor Frankl once dramatized our hidden capacity. He revealed how the human person can be sustained while suffering extreme torment, if there is sufficient meaning for enduring it.

If we were to come to recognize a previously unsuspected level of sin and guilt, we would have a better base in meaning for enduring any present and future suffering. We could stop referring to "the mystery of evil" as an inscrutable truth for which God has "his own reasons."

Naturally, our good will and sincerity of belief would be seriously challenged. And our life of meaning would depend on our response. If we were to admit an originative sin, we would receive further confirmation of what we already know about ourselves. If we were to continue denying it, our meaning for life would continue being disruptive.

Realizing that we must have sinned *with* Adam and Eve, *as well as in and through them*, would mark a deepening of the usual theistic worldview. The biggest difference, however, between the new view and the old is not the pivotal awareness of our sinning originatively and our critical need for awesome personal repentance. Deeper still is the realization of the necessarily interpersonal activity of God in creating us.

The Biggest Difference: A New Vision of Creation

The principal difference within traditional theism between the old perspective and the new supposition would seem to be the meaning of creation. The burden of this book is our need to go deeper into the heart of creation in order to find brighter light for guidance on our journey and for a richer theistic worldview.

The project, *When God Said Be, We Said Maybe*, is based on recognition and affirmation that God is both infinitely good and infinitely powerful. We can *say* God is infinite and *mean* it. God is not thought to be merely "indefinite," much less arbitrary. We really mean that God is *unlimited* in Being and Activity.

We were created immediately and interpersonally as perfect by unlimited goodness and unlimited power—not simply by "supreme" goodness and power. The real infinity of God is then affirmed and is no longer the "missing infinity." God is *infinite* actuality; we are finite (perfect) actuality.

Through prayerful reflection on our Faith, we can become more effectively aware. We can understand surely that the divine Being originally created us, "out of nothing," as necessarily perfect persons and unique likenesses of divine Personhood.

This new view of our original creation is fully person-based. It is not even partly cosmos-based, as is the usual theistic view that starts with God creating subpersonal realities in space and time.

Our *response* to being created as perfect finite persons "out of nothing" must have been immediate, totally personal, free, and somewhat failing. As a result, our minds and hearts cannot now "conceive and believe" what God had prepared for us...if we had freely, fully, and immediately confirmed the gift of intimacy with God.

We did not respond with completely personal love to the gift of being and of being-with-God. As a result, we find ourselves fixed in this *maybe*-ized, receptive world—the passively material universe, wherein we have awakened after the crash.

Obviously, we begin life in the *spatiotemporal* world by thinking about this *cosmos*-based creation. We *assume* that it is the first or only creation, insofar as we humans are concerned. In our egocentric regard for making our plight God's center of creative activity, we unconsciously regard the creation of angelic beings to be almost a glorious "side show."

But we can know better. We are, for instance, capable of realizing the relevance of that time-tested Aristotelian-Thomistic principle: that which is first in the way we come to know things is secondary in the way things really are. That is, we always know consciously that which is less important before coming to know that which is more important. So, we can observe this principle at work in our knowing of creation itself.

The world of sense and sensibility and its beginnings are known first—*consciously*. As children, we are introduced to the stars and even to the galaxies beyond our physical locale on earth and to the super-microscopic field within the simplest living elements.

Then, perhaps as we move toward adulthood, we may be led to contemplate more critical things, such as the creation itself and the meaning of our freedom. We begin to understand God's love and to increase our own care for others and ourselves.

Only at that point, if ever, are we liable to recognize—perhaps in a flash of insight—a profound truth about creation. Perfect, finite persons, with their perfectly free responses to *be*-ing, are the way things were originatively. We can begin thereby to see that the creation of this cosmic world of *be*-coming, wherein "being is coming back," is secondary—even though it may be crucial to our salvation.

The new light on creation can be understood then as a revolution in our awareness of reality. Something like what was done to our awareness of the physical universe in the Copernican revolution must be done to our awareness of the universe of *being*. We are called to undergo an immense reversal in the way we evaluate the meaning of our conscious knowledge.

In the Copernican revolution, people began to invert their vision of the relationship between the earth and the sun. They once saw the earth as the center of the whole cosmos. Then they began to see the sun as the center of "our physical world." Finally, they "saw" that the sun does *not* go around the earth at all; the earth goes around the sun.

It was "natural" at first and at length to perceive and think about the sun going around the earth and to speak of sunrises and sunsets. People could "see" it was so, just by opening their eyes. Even today we are reluctant to correct those who speak of a beautiful sunset. We do not want to embarrass them, and perhaps ourselves, by pointing out that it is really a beautiful earth-turning.

Even though we know that the sun is *not* going around the earth, but that the earth is "going around," we find truth in the old model of vision. After all, we are important; the earth is a beautiful blue planet with life and love blossoming here and there. The sun is basically a ball of flame; and it is not even in contention as a place to inhabit.

Despite the fact that without the sun's heat and light, nothing on earth would be alive, we are more actively concerned with our own predicament on this particular planet. And all the rest in space and time seems to yield to our intensive, more immediate concerns here-and-now-on-earth.

Unfortunately, we project our ego-centered vision onto God.

People today are still thinking of God the Creator simply as the Maker. Creation is unconsciously imaged as like unto an external workmanship. A created maker works, with matter and "tools," to fashion something *separate*—not just *other*.

And the creature's freedom is imaged as the power to choose from among quasi-external courses of action, such as consuming fruit, whether commanded or prohibited. The stories of *Genesis* have been interpreted emphatically from a viewpoint of "outside looking in," even though the content of these accounts pleads for at least some kind of an "inside story" as well.

The Creation Revolution

The new revolution could be identified as the Creation Revolution. Therein we can begin to reverse our vision of the relationship that the creation of the cosmos has to the creation of all *being*.

The task is immense because popular and scholarly views seem to take the accounts of *Genesis* as the central story of the creation of human persons "out of nothing." Believers insist on retaining their spatial and temporal perspective even for activity that had to be God's alone.

Evolutionist versions of creation retain and embellish the "process mentality" in which "Biblical creationists" are already inured. In some respects, evolutionist and creationist accounts reinforce each other by putting the primacy on our first, self-centric vision of reality and its dynamic of be-*coming*.

But these renditions of a gradually created world revolve around a much more central, yet missing, account of how we came to be-at-all. They fail to distinguish essentially our *existence* from our *being*. So, they do not attend to the creation of our be-*coming* as quite different from the creation of our be-*ing*.

By opening our hearts as well as our minds, we can begin to see that the creation of human persons in the universe of space and time is not the *center* of their creation. Cosmic creation revolves around another creation: the creation of all persons "out of nothing," within the infinite intimacy of the divine activity of Love. We somehow already know this, preconsciously. But now might be the time to bring it to consciousness.

We can finally acknowledge that what occurred within the creation "out of nothing" does not depend on how we find ourselves to be living now on earth. Rather, how we happen to be living on earth is totally dependent on another center of love and of being: on our *response* to our creation "out of nothing."

It was "natural" at first and at length to conceive of our creation as primarily involved in the world of matter and motion. It was also "natural" to be awed by the story of our first parents, Adam and Eve. In addition, it seemed obvious that our *personal* creation was the moment of our conception in our mother's body. Anyone could "see" that, before the year 1900, I did not exist and that, so many years later, there I was. My "being" was readily time-certified.

Today we are still talking as though existence is the same as being. We did not exist functionally, of course, in the material universe before a given time. But is our *being* circumscribed by space-time?

Yes, though only for the most limited, practical purposes, and *not* as an explanation of *who we are*.

An outside story of who we are is not enough. Our being beckons for an inside story.

So, we can begin to move to the new vision. In that light, our *existence* in time and space as children of Adam and Eve comes from our absolute, but indecisive participation in *being*. Our coming to exist (at conception) in this world is not at all the same as our personal creation "out of nothing."

Conception in this world is something that *happens to* our being; and it is in no way the beginning of the *being* that we *are*. It is the beginning of our coming to consciousness that we are—and more.

Yet, we still find truth in the old model of vision. After all, we are important here and now; and the creation of the cosmos, of plants, of animals, and of human physical existence is a powerful divine act, from which God "rested."

Besides, we do not now engage in a "face-to-Face" relationship with the Being of our Creator. If we did, we would die.

We would die not because we are finite and God is infinite, but because we are sinners, not fully recovered. If we were not sinners, our simple, perfect, finiteness would receive well—proportionately to our being—the infinitely magnificent glory of God's Being, without disruption in the slightest degree. In fact, we believe and hope that we are now being readied internally for such a responsive condition.

A supreme joy of living can be found in the truth that God created us absolutely perfect in freedom and in *ability* to love. But we are now more actively involved with the subordinate truth: our wanting somehow to survive on earth and to be saved from potential horrors ahead, in this world and in the next. Despite the primary truths of creation and our core freedom, we are preoccupied with secondary, derivative truths, such as struggling to live and to do what is good.

The Creation Revolution is like the Copernican Revolution. But there is, at least, one big difference. The relationship with God our Creator is not a distant one like the relationship we have on earth with the sun, the planets, and the vast realms of space.

God's primary creation of us, Being-with-being, could hardly be closer or more intimately related to us. We are ever giftedly and unlimitedly present to God, even though we are barely aware at times that it is somehow so. And we are quite reticent about letting God be present to us.

The call of the originative creation—gifting our being—sustains us even now, as we relate to the redemptive creation, narrated in the *Genesis* accounts. The originative creation invites us deeper within, even as we contemplate how each of us is conceived ("revived") redemptively at our own moment of time and place. The creation-call *ex nihilo* ("out of nothing") enjoins us to make renewed efforts to live in the ever-present now. We are thereby united with eternity from within space and time.

So, we can adopt the new paradigm of personal responsibility for both our struggling plight and for our efforts to cooperate with God. We can enter more deeply into the heart of creation.

The Copernican Revolution once made it possible for exploration into outer space, including the first tiny step of landing on the moon. Similarly, the Creation Revolution now might make it possible to enter communion with God in a new and deeper way.

We would be afforded more personal and profound repentance, together with deeper joy in understanding how interpersonally we were created and how interpersonally we are being redeemed and potentially saved. Our personal response to the divine is intrinsically required both in our creation out of nothing and in our ultimate salvation.

At one time, we envisioned the earth as the center of the planetary universe. And today we still regard the *Genesis* accounts of our beginnings as the primary stories of creation. We still think of the disobedience of Adam and Eve in Eden as the primary fall.

But we have changed in our perspective about the earth. And we have definitely begun to know the sun as primary—as the center of the surrounding planetary system.

Similarly, we are invited to know, as primary, both our absolute, fully Person-to-person creation by God and our immediately free, self-afflicting response, provoking the redemptive creation. But the whole vision has to shift.

Once the Copernican Revolution of consciousness concerning the physical universe took hold, people were able to understand things oppositely, but more truthfully. Also, in the revolution of Creation-consciousness, people will begin to reverse their vision of how they began to *be*.

Their relationship to the *Genesis* accounts of creation and to their own moments of being conceived—the origin of space and time, and of their individual, functional coming to exist therein—will be less important. Far more important will be their relationship to the heart of God in the originative creation of being and of freedom.

The direct creation of persons "out of nothing" by the infinitely intimate personal God will appear like a radiant sun. Contemplating this primal creation will provide a significant increase of knowable light, around and about which to live.

In the light of our originative freedom, we can see that God did not predetermine angels and humans into any one particular activity or condition. They were freely capable of loving God and themselves, immediately and perfectly in accord with their own unique essences.

Many humans—perhaps virtually all, or perhaps only a minute segment of the entire created humanity—balked a bit at be-ing and went into the "shock of a lifetime." Their condition, however, was not permanent. Their Creator gave them "space and time" to heal, within the gift of redemptive grace.

For those who can make this passage of consciousness—this shift in theistic worldview—*Genesis* is taken to describe a satellite kind of creation, needed for the redemption of those who faltered and crashed. Adam and Eve were the frontline potential recoverers.

An Interpersonal View

The new view is not simply some kind of personalism. Its essence is specifically interpersonal—*an interpersonalism*. Every actuality, including that of God creating us, is not simply personal: done by a person. It is done in direct relation to other persons. No one really lives or acts utterly alone, no matter how much he or she might try.

This new light on creation might require a difficult adjustment at first. Much of life remains utterly mundane and impersonal. We are programmed to accept and buy safely into an impersonal, cosmic-based existence. We think instinctively that the cause-and-effect ways of matter and motion, space and time, are ultimately "the way it is," rather than simply the way we first come to know "the way it is."

It is difficult to realize that the way we first come to know things is ultimately the reverse of the way those things really are. We are satisfied with our immature ways of knowing and thinking about being—especially when it comes to knowing who we are...and who we are not.

In this book, much of the reflection concerning the origin of evil pivots around the critical truth about knowing things consciously. We know the superficial and the secondary *consciously*, well before we come to know the rooted and the primary.

We realize, for instance, how automatically we attribute evil exclusively to the obvious and immediately identifiable perpetrators of violence. When a murder or rape occurs, we rightly pursue the doer and bring him or her to justice. But we are disinclined to think of how the victim got into the situation, and especially of how we all came to be in "*the* situation" called the cosmos, wherein we can be "mugged" by all manner of evil.

We take it for granted that we all start out as innocent babies. But babies only look innocent. Much of theistic tradition admits that every infant comes into life inherently vulnerable for good reason: each is affected by the sin of Adam and Eve.

Yet it remains extremely difficult to admit that the *prime* reason—though not the only one—for even everyday evils that afflict little children, as well as adults, is their own adverse doing of their *be*-ing that made *ex*-istence in this world necessary for *them*.

We childishly insist that we are not primarily to blame for all or most of the evil that we suffer. But the reality is that we are not primarily to blame according to the way we first come to know good and evil, but we *are* primarily to blame according to the way things really are—according to the way good and evil really *are*.

The way we first come to know things consciously is not the way things really are. We latch onto—as children do—the first, apparent explanation for whatever happens, even within the most profound matters of religion.

The cause of our difficulty in knowing-what-is cannot be the "way God made us," but the way *we* made us. An originative sin has blinded us from seeing how we have mistreated our originally-personal encounter with God.

From our perspective within the cosmic concentration camp that we have caused, we are almost totally self-bound to behave toward God and ourselves as we originatively did: *impersonally*. There is good reason why the opening of the "Good News" in the Christian tradition begins with "Repent, repent."

We insist on thinking of God as directly and solely responsible for the creation of the cosmic prison. While doing our insisting, we sing of its beauties and pleasures. We intend to be entertained by life's happenings. God is then inevitably regarded as *somewhat* personal, *yet largely impersonal,* in being the source of our environment and of ourselves—no matter how many *personal* names we give to God.

Yet, there remains a longing for a forthright, interpersonal basis. God *with* us, we *with* God. A merely cosmic basis, with God acting *upon* us, and we reacting to God, is not enough. But the fulfillment of our heart's inmost desires will require modification in at least some of our assumptions about human nature.

We will have to affirm that God, who is perfect in Being and in Doing, creates—directly and immediately—only persons, no things at at all. We will have to realize that the whole cosmic world would not even *be* if every human person had said *fully yes* to the gift of being-at-all.

We now need to realize an up-front, much more interpersonal relationship with God. The more that we develop such, the more we will see that all subpersonal beings—and the world of passive matter itself—result from an originative *maybe*-saying, a *maybe*-intention. Right from within the effected, fragmented energy called matter and motion—gradually organized by God for helping to heal our be-ing—we would recognize ourselves as crashed persons emerging at conception, struggling for recovery.

There at conception, everything passively material in the human would be accepted as based in recuperating human personhood. And the recovery would be recognized as coming from vastly more than what we know consciously.

The Evolution of the Sciences and Religion

With such a realization firmly in place, the physical, biological, and social sciences could acquire a redemptive dignity as sciences. They could become complementary to theology and philosophy.

The definition of the fallen human being would not be "rational animal," but "organismic person." The definition of the non-fallen human being (our originative nature) would be something like "finitely perfect receiver of being," differing from angelic beings in having a dual, rather than a simple, receptivity.

Once we would begin to see ourselves as essentially and totally persons, we could finally realize that we are in no way animals. Even though we are definitely related to animals, we "look like" them only superficially. That means that natural and social sciences could make a transition from their materialistic frames of reference into relational structures where everything material in the human—and even in the cosmos at large—refers to its base in recovering *personhood.*

Psychology would move out of its fixation on the blame chain. It would give up its superficial concept of human freedom as rooted in self-centered emotions and as largely concerned with "how I feel." There would be a transferal into the healing that makes available our sense of responsibility for making primal choices.

Psychology would become based first on truth in personhood, and secondarily on truth about emotions. The human psyche would be understood as essentially a function of the spiritual, rather than of the "animal." Logotherapy and many other forms of "meaning therapy" could take their rightful place.

Some psychological trends already show promise, especially by disabusing folks of their false victimhood and by encouraging self-determination, self-empowerment, and the like.

Yet, even there, the sense of responsibility can be thought to be grandly egocentric and impersonal. Selfhood is not quite the same as personhood and does not necessarily refer to a God-gifted nature that is the basis for a freedom, independent of the preferences and proclivities of the individual.

At present, psychology hardly recognizes any requirement for mental health through personal contrition and repentance before the awesome personal Being of God. Self-fixation blots out vision of interpersonal responsibility, such as responsibility to Another. In psychology the "missing person" (personhood) is still missing and longs to be discovered.

Also critical to the new vision would be that philosophy loosen its rationalistic grip on human nature. Then human reason could open itself to the *being* of the person. Human nature would be seen as relating to the spiritual *essentially*—not merely problematically or peripherally.

The passivity of the matter of humankind—so obvious with the passivity of human bodies—would be itself part of what needs to be healed and activated, not to mention resurrected. Our passivity and "homeostasis" would then not be obtusely regarded by philosophy and psychology as the main standard by which we evaluate so much of human behavior and potential. Reductionism could be alleviated.

Theistic religions, seeking renewal, would find more than just common ground. They would discover anew the primary creation "*ex nihilo*," to which they have long given, for the most part, merely lip service.

Then the vigorous evaluation of *Genesis* as redemptive creation ("re-creation") could take place. Scholars could come to realize that the chaos or void mentioned at the beginning of this first book of the Bible indicates a need to recover from unspeakably self-destructive, interpersonal responses to the originative creation, presupposed by the textual account. The physical universe would be seen as the sacrament of God's healing for recovering "self-aholics."

Responding intellectually to these theoretical challenges would be part of the reclamation of our being—part of a living repentance for personal and communal sin at a depth we have hardly suspected.

Theism could be truly open within itself. But not like the "open theism" of contemporary thought that reacts, in its own literalistic mentality, to the classical concepts of God and salvation. Rather, along with the Scriptural and theological dimensions, *ontological* understanding within Revelation would be given open respect.

Amidst renewal, the arts and sciences themselves could develop a new dignity. Instead of being solely interdependent, or all of them being somehow dependent on one field of knowing, sciences could interface as mutually independent. The relationship, for instance, between philosophy and theology would be independence-*with* each other.

Similarly, biology and chemistry could be conceived as not only interdependent, but also as being mutually independent. Philosophy, especially, could be seen as independent-*with* psychology, physics, and all other disciplines. The sciences and branches of knowledge would be raised to the dignity of having, at least, a partially shared independence.

The Personal Challenge

The main challenge, however, would not be scientific or scholarly. It would be personal and communal. For every authentic seeker of meaning, this new consciousness-of-creation could become deeply freeing and life-gifting.

By meditation and prayer, we can break through our egocentric resistance to having our repression exposed. The result could be an ever-deepening revelation of God's absolutely intimate creation of perfect persons.

Our self-created volitional smog could be steadily burned away. Out of the clouds of our present perceptions and conceptions, the living God who is infinite Love could appear more readily.

A new horizon of personal meaning and joy would be gained. By admitting that creation is an interpersonal act of God and that our response was fully ours, we would be crossing a new threshold of hope. We would be better prepared for loving God with our whole hearts and our whole minds. We would be able to respond more freely and intimately when God says, "Come."

Some final words, from the three theistic testaments:

In the Christian Testament, we read that despite God's great love for the world,

> "...(T)he light is come into the world, and men loved darkness rather than the light: for their works were evil.
>
> For every one that doth evil hateth the light, and cometh not to the light, that his works may not be reproved.
>
> But he that doth truth, cometh to the light, that his works may be made manifest, because they are done in God"

John 3:19-21

From the Quran:

In Sura al-Baqarah, Allah is said to love those who turn to him in repentance and to love those who keep themselves pure.

Quran 2:222

With the Hebrew Testament, we can all pray:

Psalm 50

"Have mercy on me, O God, according to thy great mercy. According to the multitude of thy tender mercies blot out my iniquity. Wash me yet more from my iniquity, and cleanse me from my sin. For I know my iniquity, and my sin is always before me. To Thee only have I sinned, and have done evil before thee: that thou mayst be justified in thy words and mayst overcome when thou art judged. For behold I was conceived in iniquities; and in sins did my mother conceive me. For behold thou hast loved truth: the uncertain and hidden things of thy wisdom thou hast made manifest to me. Thou shalt sprinkle me with hyssop, and I shall be cleansed: thou shalt wash me, and I shall be made whiter than snow. To my hearing thou shalt give joy and gladness: and the bones that have been humbled shall rejoice. Turn away thy face from my sins, and blot out all my iniquities. Create a clean heart in me, O God: and renew a right spirit within my bowels. Cast me not away from thy face; and take not thy holy spirit from me. Restore unto me the joy of thy salvation, and strengthen me with a perfect spirit."

Psalms 50:1-12

Chapter 18

Questions and Responses:
Creation, Evil, and the Suffering of God

Sample questions and focused responses are offered with emphasis on creation, evil, and the suffering of God. These considerations might afford further perspective and serve as a kind of summary of the proposed theistic view. Except for several select repetitions, the questions add to the battery of questions and responses in volume 2, *God Says, We Say.*

The Two Kinds of Beginning and Our Repression

Question. You say we have two kinds of beginning with no time between them. How can this be so?

Response. Our time-bound minds are insulated from the meaning of being. So, first, we ought to distinguish existence from being.

"Existence" is the *manner* of being, by which we "ex-ist" (*ex-sistere*). Somewhat in accord with the roots of the word, we stand outside ourselves and we are attempting consciously to make our choices. Within the gift of our be-ing, originative sin has been the specific act whereby we passivized ourselves into an *ex-istence.* We "flattened" our be-ing, and we are now attempting to "peek out from under it."

Ex-istence is the result of a self-determination about sheer *be*-ing. This standing-outside kind of being applies to everything in this world of time and space, but especially to us fallen persons with our "cast out" spiritual, mental, emotional, and physical selves.

Non-persons also *exist*, but in a partial or fragmentary way, with no capacity for a truly self-conscious reflection and choice. These subpersonal creatures are, as it were, energy-remnants. They are fashioned by God out of the dire results of the originative crash of human personal freedom.

This formative actuation of all subhuman creation—whether it developed by creationism or by evolution—is a major dimension of our fallen human origination. It is clearly derivative; a second kind of beginning.

All subhuman realities might be called *excidents*, since they "fall out of" or away from (*ex-cadere*) the human be-ings that exist. Animals and plants, as well as all organic and inorganic substances, are creations of God out of the energy caused by the originative crash of our sheer *freedom*. (Our freedom had exploded into bits.)

These subhuman entities are fashioned from the energy formed by the self-fractuation of originatively sinning human persons. They provide paradoxically a remedial base for the redemption of fallen human persons, who eventually come to be conceived and rooted among them.

These excident entities—from molecules to monkeys—are partial beings. They are not *whole* beings because they do not exist with the powers or potential for self-reception and self-identification. But they are all related beingfully (ontologically) to us human persons who have crashed originatively. Originative sin affected not just human wills, but *caused to be* every atom in the universe, through the defective activation of those human wills.

In order to surmise the character of subpersonal (partial) beings, one might imagine animals as "partial humans." Animals would be appreciated as something like fingers without basis in a hand. These "detached" fingers would wiggle and point and react similar to "real" fingers on the hand of an integral human person. These partial beings—from animals to subatomic particles—are fashioned to be as humanlike as the intensity of their energy-constitution (fallen-off human fractuality) affords.

Excidents are elements that are material, incomplete substances and that are extrinsic to human substances. In contrast, there are what the traditional philosophy has called *accidents* (*ad-cadere*, to "fall toward"). The term accidents, in this usage, does not refer to a "fender benders on the boulevard," but to everything about a person or thing that truly belongs to it without being the reality in itself.

Accidents of a person include powers to think and to walk, as well as the individual and collective acts of these powers. Examples of accidents, for instance, would be both the power to talk and acts of talking by a human substance (person), both the power to bark and acts of barking by a canine substance, and both the ability of a bush to produce or to grow roses and the roses themselves. These features of a substance exist *in and through* the substance and cannot exist on their own. They are not "little substances."

As a wag once put it, "I have seen many faces without smiles, but never a smile without a face." The smile, and even the face, of a human person are accidents: features that cannot be without existing in and through some particular person or thing. No one has ever encountered barking without a barker or thinking without a thinker. Nor even a face without a "facer." Accidents stand as *parts* of the substances in and through which they exist.

In contrast, the manner of existing of a substance is *in and through itself,* and *not in and through another.* The substance might be dependent for its existence on many other substances, but as such the *way* in which it *exists* is in and through itself, not in and through another.

You and I are not accidents any more than a tree is an accident. People, animals, plants, and so forth do not exist in and through any other substance. They indeed *depend* on many other substances *for* their existence; but the *manner in which* they exist is *in and through themselves.*

Both excidents (in the way the new view conceives subpersonal substances) and accidents (features or parts of existents) emanate from the fragmental nature of fallen human persons. At the moment of *immaculate* creation, these persons self-defected.

Excidents are "breakaway energy" that is developed or matured through divine power in the recovery process. They comprise all subpersonal substances and their accidents.

Accidents of *human* substances in this world comprise all of the "extended or distended energy" that helps to form the recuperative powers and the actions of the redemptively recovering persons. We might say that accidents are developed within us from fragmentive human energy that did *not* "break away." That energy had *imploded* upon us and remained within us and of us. It was not lost by us, but existed in us and for us.

Strictly speaking, all things resulting from the second beginning, the beginning of be-coming, both are and exist. They are, but in a "cast out" manner of being—that is, they *ex*-ist. They are beings, but they *are* in a way that is "outside themselves within themselves."

God and the postitively responding angelic and human persons, however, do *not* "exist." They simply *are*. Lots of false problems would be wiped away if theists came to realize that God does *not exist*. God simply *is*. God is the infinite presence, to whom we have given, and are giving, incredibly little response.

We fallen persons are full beings that exist. We are, *and* we exist. Our egocentric consciousness impedes us and we think existence, the "cast out" manner of being, is the same as being. God is even "honored" sometimes as the supreme *Existent*, rather than as the supreme *Being*.

Moreover, we surmise unconsciously that being is in a temporal framework; that being is somehow framed by time. But it is not a mode of time. Rather, time is a mode of being—a defective mode—consequent upon our dive into ex-istence.

Both time and being are real, without any "time" between them. One must not be played off against the other, as is the inclination in Platonic, reincarnationist, and even Origenistic thought.

When people think that there must have been a pre-existence—a kind of "time before time" or "being before being"—they are, perhaps among other things, trying to develop room for the idea of our pristine, radical freedom. A "pre-existence" might sound like a good platform for a totally free self-determination, because we can hardly conceive of any such thing occurring under the conditions of space and time.

But, in order to postulate perfect human freedom, there is no point to a "pre-existence" as functional before the existence we are now living. The unity and the integrity of God's perfectly created beings provide "all the room in the world" for those perfectly free persons to respond and either to consummate or to mess up the gift of total union with God.

The term, "pre-existence," however, might apply to the crashed condition resulting from our act of flawed response to the creation *ex nihilo*. It would be actually something absolutely "pre" or prior with respect to our existence at the moment of conception. It would constitute the duration "between" the timeless act of creation *ex nihilo*—including our timeless, bad response—and our personal conception by our parents' gametes: the start of formal time for us as individuals who are actively responding to being redeemed.

At the moment of creation out of nothing, we crashed or collapsed into a state of passive existence where we "waited" until we could attain active existence in space and time on planet earth. We are now ex-isting (*ex-sistere*, to stand outside) actively, having been actually brought into active existence by way of our parents generating us.

In those vast ages, before we were conceived at a particular time and place, we were "pre-existing," that is, passively existing or being in a crashed manner prior to conception. With conception, we became formally existent. Our active existence began functionally at conception. Our *be*-ing badly—the immediate result of originative sin—might be called a "pre-existence" that had no active existence; it was really a faltering form of being—and of being our "plunged" self—strictly before our active ex-istence.

We who "messed up" caused the need for existence—for time and space to be. We are now trying, here and now in formal time and space, to "wake up" and to decide whether to admit our need for redemption and sanctification. The decision to admit is likewise a momentous activity of freedom, in which we are *now* engaged.

Having botched our creation in be-ing, we are now charged in this life—this ex-istence—with the opportunity to "come back to" sheer be-ing—to receive fully the gift we partially rejected. Our space-time life has been caused *both* by our crash *and* by God's infinitely merciful attempt to recover us, despite our profoundly unconscious resistance. God creates our *be*-coming, too.

We are subjects of the two kinds of creation, the two beginnings. Both creations—our creation in be-ing (creation out of *nothing*) and our creation in becoming (creation out of *something*, out of the mess)—began at the same *timeless* moment.

In being created, we immediately failed to receive fully our be-ing. This caused the crashed condition and we were thereby immediately in dire need of be-*coming*, and of another creation.

That other, derivative creation *began immediately* to be effected, but only through the saving love of God. This second beginning—at the same *timeless* moment as the first—is the redemptive creation that is continuous with the first. The originative moment was both the absolute beginning of our being and the definitive beginning of our redemption. It is no wonder that we conflate these two creations.

Jews and Christians, for instance, believe firmly in the coming of the Messiah or the Savior. His mission is to crown personally—right in our face, so to speak—the global work of God: redemption itself in space and time. For Christians, the definitive culmination of this liberation from sin comes in and through the death and resurrection of Jesus Christ.

In effect, all theists can come to appreciate how it could be that, *in one non-durational moment—freely and immediately—God created us out of nothing, we responded defectively, and God responded to our response by lovingly and forgivingly beginning the work of our be-coming (our "coming back").* This did not mean that we were necessarily going to be saved, but that we were necessarily being redeemed.

Our redemption is effectively the work of God incarnate alone. Our salvation is effectively the work of *both* God *and* our repentant hearts.

Q. You seem to be using the term *energy* as applicable only to creation *out of something*, but not to the creation *out of nothing*. Did God create energy only within the second kind of creation and not in the first?

R.   *Yes.* Energy is *the capacity to do work*, and the redemptive doing takes effort.

(For Christians, the incarnation of the Word of God requires that the incarnate One be part energy—even though there is no energy in God as God. "Divine Energy" is a metaphor. But the Word-Person of God acts in, through, and with human energy in effecting the redemption.)

There was no effort at all for God to create all person-beings "out of nothing." Nor was any exertion intended for the created ones in their *receiving* of this gift of be-ing at that pristine moment.

We could have received, freely and effortlessly, our own be-ing and exercised it by perfect freedom in uniting with God. Our gifted independence-*with* God affords us no scope for work and energy. Struggle, striving, and any other form of effort have come from the *passivity* that *we* effected by causing conditions of independence-*from* and dependence-*on*.

Salvation, however, is *work* on our part and, in a sense, on God's. Infinite power respects our activity of finite freedom, even though we exercise it resistantly. Christians, at least, regard redemption and salvation as the *work* of God, quite particularly through the passion and death of Jesus, the Word-Person of the divinity. In addition, many theists recognize the *work* of the six days of creation, touted in the first passages of Genesis.

In the new perspective, the forming of the earth and its creatures is a central part of the second or redemptive creation. However long it took, this world was created in and with time. Time is required for the actions of effort.

We redeemed persons, however, are not just "doing time." We are integrating time. Moreover, that endeavor is part of our work, done by means of the expended energy caused by our fractuality. We need time in order to awaken from the shock of being self-wounded, as well as time to receive our being to an appreciable extent. In short, to "wake up."

At the instant of creation out of nothing, rebelling human actuality split itself, resulting in two basic kinds of energy. From this primal fracture, one kind of energy was extrinsic; the other, intrinsic.

Subpersonal matter is extrinsic *human* energy. Yet this extrinsic energy (fractuality) ("alienated actuality") in its super-multitudinous forms of animal, plant, mineral, and so forth, provides grounds for the attempted human renewal. While it represents a primal effect of our originative sinning, this extrinsic human energy is also *gifted* (*ex aliquo*) by the divine activity on behalf of our recovery.

Extrinsic cosmic energy forms the matrix for the conception, birth, and development of sinful human persons, including their potential contrition, conversion, and repentance—the quasi-placental life of becoming redeemed.

But proper to us, as self-fractualized human persons, is *intrinsic* cosmic energy. Within the spatiotemporal matrix, whole human persons—bodily, emotionally, mentally, and spiritually—work by exercising their own personal energy. This energy is intrinsic only to humans-in-recovery. It comprises the human body and the functions of humans who are undergoing redemption and potential salvation.

So, we can say, again, that there are two basic kinds or forms of human energy, as the result of the prime fractuality within our fallen human personhood.

The first is fragmentive energy: energy of the whole cosmos that is functionally other than that of the integrative human persons who are struggling to awaken and to convert from within it. God formed into non-primal substances this extrinsic human energy that had been caused by the initial human cataclysm, the big bang of being. Coming from the fractualization of human freedom at its primal moment of irresponsibility, this crucial energy or reactive actuality is extrinsically related to the human persons who depend upon it for cosmic or earthly sustenance.

The second kind of energy is integrative energy: the intrinsic energy of the individual human person that includes the person's own bodily, mental, emotional, and spiritual condition.

Intrinsic energy represents part of the nature of the human as God physically constitutes the person in the world. This auto-energy of the whole individual person has not been explosively fragmented by his or her originative sin. But its effectuation represents a kind of bloating of being—a significant distortion of originatively gifted being. This kind of energy is actively, if constrictively, exercised by the individual person. By means of this intrinsic source of total endeavor, the redeemed person copes with the cosmic struggle to awaken and be saved, all the while interacting fluently with extrinsic human energy (the energy of the cosmos).

Our life as a prebirth child might serve to suggest the situation of our energy in the larger womb of space and time. In the mother's womb, the child's placenta is a kind of necessary functional part of life: serving as a kind of extrinsic energy or self-environment that came from the same unitary source as the intrinsic energy that forms the child's body. The fetal body itself represents a kind of intrinsic energy on the way to maturation. Upon the "death" of being born from the womb, the child loses its placental (extrinsic) energy and goes into extra-uterine life with the same intrinsic energy, ever manifest in the growing bodily self.

Paradoxically, these two forms of human energy—extrinsic and intrinsic—can be understood as dramatically interactive at death. The dying person can be seen to be "in touch." Not only in touch with cosmic energies, but with the timeless dimension of his or her being, wherein originative failure occurred.

And at the moment of death, there is a kind of recapitulation of the activity that caused the need for death. The *maybe*-saying that was responsible for originative fractualization of being is manifest in the that very mega-*maybe* of death and in its impending collision with everlasting destiny. No one escapes this major measure of self-immolation.

Death has been rightly called a substantial change, quite different from, and transcendent to, all the motions and actions of the person in this world. Amidst myriad accidental or secondary changes of the human being, every substantial change in this processing world happens in an *instant*. In this *instant* of substantial change at the death of a person, there is "contact" with the timeless from which we are normally self-blocked; yet we move inexorably toward it.

When the human being is seriously ill and dying, there comes a point at which the whole human being ceases to ex-ist in space and time. What remains observable to us after the *change* that we call *death* is non-living ("dead") matter that is a being-based residue (the corpse). At the point when a human person no longer exists in this world and when only multiple non-living elements such as carbon, nitrogen, and other cadaverous substances exist as remains, there has been a substantial change.

The multitudes of accidental modifications of the living human as he or she is sliding toward death are features of the human substance itself. Yet at the instant the person "loses life" in tangible space and time, there remains only a complexus—an extrinsic unity—of non-living substances. The person no longer exists in this world at that point. And the new substances—particles of the corpse, the dead "body"—start to exist. They are *not* particles of the living body, but multitudinous new elements. They are inorganic substances *caused* by the death itself.

So, that instant constitutes a break in time—a timeless moment. Such an instant is *not* a part of time. The instant is a non-temporal divider: right within time, dividing absolutely all that is past and all that is to come.

In order to appreciate this, we might consider a simple geometrical analogy. Draw the line AB. Place an X somewhere in the middle of the line. This point X on the line AB is a *not* a part of the line. The point X marks the end of the AX part of the line AB, and it also marks the beginning of the XB part of that line.

Similarly, the instant of death for the human substance marks its end in this world. At once, there is, in this world, the beginning of wholly new substances. Their array might "look like" the original. The corpse looks like a living body without being one. But every molecule in that corpse is substantially quite other and is *not the same* molecule as its living "look-alike" counterpart that was there the moment before death.

In the world of space and time, the timeless intrudes at every "point." Every instant is *not* a part of time, but itself is timeless: serving as a division of past from future.

From a more fundamental point of view, however, the whole of space-time happenings can be seen as within the "larger" realm of the spaceless-and-timeless. Space itself forms a wounded condition within the spaceless. And time itself is a wounded condition within the timeless. Space and time also serve redemptively as windows in our longing for union with a spaceless and timeless destiny.

If fulfilled, that destiny is to be a pure finite act of love. When a person comes into full union with the divine, energy will be literally useless.

Q.   In recent years, there have been many people who claim to have had near-death experiences. Some report that, in their out-of-body experience, they were told something about the meaning of life, but that they would actually forget the message when they reentered their normal earthly existence. Could it be that

they were informed about their bad response to creation out of nothing, but that the shock of knowing was so immense that they were unable to recall it once returning to ordinary life?

R.   Possibly. But I do not intend to place much stock in "private revelations."

The idea that something would actually have to be forgotten is not surprising. One of perhaps many "forgettable truths" might be that these returnees and the rest of us have committed an originative sin that caused all of the passivity of redemptive creation.

The originative encounter with God that resulted in sin and that caused the actuality of repression would have made the redemption necessary. And it would have required us to participate personally in our salvation.

At least, the idea that to live in this world is to live in a world of "forgetting" major truths should not surprise us. Our actions in this world might be likened to paralytic behavior; they are freighted with the conditions of passivity and dependence.

Perhaps we could regard our miss-exercise of originative freedom as creating quasi-hypnotic suggestions.

We know that in the ordinary world the person under hypnosis might be given a suggestion about not being able to do something and, after coming out of the hypnotic state, he or she is completely incapacitated in that particular way. Somewhat similarly, at the originative moment of sin we might be said to have done something similar to ourselves spiritually: we could have actually caused a self-suggested incapacity.

In any event, we could say that our present essential dependency and passivity was caused by us at that unprecedented moment.

Our present ontological paralysis is not directly caused by God, but is directly self-inflicted. It is as though we are victims of our own self-suggestion at the originative level of freedom. Only divine compassion and power—infinite and eternal—could support us after our break with our be-ing by means of the "self-hypnotic" condition, if we permit this divine "help."

Nevertheless, even the breakthrough of salvation itself could only occur if we come to the point of admitting our originatively self-distorted condition. Such a point, for most of us, apparently comes at the moment of death, or not at all.

Q.   You do not want to rely on merely private revelations and on intuitions. Nor do you wish to make irrational suppositions. So, are you claiming that your hypothesis is logical or rational?

R.   The hypothesis of originative sin would seem to be genuinely an ontological inference based upon several main truths about God and human creatures. It is likewise intuitive for those who are willing to understand.

For instance, the hypothesis acknowledges God as both infinitely powerful and infinitely good. So, there is no way we can attribute to God any evil, nor even the slightest imperfection and arbitrarity. The reason for evil and suffering lies in created persons themselves.

For Christians, Jesus as the Redeemer is the obvious exception, suffering without having committed an originative sin or any other sin. Another type of exception would be any created person who might be originatively free of sin, but who freely consented to help in the redeeming activity by suffering with those who had sinned.

To all of us, and particularly to Biblical archetypes like Job, the traditional view says this: God's allowing evil to afflict the innocent is a great mystery. It is beyond our powers to understand. So, we are called to live within this mystery in fear of the Lord, knowing with the certainty of Faith that God is kind and merciful.

Such a response is good as far as it goes. But if there is a more intelligible way to understand God allowing evil, are we not obliged to accept it—at least provisionally?

Originative sin—taken together with original sin—offers a more reason-worthy perspective. When developed, this supposition would seem to be more attuned to the fear of the Lord and an acceptance of the great mystery of evil than the usual interpretations have been. It provides a reasonable—if shocking—account about how and why we must have sinned originatively. As a result, the questions about the origin of evil and suffering, and about the reason for both, finally have answers that are basic, if not "fully detailed."

Moreover, as far as our origins go, the standard interpretations that effectively regard us as sheer victims of the failure of Adam and Eve are hardly worthy of the sons and daughters of God. And when some people regard God as the foremost Abuser, as does the theology of protest, there is a tragic failure to see how infinite Being is and acts, and how God is infinitely different from being and action that is finite and defectible.

Traditional defenders of God's ways as not being our ways often say that the problem of suffering is not something we can solve, but that it is a mystery to be lived. Unfortunately, they often neglect to indicate that living the mystery of evil and suffering is something that can be done with ever-increasing insight and understanding, to which all are called as part of their authentic living.

The hypothesis of personal responsibility for originative sin would seem to move us deeper, yet more understandably, into the mystery. By recognizing personal responsibility for evil's origin in our own lives, we are invited to be much more at home with the mystery.

We do not have to assume the usual theories saying, in effect, that we must simply believe. The basic idea of these theories is that we cannot reasonably see why an infinitely perfect God would allow any suffering at all, including the peril of permanent punishment, to inflict obviously innocent children. The pivotal premise seems to be that sinning was initiated solely or mainly by others (Lucifer, Adam, Eve).

Yet we do not have to play this blame game.

We can definitively affirm that God is truly infinite, through both power and goodness. We were created as perfect finite persons, creatures of the infinitely perfect God. We were not simply the second level project of a super-creator, who acts like an artisan in creating the world through a process, lasting mere days or many aeons.

We can understand that our immediate and fully free, if partial, deformation of the gift of perfect freedom has placed us in danger of perdition and in total personal need of a divine Savior. With respect to our original condition of sin, we ought to take Lucifer, Adam, and Eve off the hook of ultimate responsibility. And God, too.

Our repression can be eased considerably thereby and we can be moving toward much more effective healing through a significant increase in meaning. The new supposition would seem to afford better meaning for better healing.

Q. You seem to think that holy ones have a kind of preconscious recognition of their failure in be-ing. They are so ready to accuse themselves of a deeply sinful condition. So, do you know of any saints who have confessed consciously an originative sin such as you describe?

R. No. But that does not mean that there are none. And my claim is that we all know, at least in a spiritually unconscious way, our originative failing. I am claiming that you know it. Now, are you going to admit it?

We are called to realize that we did not begin to *be* at the moment of being conceived or rooted in this world. We cannot remember empirically, of course, our existence prior to conception. But that is because this "duration" is rather a kind of pre-history and is, as it were, the "precursor of spatiotemporal history." A fuller account of our be-coming here in space and time is founded upon the story of our be-ing—why we are in this condition of being.

Since we do not know to what extent we have been originatively self-deceptive in be-ing, we should be all the more attentive to our beingful responsibilities here in the *maybe* world of be-coming. The uncommon sanity of saints arises from their acknowledgement of, and corrective attention to, good and evil in their own selves.

In the Christian tradition, even a great "little soul" like Therese of Lisieux must have had particularly divergent elements to her being. Prompted by her originative sin, these features of fractuality show up obliquely in her earthly life, such as in her last year when she was constantly tempted by atheism.

Mother Teresa of Calcutta suffered a great emptiness during many of her years of missionary life, bereft of spiritual "consolations." Was she not profoundly living out the consequences of her own originative sin, even as she consoled and comforted her companion sufferers?

Holy ones in the Christian tradition have always identified with their Savior's apparent abandonment on the cross. Their strength comes through appreciating, and identifying with, a kind of divine "emptiness" (receptivity) that was required to redeem and save a sinful world.

Even more so, Christian saints testify to God's redemptive love as truly infinite. They really believe that the love of the Word-Person of God was not just perfect, but infinite. Infinite love acts to effect the triumph of salvation, but accomplishes it through weakness and self-abandonment, rather than through aggressive conquest. Only infinite love could do it that way. The finest of finite love could not have redeemed or saved us.

All are called to live the burdens of existence as a consequence of sin—both the originative and the original. To attempt "verification," it might be helpful to try to deny a particular supposition of this book, namely, that "I could have committed an originative sin at the moment of my creation 'fresh from the heart of God.'" See whether you can honestly say, "No, that *could* not have happened. The idea is absurd!"

Next, keep yourself honestly aware that God always acts—in creating, redeeming, and in any other way—with infinite goodness and infinite power, and as well with infinite justice and mercy. Then ask yourself how your predicament in earthly life—not immediately knowing where you came from, nor where you are absolutely headed upon death—could have developed *in any way other than by an irresponsibility that was fully personal.*

Q. You said that Origen, in the early Christian Church, did not have access to the systematic concept of the unconscious and of repression. But, even if thinkers in and beyond the 20th century do gain leverage, how can anyone then reasonably take the idea of repression that clearly comes from the psychological realm and project it onto the vastly different realm of the spiritual?

R.   As indicated in my books, the psychological does express what is spiritual, and not vice versa, even as the physical expresses both. *Everything* in the human being is similar to, though different from, everything else. We can take our first awareness and early study of something, such as the phenomenon of psychic repression, and see whether it has analogous—not univocal—application to other areas of human life.

Such is the way the human mind seems intended to function. For instance, before we can know about divine creativity, we first know something about human makers of products and art pieces. And then we must be careful to notice that the order of knowing is the reverse of the order of being. So, even though our ways of knowing are a bit like God's ways, God's ways are not "like" our ways.

Similarly, there is a reversal in meaning when we study levels of activity within ourselves as doers of *be*-ing. We know about human psychic repression first; but we can come, at least later, to surmise human spiritual repression, which is prior in being.

In other words, psychic repression is *consciously known* first, but is far less important with respect to being and truth than the spiritual repression that creates part of the originative cause of all spiritual, psychic, and physical defects. And we ought to allow that, while psychic repression is somewhat like spiritual repression, the latter is not at all the same as the better-known, psychic repression. Yet it is vastly more real in itself. (In addition, it is immensely more difficult to admit.)

Correlative to the psychic and spiritual *unconscious* we ought also to acknowledge the *physical* unconscious: that massive physical structure of our being that underlies our bodily anatomy. What we call our physical body is the *consciously accessible* structure of our *physical* being.

The overtly sensible part of our physical life (body) is what is susceptible to death. But its sustaining counterpart, our unconscious body—together with the depths of the emotional and the spiritual unconscious—does not *die*; it dislodges from empirically detectible space and time at the moment of physical death.

Our unconscious life awaits redemptive transformation, upon the release of our hold on cosmic existence. In *this* world, we are not so much conscious beings with an unconscious life; rather, we are unconscious beings with a conscious life.

Once we can appreciate this reality, we will have effected a critical transformation of vision. And we will have acted according to what I like to call the Aristotelian reverse principle: our way of conscious knowing is the *reverse* of the way of being. The cause of knowing something is not at all the same as the cause of the *being* of what we know

Creation and Evolution

Q.   You definitely differentiate between two kinds of creation: the originative and the redemptive. Within the latter creation, however, you do not seem to take a stand on the controversy between theistic evolution and creationism. Why not?

R.   Did the human community originate in space and time through a direct and complete act of God's making (creationism)? Or did we evolve from lower forms of life—through mediated activity of God (theistic evolution)? This issue is important. But, at this point in the history of reflective consciousness, it is probably not resolvable.

On one side of the issue, the side of creationism, God could have "miraculously inserted" into this material world a fully developed Adam and Eve at a particular point, with or without a preparatory "evolution" of lower forms and conditions. But such a couple could not have been a creation "out of nothing." Their origin in this world would have to be a "making endeavor" of God, fashioning them out of the "remnants" of their crash in freedom. The "dust of the earth," perhaps?

The creation known according to the theory of creationism is a process—albeit a "quick" one. Energy can be emitted in bursts of creativity. But the creation of such energy is out of *something* (*ex aliquo*), not out of *nothing*. Energy is necessarily an imperfect form of being.

God creates directly, however, only perfect creatures. Only the perfect can come immediately by virtue of the perfect. That is, the origination of the perfect finite can come only through the activity of the infinitely perfect.

We must begin to admit that the story of the Garden, as such, is not of a *perfect* couple, even though the conditions are described as approximating perfection—or seem to hint at the state of perfection underlying the story. Yet, not even *God* can create a perfect being out of dust or passivity. Passivity would be a kind of constitutive imperfection in the result. God is the *infinitely* perfect Creator who creates out of *nothing*.

God is not a magician, producing fantasy. The perfect comes "out of nothing." That which is originally *not*-perfect cannot be a base for the coming of the perfect.

On the other side of this issue, the side of evolutionism, it is impossible for the human community to have come through merely "natural causes"—without divine power and activity. So, evolution without God is impossible.

And while the very process of evolution through God's power, despite the lack of "empirical evidence," is possible theoretically, it could *not* be the *same* as the original creation (*ex nihilo*). Its whole meaning is *existence*: a manner of *being-out-of* something lower.

Thinking that evolution could have been God's original way of creating (*ex nihilo*) was one of the big mistakes made in the 20th century by the renowned scientist-philosopher Teilhard de Chardin. His dynamic worldview has inspired an utterly massive evolutionary perspective and discussion. It might contain merit, but only by way of partly explaining redemptive creation.

Evolution, taken fully into account, is an inherently flawed activity and could *not* have come *directly* and *solely* from God's activity, nor from creatures who were perfectly responsive to God's will. An evolution of consciousness could perhaps be part of the dynamic "natural cooperation" with God done by *maybe*-saying creatures, by created persons who are being in the process of actual redemption and potential salvation.

Contemporary theology is laced with attempts to explain origins through evolution. Many religious scholars have even been impelled to re-think the nature of God in some respects. The burst of thinking known as "process theology" represents a systematic account of God and cosmic creation that tends to conflate the divine and created worlds, while trying to make God more dynamically relevant. The Creator-creature relationship is truncated in an over-reaction to the deistic and creationistic postures of the past.

Theology is ever profoundly challenged. Some evolution-inclined theologians within the Christian tradition have developed important reflections concerning the proposal that God expresses vulnerability and is engaged in a self-kenosis or self-emptying toward all creation. They claim that the divine omnipotence is compatible with genuine humility and with a divine activity of love that is defenseless (not powerless) and vulnerable.

Christians, of course, believe that the Son of God endured an excruciating torture and death by crucifixion. So, from that point of view, the claim of God's susceptibility to being violently resisted seems unassailable.

Redeeming corruptive people with incarnate love is a "task" even for infinite power. Infinite love is faced with the absolutely gifted freedom of created persons. These fallen persons are actively resisting God, through the dynamics of the subhuman world—to which they "contributed" originatively—as well as through their own consciously contemplated choices.

But there is no vulnerability involved in creating perfect persons with perfect freedom to respond. Only the imperfect response of those created persons who are freely reluctant could "make God vulnerable."

The notion of an *immaculate* creation *ex nihilo* is far from being acknowledged by theistic evolutionists. And so, by an inner logic, many of them regard God as acting in the manner of a mega-creature or mega-maker who is self-abandoning, under the chaotic moves of matter in motion.

Actually, self-abandonment is not anything that God does. But it is something that we *think* God might be doing because we continue to deny that we are the one's who have abandoned God in the most radical manner.

We are inveterately inclined to make it appear that God must do something extraordinary "even for God," so that we are redeemed and saved. Projection onto God serves as the hobgoblin of personal irresponsibility.

While they fancy themselves as rejecting the "metaphysics of the past," process philosophers tumble into the trap of advocating a "metaphysics of the future." But the change of focus from past to future is largely an escape. Theological "Darwinists" continue to work from the unconscious framework of necessarily spatial and temporal perspectives, even as their creationist opponents do. Both sides seem to be—rather unconsciously—locked into the framework of space and time.

Theistic evolutionists, moreover, are quite inclined to subscribe not simply to the intriguing data of biology and anthropology, but to the dynamics of evolutionary biologism. They are apt to find support therein for the grand impression that everything past and present is "explained" by whatever might turn out to be.

Biological determinism makes it impossible to escape a kind of metaphysical "teleologism" (subverted teleology). In the present climate, both theological and scientific minds are inclined to deal with purposes that are inherently natural and then to reduce them merely to "outcomes." Results-oriented consequentialists have their own propensities for denying the primacy of originative being.

The idea of "natural selection" is highly selective. Process thinkers almost inevitably transfer to the future the meaning of existence and their ultimate sense of responsibility for who they are, both now and forever. Going from being hobbled by the past to being held hostage to the future is hardly an improvement. *Becoming* thereby trumps *being*. We remain inherently meaningless in our *being*.

Q. Suppose, as theists generally believe, that there was a single couple, Adam and Eve, who became the father and mother of all humans on the planet earth. How could the human community get its start without the children of this couple engaging in incest?

R. That is a good question and it displays one of the reasons I do not think we have developed sufficient knowledge regarding the "mechanisms" and timelines of human origins in space and time.

The "one and only first couple" idea (monogenism) would seem to involve some kind of necessary incest, at least at the beginnings of human existence. But the notion of there being "more-than-a-single-couple" (polygenism), taken for granted by many evolutionists, would also likely involve incest.

That the human community would have to start out mired in incestuous relations provides a testament to the punishment for both originative and original sin. Even if Adam and Eve had not fallen and had begun to procreate within paradise, would not incest be inevitable?

This predicament is especially symptomatic of the prime sin at the moment of the *originative* creation. Therein we freely, if partially, engaged in direct intercourse with ourselves, an ontological incest, instead of uniting completely and ecstatically with God.

Moral Law and Subhuman Creatures

Q. If nature is so crippled, then what do you think about the natural moral law?

R. I firmly assent to the meaning of natural moral law as developed by Aristotle, Aquinas, and many others down to our day. But it is, of course, not the *complete* natural law given by God with our *being* "out of nothing," with its finite perfection.

As it is now, our knowledge of the natural moral law is immediate and intuitive, as well as rationally derived. But it is still shortsighted and could be given further development in its roots by cooperation with God's grace.

Something more is needed. Our being longs for *essence law*: the structure of created love itself. God redeems us, in part, by gradually restoring us to ever deeper unity with essence law—the originative natural law of love given in the *first* beginning.

In creation out of nothing we were gifted with the pristine, natural law of grace—gifted directly by the personal power of God. What we now call natural law is good, but incomplete. It ought to be regarded as natural law truncated by sin. Or, perhaps, the law of grace denatured.

The prime principle of natural moral law, as we live it in the spatiotemporal world, is "do good and avoid evil." This precept serves for a world that is suffused with good-and-evil. It rules in the world of our *second* beginning.

However, "do good and avoid evil" is the dim reflection of the originative principle of perfect freedom that is contained in God's absolutely loving command to "Be": "Be fully yourself, you are entirely good, just as you are and are gifted to be!"

Here in our redemptive life we come to know principles of natural moral law, such as "do not lie, do not steal, do not kill, do not covet," and so forth. These injunctions and others serve us in a manner proportionate to our present condition, estranged as we are from the originative gift.

Furthermore, the self-deconstruction involved in our response to our first beginning is critically significant. It means that all of what is now natural to us—eating, sleeping, choosing one course of action over another, and so forth—is only a provisional or secondary aspect of our originative nature.

This secondary nature is both good and deprived: both God-given and self-driven. It is profoundly egocentric, as anyone can see in the ways all babies behave—no matter how aged they become.

By our *ex*-istence, we are inclined stubbornly to accept human nature the way we find it and to call it "natural." But, in doing so, we allow ourselves little room to understand the deeper nature that flows immediately from our essence. That nature was wounded and deprived *by us* in our first response to God, at the moment we came to be, immediately and interpersonally, within the divine Heart.

That deeper natural way of being human would have been to relate with God immediately, fully, spontaneously, and finitely without end. The humanly natural and the divinely Natural (supernatural to us) would have been wedded together perfectly forever.

Our essence as finite persons is to be able to unite interpersonally with infinite Personhood. But now our nature involves a disposition to do that uniting rather badly.

We are virtually unaware of this originative prospect. Therefore, we often find it difficult now to acknowledge the need for a really personal Savior—wherein not only the Savior is received as fully personal, but so are the saved. We are called to receive ourselves as persons and to be personally involved in countering the originative evil from which God attempts to save us.

Theistic Revelation on earth is rooted in the divine covenant with the chosen people. Revelation declares both our natural, impersonal resistance and God's interpersonal effort to bring us into a spiritual condition that repairs the originative divorce in the marital covenant of creation.

We would do well to apply to the meanings of nature and grace the classical principle of reversity: the way we first come to know anything is the reverse of the way it is. We first come to know nature (our defective kind) and only gradually, if ever, come to know the grace of being-*with* God in which we were originatively created.

This latter reality is *first*. The nature that we more readily and immediately know was caused by a rupture that we effected within that very interpersonal grace of primal creation.

We begin to understand ourselves consciously first as beings of nature—nature that is good, but severely injured. Then we work our way toward seeing things more as they are in themselves. We go from knowing them unconsciously to knowing them consciously.

Originatively, all beings were beings of grace: perfect gifts of the infinitely perfect Gift-Being who is God. The life of God is grace. But, in an extended sense, our originatively intended union with God is also grace: the grace of gifted being-at-all (creation). To a large extent, that grace is still being deferred, and can be rejected.

Q.   I seem to hear you saying that plant and animal life are somehow effects of what you call our primal sin and, at the same time, are effects of God's redemptive creation. Do you really mean that we are partly causes of the *existence* of plants and animals? Frankly, this seems preposterous.

R. Bacteria, viruses, fungi, parasites, mosquitoes, snakes—in fact, all plants and animals—would not exist, I think, if we had all said *yes* to God instead of *maybe*. In that sense, we are originatively conditional causes of their existence.

Our sin occasioned their existence. But even so they would not exist at all without God's redemptive response. They are created by God *ex aliquo*: out of the breakup and fallout of our originative nature. They are thus *excidents* of our fallen human personhood.

In redemptive creation, God is forming these non-human creatures out of the primordial chaos that we caused within the originative creation that was fully and exclusively personal. *All of subhuman creatures—including simple atoms and molecules—are human-like in various degrees; and they anticipate, somewhat supportively, the decisively spiritual likeness to God that is realized specifically only in humans.*

Subpersonal creation "groans and gropes" toward a resolution of the massive energy, originated and dissipated by the fractuality—the fractured actuality—of crashed human persons in their originative miss-reception of *be*-ing.

Creatures and a Perfect Creation

Q. But this approach seems incredible. You think that only beings who are persons can really be perfect creatures. Are other creatures imperfect not only *de facto*, but necessarily so?

R. *Yes*. Creation *out of* not*hing* by divine being is necessarily an inter*personal* act.

Subpersonal creatures are naturally incapable of actively receiving the gift of being as a gift. So, they are necessarily imperfect. Plants and animals are so passive that they cannot actively and self-consciously receive. They cannot receive at all; they can only be "done to"—never "done with," never interacted with, *spiritually*.

Some are much more passive than others. Subhuman creatures exist along a continuum of "holistic passivity"—from the greatest to the least—as *part* of the redemptive or remedial universe.

There could never be a perfect tree. Treeness itself (the essence of being a tree) necessarily includes passive matter and quantitative features like length, height, and weight, of which there is *no* possibility for absolute perfection—for perfect union with God. There is, in itself, *no* "perfect length," "perfect height," and so forth.

Besides, there can be no perfect tree because to be a tree is to be part passivity as well as part activity. Speaking of a "perfect tree" or a "perfect cloud" is quite like speaking of a "square circle." These "entities" are impossibilities "even" for God, and represent, at best, figments of our egocentric preferences.

All subpersonal entities are quite incomplete; they are partial beings, essentially incapable of receiving and giving themselves. Some, like chimpanzees, do reflect beautifully and emphatically, through their "imitative" physical and emotive behavior, a peculiar likeness to the spiritual intentions of specifically human behavior in space and time. But they cannot really know themselves as selves, reflectively and intrinsically independent of all matter and motion.

Aristotelian-minded philosophers and theologians realized that a kind of qualified perfection remains possible among humans. Such a condition, they thought, obtains only when passive matter and its intrinsic qualities are not essentially a part of the activity. And so, they recognized that the *idea* of even the most mundane physical substance is *not* physical at all—*as idea or concept.*

They could see that when we cause an idea as such, the effect, the idea—as well as the activity strictly causative of it—is not itself time-bound or space-bound, even though it is cooperative with a particular temporal sequence. They were able to distinguish the extrinsic dependence of the intellect upon sense activity from its intrinsic independence with respect to the sense activity with which it *de facto* cooperates.

This realization also means that knowing your favorite tree in its *treeness* is knowing something of space spacelessly. Unlike that of even the "highest" animals, human knowing remains intrinsically independent of matter and motion, even when extrinsically quite dependent. Human senses are necessary, yet extrinsically so, relative to the specific acts of knowing the essences of things in this world. While mightily cooperative extrinsically, the senses cannot help intrinsically.

Many philosophers recognized that non-sentient knowledge and love—found only in persons, including humans—are essentially free of matter and motion in themselves, even when their objects are material things. Knowledge and love can be perfect, specifically as powers and acts of personhood, not of animality.

A big problem, however, is the traditional notion that substantive perfection can include passivity. Spiritual creatures such as angels, and humans with respect to their spiritual souls, are regarded as passive in the essence of their being. Even the good and sinless angels are thought to be constituted by essences that are passive, relative to their actuality of being. So, in the common understanding, only God is perfect and is known as Pure Act: Actuality without any passivity.

This is a monumental mistake. It confuses purity of actuality with infinity. God is not just pure act, but *infinitely* pure act. By contrast, the prime intention of God in gifting persons with being had to be to create finitely pure acts. We were originally intended by God to be pure actualities—limited, specific, perfect (personal) creatures. God cannot create "out of nothing" any passivity at all.

Each created person—whether angelic or human—is "more or less" a likeness of God. Some angelic beings are much more "God-like" in their essence than others, but each one is a perfect likeness at its own finite, yet perfect, level. We, however, who are human persons were created to be not only perfect likenesses of God, but perfect images—perfect complex essences. We became imperfect images through our own defective act of first freedom. (The word "image" here must be taken figuratively and symbolically.)

Strictly speaking, finite persons cannot be "more or less" like God, since God is infinite in perfection. While the finite is related to the infinite, it cannot be related comparably. There is no *formal* basis for *comparison* between the finite and the infinite.

The whole realm of the finite nonetheless might be said to be related comparably within itself. Although some finite beings are not "more perfect than others" originatively—since they are all created absolutely perfect at their own level—some might be considered superior in kind of finite essence (perfection) relative to others. One finite essence can be of a higher kind than another can, while both are perfect in their own way—in their own unique likeness to God.

When the finite is considered in relation to the infinite, however, there is no basis for comparison. Yet there is unlimited basis for *relationship*. God is infinitely related to us, even as we are finitely related to God. As persons, we are *capax Dei*, that is, we are able to relate directly with God.

The relative or comparative character in our being applies strictly among ourselves as finite persons. We are more or less like each other in the finite essences with which God gifted us. And we are originatively related with God, not as imperfect to Perfect, but as perfect finite (unique individual and communal) ones to the infinite One.

Because many philosophers and theologians in the past have not adequately distinguished *finite* being from *imperfect* being, they have often held that while we are related to (read: dependent on) God, God is not related to (read: dependent on) us. They have confused being related with being dependent. And they have not adequately discerned the difference between saying God is perfect and saying God is infinite.

There might be some reason for thinking that perfect being cannot relate to ("depend on") imperfect being, even as the imperfect desperately needs (depends on) the perfect. But this thinking misses the distinction between perfection and infinite perfection. God's perfection is not finite perfection, but infinite perfection—relating to all being in an infinite way.

Q. You say it many times in this book: God originally creates only perfect beings. But there has been so much theological and religious discourse that, in effect, denies this kind of claim. So, it sounds like you are saying God creates God. Is not God the only perfect being that there is or could be? Is not every creature necessarily, *in some sense*, an imperfect being, otherwise the creature would be God?

R   No, indeed. As mentioned, a perfect being created by God would not be God, because God is not only perfect, but infinitely perfect. (There could be, of course, no imperfect infinite being.)

Every creature that is immediately created by God is perfect finite being, capable of fully responding to God with knowledge and love. Such is a person.

Imperfect finite being, such as ours, is caused by free finite persons degrading their own perfect freedom in their very first act of *be-ing who they are*. (If they do not degrade themselves by their first act of be-ing, they necessarily confirm themselves as perfect. Every act then flows from confirmed perfection of be-ing and would be 'untemptable.')

This means that the whole spatiotemporal material universe was brought, not directly "out of nothing," but really out of "something" caused by us: out of our *may-be* response to be-ing. Every element of the cosmos comes, through the redemptive efforts of God, out of the void in *our* self-frustrated human natures.

The infinite Being of God can only create (bring "out of nothing") finite beings. Yet, these perfect finite beings (finite pure acts, without passivity) cannot bring into being *out of nothing* anything at all.

However, by perfect, God-gifted freedom, and within the infinite grace of God, a finite being *can* and *does* bring into being *out of itself* its freely chosen destiny in the covenant of God's creation.

We are originatively God-like, but are not God at all. We are not like God in being finite, but in being perfect. We are like God in a finite way—that is, limitedly and perfectly—but God is infinitely other than we, in being and ability.

Moreover, God's infinite ability is not in any way arbitrary, as our defective, projective understanding readily takes it to be. Christians, for instance, are often awed at Jesus saying, "Be you therefore perfect, as also your heavenly Father is perfect." (*Matthew* 5:48). They wonder how they can be "equal" to God in goodness.

But when a finite being acts perfectly in accord with his or her finite nature, this being is "just as perfect" as is God, who acts in accord with infinite nature. Both created and uncreated persons can be perfect relationally and proportionately—finite to infinite.

All theists need an awakening to reality: God's originative act of creating has caused an *immaculate creation*. The originative creation could not have resulted in any imperfect persons. If there were the slightest imperfection of originative freedom in the created persons to respond perfectly and immediately in knowing and loving, then there would be no hope for ever attaining full intimacy with God.

From the imperfect, only the imperfect can come. An imperfect ability to love, as an original gift of God, would be an absurdity.

Unless they have perfect natures from the start of their being, sinful creatures have no perfection to "return *to*." Not even God could *restore* what is *not* there originally to *be* restored.

God is not a kind of "value-added" creator and redeemer: adding perfection on top of what is already imperfect. Redemption restores the ability of each fallen human person to unite perfectly with God as originatively called to do. God creates only perfection from the beginning. There can be nothing for God to "add," ever.

In the very act of *salvation*, God then will restore perfect being-gifts to their original relationship. But only if these gifts offer their consent, fully and perfectly, by virtue of the God-given power of that original relationship.

Theologians and philosophers from the beginning have tended to subvert theology itself by treating God merely as a perfect Being and created persons as somehow not only limited, but imperfect, even as coming immediately from the heart of God. Until the admission is made that God creates originatively only perfect finite persons, theology will be self-hampered even in its most critical contributions to Faith, and it will limp along many fruitless byways of ultimate meaning.

One is reminded of a predicament not dissimilar in the world of science. Over the last several hundred years, the interpretation and valuation of empirical science has largely undermined itself by its own presuppositions. Short-circuiting has occurred, especially by the idea that only atomistic materialism is worthy of consideration as the ultimate base for scientific explanations. Such an assumption is unverifiable by its own scientific, methodological, and procedural determinations. It undercuts the nature of science itself as a free-ranging inquiry into the meaning and the dynamics of the physical universe. Science turns into *scientism*.

Similarly, theists constantly undermine themselves by the blatant, or often latent, avowal that created persons are necessarily imperfect and that "only God is perfect." All the promises of life with God in unending bliss are undercut by thinking that God's infinite love *could* not, or *would* not, create every person as perfect. Theists suppose blindly that created persons would not be perfect in being, freedom, and responsibility to love fully from the first moment of being.

Despite the rhetoric about "infinite love," "miracles of grace," and so much more, believers continue unconsciously to wrestle with, and rebel against, the supposed imperfection of God's act of creation. God's creation is taken to be maculate, stained.

Theology then becomes latently the study of a finite God. And many somehow know it, even if *not consciously*. God is practically turned into a kind of grandiose mega-creature. Theology turns into creaturism—only creatures need "apply" as candidates for study. A cryptic *theologism* undermines further development.

Even as scientists can take their own methodologies too seriously, theologians can miss-function similarly. Scientism is the arrogance of really disregarding physical nature as a redemptive gift of God. It overlooks material substance as being susceptible to study by both empirical and theological means. Similarly, theologism is the *hubris* of thinking that we would actually be God if we were perfect, and of overlooking God as being truly infinite in goodness and power, susceptible to study by both ontological and theological means.

Q. Are you sure that what we think is arbitrary is really so? Maybe what looks to us capricious is not really that way to God. Why, for instance, could not God create imperfect creatures immediately "out of nothing," even though it looks arbitrary to us? Could it be that the act is not really random to God in the infinitely powerful divine vision?

In other words, we can *say* that God definitely does not do anything capriciously or whimsically, but we might misevaluate and consider arbitrary something that looks overwhelmingly so to us, without it actually being so.

R. That is true. Nevertheless, if something is not arbitrary in itself and only appears so to us, then the proof that such is the case is the burden of those who claim it is not *really* arbitrary. And it is not sufficient to say that God does it, so it is not arbitrary. That simply begs the question, "Is it really God who is doing it?"

Is God the adequate, sole, originative cause for the world of becoming and of process? No, that world is inherently imperfect.

The message of this book bears upon our defective propensity to consider God as "the most powerful" or "the most good" (the best being) and to confuse that consideration with God as unlimitedly powerful and good. The latter idea is not the same as the former.

God is not merely all-powerful or all-good, relative to any other manner or kind of being. God is simply infinite power and infinite goodness. And one main, inexorable, inference from this truth is that God does nothing arbitrarily or imperfectly, such as the creation of something imperfect "out of nothing."

If God were simply more powerful and more benign than all the rest of reality, then God might be seen as possibly "outsmarting" creation on occasion or even at every point. Such a meaning for God—whether conscious or unconscious—demeans the divine.

God would be regarded as a kind of mega-creature, the biggest potential bully that there is. We are quite prone to think like that, granted *what we have to hide from ourselves*: our unwillingness to receive being, truth, beauty, and goodness with a finite, full, and perfect spirit.

God is *want*-less, *whim*-less, but infinitely *will*-ing. God ever wills what is the truest and best for every being in every way. In our painfully dependent, needy nature, we might like to think otherwise. After all, having sinned originatively, we are ontologically "on the defensive."

How can we expect to increase our intimacy with unlimited love when we refuse to recognize what unlimited love is *essentially*? By our refusal, we are systematically ignoring God as infinitely perfect love in being and activity.

Limits and Our Likeness to God

Q. You acknowledge that we are like our Creator. But you also say that we are not dependent on God originatively. Surely, our being-limited necessarily means that we are dependent on the unlimited.

R.   God is the infinitely independent Being, who creates us to be as finitely independent beings. We are not like God in our being finite. But we *are* like God in our being-at-all and in our being independent (independent-*with*).

At the moment of creation, we now-earthly humans, freely and independently, asserted ourselves to be partly independent *from* God and God's grace. We failed to be simply independent *with* God, gracefully. That defective exercise of independence damaged our God-graced beings and so we caused ourselves to be structurally weak and dependent on God.

Our originative gift of independence-*with* God *remains*, but it is rendered naturally ineffective to some extent. We now depend on God to free us from this added, self-caused, servile condition of dependency.

We who caused our dependence on God through our free and partial assertion of independence from God now come along and say something profoundly ironic. We assert that we are completely dependent on God; as if that is the way it is originally supposed to be. This claim amounts to another unconscious, incredibly subtle way of blaming God for our basic plight.

We treat our interface with the Creator of our being as though this relationship were a question of finite being relating to finite Being. We refuse really to acknowledge the unlimitedly *gifting* act of God's infinite Being. We will not *let* ourselves realize the gift of being *as a gift from the Infinite*—and not simply from some finite mega-being.

God is the source of absolutely no dependency whatsoever. There is no dependency *in* God nor *by* God. If there were, God would be defective. Even for us who are created persons, it is defective to be dependent. But it is not defective to be finite.

We make it a virtue to be dependent on God for our being, instead of acknowledging that our real dependency on God is for our be-coming—for becoming redeemed and saved. And we keep failing to recognize that *we* originated the condition of dependency by our self-brokenness that dishonors our infinitely gifting Creator.

Many are the ingenious ways by which we defend our deepest spiritual repression. But one of the most subtle is the common way we attribute dependency to our relations with God, being-to-Being. *We* caused every bit of the dependency on God that we find in ourselves; but somehow we conveniently think that God could not *gift* us into being in any other way than as dependent. God must act as we do.

Yet the opposite is the case. We could not *be*, and be *persons*, without being essentially independent-*with* God. Not *equal* to God; but essentially and intimately related with God, heart with Heart.

God could not create us as really being dependent beings. God creates originatively only independent beings, fully apt to be-*with* God as beloved friends forever.

We might get a glimpse of what this relationship could mean when we contemplate the best in relationships between parents and their adult offspring, whose growth within mature interactions reveals a primary relationship of shared independence of life. Adult to adult, parents and offspring can relate beyond (though not separate from) the parent-child dependencies of existence that led up to it.

Friendship provides a culminating touch to any healthy, natural relationship. Moreover, that friendship is structured by the kind of relationship that is "independence-with" among all concerned, even among parents and their adult offspring.

But we tend to insist that this could not *possibly* be so with respect to God. Thereby we keep revealing our own hardness of heart and unconscious willingness to be no more than minimally intimate with God's heart in gifting us to be. We complacently think of ourselves only as dependent be-ings. But such thinking is a prime result of our originative sin. We are unaware of how independently gifted we really are as potential friends of God—gifted to *be* out of nothing.

Q. Do you not accept the dependency of an effect on its cause? It seems that we must be dependent on God as the *cause* of our being.

R. Here, again, we must deepen the roots of our thinking. Creation from nothing is such a unique kind of causality that it transcends what we think of as the ordinary relation of cause to effect, and of effect to cause.

Creation is the gift of *being*—not the fashioning or the production or the delivery of goods. It is not at all the same as the causality of bringing one thing to be from another. God's power to give us being is infinitely other than our ways of causing, though our ways are somewhat like God's way.

In this world, we humans cause both finitely and imperfectly. We necessarily render the effect dependent upon the cause, since we who cause are ourselves dependent. But God's infinite way of causing transcends dependency. God's way of acting knows nothing of dependency or of dependency-rendering. God is not the least bit insecure about other beings *be*-ing. There could be zillions of finite beings who are independent-*with* God and are infinitely "delightful" to God.

We ought to ask ourselves a few questions. Are we really ready to demand that God not cause any persons to be "out of nothing" unless the act of creating is dependency-rendering? Are we going to insist adamantly that God necessarily depend on the laws of human logic for doing anything? And furthermore, must God act according to the laws of cosmic dependency?

Our typically "logical" minds chronically seek a univocal ("one and only one"), self-centered kind of meaning. We demand that God's infinite being conform to our logic, a cosmologic—a logic that is finite, defective, yet critically needed by us, especially for knowing things in space and time.

We cannot, of course, consciously think about the relationship between creature and Creator as anything other than dependency of the created on the uncreated. But that is because we project, and insist upon, our cosmic framework of rehabilitative causality as the base for understanding all causality.

And that is also why it is so difficult for us to distinguish the two kinds of creation from each other: the creation out of nothing that is absolute, originative, and celebrational from the creation (*Genesis*) out of something that is relative, supplementary, and redemptive.

We need to think "outside the box." The box is our dependency-ridden, totally-in-need-of-redemption kind of life—after the crash and the fall. In our passivity of knowing, we instinctively try to measure the efficacy of God's activity by the defective standards of our own activity. Our personal *maybe* response to God's immaculate creation—resulting in a heavy fixation on ourselves—tends to lock us out of the freedom of friendship.

But we must make the effort to conceive of what we might have been had we initially received the Creator's gift of being—*fully receiving* our perfect finite being.

We would not be dependent on God at all, but we would be super-grateful. Our appreciation would not have the aura of dependency about it, since we would not then also be under the conditions of requiring redemption, as we most certainly are now. The framework of dependency would not exist. There would be nothing to haunt and inhibit our finite (perfect) consummately grateful activity.

Infinite Love is the cause of *being—created* being. Not of any action upon bodies or even upon souls. We were loved into being by *infinite* love. This Creator-love is not dependent on us, and is not like creators in space and time, dependent on the matter of their effects.

Our Creator is *not dependent* on us at all. But neither are we dependent on infinite love for our *being*. We are gifted with being, by *gifting* that is an *infinite act, incapable* of effecting dependencies. *Yet we are wary of seeing this because we would then uncover the heart of our sin and the depths of our self-alienation from God.*

As causes, we are, of ourselves, nothing. We could not create ourselves "out of nothing." Nothing means nothing-at-all; not even the ability to be acted upon (passive potency). Since we do not have a passive potency to *be*, but are totally *gifted* to be "out of nothing," our *being* is not caused in the usual sense.

Within the gift of our being, we are given an active (not a passive) potency: a purely active ability to receive (or not to receive) the gift. This potency or capacity to receive is our essential freedom: our independence-with God that is constitutive of our very act of being as gifted.

When people contemplate our primary relation to God, they are almost inevitably inclined to think according to a flattened logic. Knowing that we are brought into being from nothing, they conclude with sureness that we must depend on God for this to "happen."

But "before" it happens we are *not*, and so cannot de-*pend*. And "after" it happens we are gifted with a perfect finite being. This gift is independent and quite able to confirm its finite independence with God—or gracelessly to reject it (totally or partially). If we reject totally or even slightly, we thereby *render ourselves dependent* (hopelessly or hopefully) on God.

If we reject totally, we establish ourselves as really independent *of* and *from* God, definitively and forever. We are also, thereby and paradoxically, dependent on God, but hopelessly so, since God infinitely respects our finite will.

If we reject partially, we thereby establish ourselves as partly independent of God, at least for a "time." But we are also thereby dependent on God, definitively and hopefully, for redemption and salvation.

Thinking of ourselves as originatively dependent on God in *being* is one of the more subtle ways that we can hide, at least unwittingly, from ourselves. We thereby repress the sheer gift of being-at-all and of being-with-God that we have "already" partly denied. And we are setting ourselves up, at an unconscious level, for the pantheistic belief that we are part of God or, at least, that God is a part of us.

If I cannot be "without depending on God," then, as long as I am, I must thereby be a functioning part of God or else God must be a functioning part of me. However we think about it, we are subtly regarding God as a *whole*, of which created persons are functioning *parts*. God is our benign possessor; and we are forever possessions and thereby impossibly friends.

Instead, we can come to the realization that our being-*with* God, our independence-*with* God, is truly God's primal gift of grace and friendship.

Neither heaven nor hell is possible unless created persons are ontologically free to determine the receptive side of their everlasting structure of being and of their being as related to God. Heaven and hell are not simply "moral conditions"—based on the functioning of passive intellect and will alone. They are being-based conditions, constituted by the whole being of the finite person, forever.

If the created person (angelic or human) were structurally or essentially *dependent* on God, there would be no *possibility* for either full intimacy or total defiance. And theologians like Origen would be right to think that perhaps all will be saved eventually, even Satan, since these created persons cannot extricate themselves from some kind of real dependence on God. God would have an everlasting lien on them. And, granted God's infinite power and goodness, every creature would have been destined finally to "come around" to God's holy Will. So much for real freedom.

Such ways of thinking represent a dearth of meaning for freedom and love in the theological mind and heart. God is then regarded as not *secure enough* to let created persons work their will definitively for now and forever.

Q   You say that our dependency on God is to be founded on the passivity that we ourselves created by our sin at the moment of creation out of nothing. Rather, is not our passivity founded on our inherent *nothingness* that is the *essence* of the creature as a creature? Every creature as created being is, of itself, nothing. Only God is being-in-essence.

R.   Not so. "Inherent nothingness" is a foundation for nothing at all. There is nothing inherent about nothingness and so no basis for anything.

Created persons, too, are being-in-essence; but they are being of and in created (perfect) essence, not uncreated essence, as is God. Uncreated essence is not the only essence that *really is*—thanks to God. Thinking otherwise is tantamount to pantheism.

We continue to confuse being with infinite being: a quite subtle form of pantheism in action.

The inherent attributes of created being are not the same as those of infinite being. Yet, for the sake of "honoring" uncreated being, we readily overlook the efficacy of *created being in itself*. In a most subtle way, we thereby "identify ourselves" unconsciously with the infinite being of God. We think that whatever is inherently positive about us is divine. We are lamely grateful for the gift of intrinsic worth, given to us—not loaned—by God. Not out of God, but "out of nothing."

We are likewise readily fooled into treating "nothing" as though it were something, however subtle. But we should not permit the requirements of grammar and of "logic" to dictate reality.

The being of a created person is inherently "something"—namely, this whole unique person-being. Everything about the created person is real, as God-gifted absolutely out of nothing.

There is no *basis* for dependency on the part of the created person inasmuch as, by the infinitely perfect act of God, he or she begins to *be*. God is not the only "really real being," thanks to God. And God is not the only "really independent being," thanks to God. ("Thanks" here does not necessarily signify dependency on our part, but rather a relationship of gift and gratitude that comes only by responsibly exercising one's independence-*with* God.)

We continue unconsciously to misconceive the dependency that characterizes all of our "logical" activity and to confuse it with the non-dependent, ontological relationship between all person-beings.

Every interpersonal relationship is chiefly one of independence-*with*: whether the relationship is one of created person to created person or of created person to God. Dependent relationships stem only from the originative sin and self-caused dependency of the dependents, who were originatively *not* dependents, but essentially super-related independents.

God is *not*, therefore, the only "being-in-essence" or essential being. God is the *only necessary* being. We did *not* have to *be*. God simply *is*.

But once we are *gifted* to be, we are being-in-essence: created essence. We are our *own* being. But *never* can we be said to *be necessarily* or to be necessary beings.

Q. Why have philosophers and theologians supposedly failed to see what you are asserting? Are you sure *you* are not the one being deceived about God, creation, and sin?

R. No, I am not absolutely and unqualifiedly certain. How could I be? I am just another defective seer who claims to discern something different from, yet quite similar to, what the others assert.

Due to our originative sin, we all stand at an immense distance, mentally and spiritually, if not *beingfully* (ontologically), from the act of creation. To a considerable degree, we are even alienated from acts of causality done by us and by the beings around us. These activities of creation and causality are *too close* for us self-disrupted, self-thrown knowers to know with the degree of certainty we desire.

By our originative distancing from both self and God, we have ejected ourselves from intimacy with the first truths of being.

I am simply offering a philosophical-theological hypothesis for further testing in the lab—the laboratory of our ability to think of being and of God. Everyone naturally has such a lab: one's holistic consciousness and one's consciousness as a whole, including all the data of natural and supernatural revelation.

I am trying to be true to what I have seen in my "lab"—with the help of others. You ought to attempt to be true to what *you* have seen in *yours*—with others' help.

Does God Permit Evil?

Q.   In your "lab" have you tested the response to evil given by many theologians: 'God brings good out of evil'? And is it not true that God permits evil for the sake of a greater good?

R.   The traditional idea of God "permitting" evil has a sound base. But God does *not permit* evil, as though making an exception to someone for abrogating a rule or law. God *allows* evil, and does *not* impede it under normal conditions. These conditions do contain a degree of good and bad, proportionate to the cumulative good and bad exercise of the freedom of all the created persons involved. The wheat and the weeds are allowed to grow together until the harvest.

Understanding God's relationship to evil is necessarily difficult. Extremist views are inevitable. For instance, the notion that God creates evil as well as good. Alternatively, the opposite is a common idea (expressed by the question) that God "brings good out of evil." Both extremes distort.

God does not literally *create* evil—that is, bring evil "out of nothing." Some religious people take entirely out of context words like those of Isaiah: "I form the light, and create darkness, I make peace, and create evil: I the Lord that do all these things" (*Isaiah* 45:7).

The Scripture here is not referring to the act of creation as such, the bringing into being of something "out of nothing." As in other contexts, the idea is that by infinite power God knows and allows good and evil acts and their consequences to come forth from the freely self-determining creatures that God brought "out of nothing."

God "allows" both good and evil as the result from the fallen creatures' exercise of God-gifted freedom. God can "create" evil and darkness and ignorance only in that sense. (If the Creator were not going to allow evil, then creation would not *be* at all. God creating puppets makes no sense.) Again, we interpreters project onto God our ways of causing and creating.

Sadly, in a kind of opposite way, a similar misunderstanding has often permeated theologians when talking about God acting for the sake of "the greater good." Yet, there is no greater good for us that could *possibly be* than the immediate, full-hearted, ecstatic union with God that was offered at the moment we creatures were gifted to *be*—in the *immaculate creation*.

This good would now be ours had we given our total *yes* to God, to ourselves, and to one another. Our immediately interruptive sin, however, was instantly given divine response by the beginning of a redeeming process. And, according to Christians, it culminated in the death and resurrection of our Savior, the living and true God. As immense as this latter gift (redemption) really is, it could, at best, "approximate" the original gift of God within the most intimately personal covenant of creation.

People who sometimes refer to original sin as "Adam's happy fault" are trying to affirm the supreme generosity of God. By the act of redemption, however, this beneficent God could give us no *greater* love than the *infinite* love gifting us our being-at-all in our creation "out of nothing." Redemption is not a "greater love."

We may fail to see the parity between infinite love creating us and infinite love redeeming us. But that is because of our commission of the sin—and our denial of it—that really got us into the redemption-needing condition right from the beginning.

Besides, bringing good out of evil as evil is definitely one thing God "cannot" do. No one can do it. Out of evil can come only more evil. Evil is the very taking away of good. So, there is *no* good in evil *as evil* for God or anyone else to "bring out."

Nevertheless, out of the muddle of good-and-evil situations and conditions into which we humans get ourselves, God can and does bring the best outcome—not just any good outcome. God shepherds an outcome compatible with the good that is already there and with the ongoing abuse of the gift of freedom that the sinful persons, human and demonic, have perpetrated, at any given moment.

God brings good out of the world of good-and-evil, not out of the world of evil. Redemption works with the *yes* in the *yes-no* that originally constituted the world of good-and-evil.

God allows evil. But it is not mainly for the sake of obtaining a so-called greater good. The reason is that originatively-created persons are fully free and yet so many have chosen to exercise their freedom badly. God fully respects the gift of freedom, including our ability to resist redemptive love.

We are able to resist and to deny goodness; but we are not *free* to do so. The expression "freedom to do evil" is figurative. Such an exercise of freedom-power necessarily diminishes, and can even shut off, any real freedom itself.

Some Christian apologists have touted the idea that God allowed Adam and Eve to sin in order to launch into the world an even "greater good," the Savior. Such could be true only if God is the "great Utilitarian." Analytically, that somewhat cherished notion would make God out to be the "Great Behaviorist in the sky," the divine Manipulator.

God should be seen as sending the Savior into the world to reveal unconditional love to those who have "conditioned" their own love. God comes to give sight to the self-blinded, and to promise divine and everlasting union with humans who have fallen and are willing to admit it with their lives. By receiving the Savior with their whole heart, self-crippled human be-ings become sacramentively united with the new covenant—the covenant of redemptive creation.

The union of the originatively-free creature—immediately with God at the moment of immaculate creation—would have included "all" the good that is done by the redeeming activity of the infinitely loving God and Savior. God rescuing us from our sins cannot be *literally or analytically* a greater good than God creating us to be perfect persons able to love freely and fully.

What makes redemptive relationship to God *seem* greater is our present self-centric, largely repressed position—from which we receive divine revelation. If we had not originatively sinned—if we had fully and immediately loved—we would be overflowing with divine union and knowing it.

How could we honestly say it is better for us to have sinned—or for Adam to have sinned—and been forgiven than never to have sinned at all? Only a lack of humility, tied in with our perennial misunderstanding about our origins "out of nothing," could prompt sentiments of this sort.

Above all, by such thinking, we do not evince awareness that God is more than "all-good" and "all-powerful." We are really avoiding the truth that God is infinitely good and infinitely powerful *in every act of love, especially the act of originative creation.*

Even when theologians say that God is infinite they might not really mean it. The habit of misunderstanding what *infinite being* means is deeply engrained.

It is a bit like a teen-ager saying, "Everybody's doing it" or "I'm never going to graduate." They do not mean it literally. They mean that "most people I know are doing it" and that "graduation seems like an ever receding goal."

Similarly, theologians might even *say* that God is infinite, but practically they could be *meaning* that God is all-good and all-powerful—perfectly so. Or they could be thinking that God is "the best ever" without effectively recognizing that God's goodness and power are absolutely unlimited, incomparable, and "beyond" the best.

What is the best is the originatively created world of persons. God *could not create anything but* "the best possible world."

In the same vein, Christians often think myopically. Their scope seems to include only sinning in *this* world, as though this is the only "world" in which they live.

Yet they might well surmise that deeply repentant sinners love much because they have been forgiven much (*Luke* 7:47). Perhaps they have been forgiven of much more than even they know. Jesus spoke directly of a this-world level of sinning and loving. But more was implied.

All of us theistic observers ought to learn more about how the reality of sin applies to ourselves and to all humans on planet earth. The "children of Adam" should love whole-heartedly the God who saves them, not only from earthly sins, but also from the sin of sins: originative sin—the most deeply personal sin of all.

Without that sin, we would not *be* in the "sinning business" at all. God's forgiving us of that sin is a basis for us loving God in this world so much more than we could ever imagine or conceive. And if Christians would realize the decisive truth of this originative sin, their meaning for sacramental baptism could receive an immense increase.

Unfortunately, most theists seem to think of themselves as victims of other people's attitudes, instead of resisting and taking full charge of their own originative attitude. Today, however, there is a wave of psychological realization that we are chronically and unnecessarily blamers of others. People are being urged to throw away negative thoughts and self-doubts, and they are encouraged to realize their own power within: the power to believe in, and to make happen, whatever they desire. They are told to recognize and reject the self-defeating attitudes under which they normally live.

But, despite significant truth, this psychology is virtually Godless. Self-empowerment or self-powerment is still a fixation on *self.* The present practice of most depth psychology—like the modern post-Cartesian epistemology—has nowhere to proceed on its own, except deeper into spiritual narcissism.

We must first admit the roots of our spiritual self-victimization and start allowing God-powerment really to occur. Only by our heartfelt exercise of completely repentant receptivity will we escape from becoming hopelessly *more* deceived.

This God-power is not a secretly nursed pseudo-transcendence that extends the ego into its own unseen sources. Rather, it is the power of a real, personal *Other*, who freely redeems and saves.

We have to confront our fallen preoccupations that are exclusively devoted to some of the remedies of sin in merely cosmic existence. We desperately need awareness of the realm of primal creation.

In that creation out of nothing, there were multitudes of created persons, at least angelic ones, and probably human ones as well, who received immediately and fully their own created power to love and exercised it to the maximum. For them, contrition is literally uncalled for and not in play at all.

In that light, from out of the cosmic creation of be-coming, our contrite love, at its best, can only approximate the love we could have exercised had we fully and freely said *yes* in the creation of be-ing.

"Happy fault" sentiments, if taken somewhat literally, do honor to neither God nor creature. God is infinitely loving, just, powerful, and so forth, whether God wills to create or not. God is infinitely loving, whether creatures determine to decimate their "creation right" (their freedom) or not.

Forgiving sin, sending a Savior, and showing compassion are acts of God that to us seem greater than God's "merely" creating us "out of nothing." That assessment, however, occurs because we are so self-centric in our spirituality as we come to consciousness in this world. We are lacking in gratitude for being created at all, and we are profoundly unaware of what originative creation actually offered us. Indeed, *we* are the ones who balked at it and now refuse to look.

Perhaps we think that redemption is a greater good than not having the need for redemption because it makes us feel more loved. But are we more loved by God for having been redeemed than we would have been for having been received fully and ecstatically into God's heart in our absolute beginning? Only gross unawareness and denial of our originative, God-gifted freedom could make us accept such a self-gratifying rendering of our creature-to-Creator relationship.

We tend to base the idea of God as Creator and Redeemer on a defective notion of how Adam and Eve lived in Eden before the actual temptation and fall. We assume that these first parents were somehow living *perfectly* the way God originally intended them to be.

However, throughout this trilogy, we have tried to realize how the scene before the coming of the serpent was anything but perfect, and could only be thought to be so by a very imperfect interpretation of it. Among other things, we asked, "Where was perfect love in the Garden? Where was a Creator of Adam and Eve out of nothing, and not simply a Maker?"

We tend to think of the "naturalistic perfection" of the Garden scene before the fall, as commonly conceived. We then compare that "pre-fallen state" to our being redeemed from sin by God and to the raising of us fallen beings to the divine life of communion. When we contrast these conditions, the redemption and sanctification indeed are a "greater good" than the condition of Adam and Eve before the coming of the serpent.

The new perspective, however, proclaims that this union with the very life of God could have been ours immediately, fully, and freely. We could have simply given one totally free and positive response to the gift of being and to the Giver at very the instant of *pristine* creation.

There could have been "nothing greater" that God could have "done for us" than to create us with perfect freedom to love God wholly. The only reason we did not attain full communion with the life of God was our own adulteration of the gift that we are to ourselves—a defilement rendered by us in partial defiance of the Gifter.

In this light, it is cynical that we sinful creatures come along "later" and claim that the redeeming action of God was so good compared to what could have been if Adam had not sinned.

The notion of the "happy fault" of Adam, if taken too seriously, is a way to hide from ourselves our own self-blinding irresponsibility that resulted in our cosmic fixation. It becomes (quite paradoxically) another manner of denying how radically we are in need of God, our *interpersonal* Savior.

Q.   What about the torture and murder of a child? Does such great evil indicate that this little child, originatively, even as an immaculately-gifted person, freely said *maybe* to God by way of a particularly negative emphasis, and is now receiving proper

payback? You seem to be claiming that there is no such thing as injustice, if we go back far enough: to an originative sin. But that surely seems like an impossible stretch.

R.   That "stretch" is just as possible as another apparent extension: making the effort to know God as infinitely good, loving, and powerful, and not just "as the most loving Being of all." We can know God's unlimitedness (infinity) as not limited, and thereby as different from all finitude. And we can do so without stretch or strain.

Moreover, neither case requires an impossible reach. No historical perspective is necessarily involved. Both the infinite love of God and our failure originatively to receive it are as close as the depths of our hearts, wherein both truths can be immediately, if confusedly, known. (And for that knowing, no "stretch" is called for, only a profound reception of what is and is so.)

In the world of space and time, the torture and murder of anyone is a grave injustice. Heaven itself cries for retribution.

But the enormity of each person's originative, untempted act of sinning is monumentally greater. This act was *entirely* free in its power. It was also more lucid than the ordinary choices we make in this world. We need not "go back far enough." We need to go deep enough. Right here and now. The torture and execution of a child is both undeserved and deserved, both unjust and just. Such is the ironic product of the originative personal *maybe*.

Any injustice done within this world pales by comparison to our originative personal sin—however slight it might have been on the negative side of *maybe*. Each one's originative sin was done in the brilliant light of God's infinite goodness and truth, as well as in the reciprocal light of our God-gifted finite freedom, goodness, and truth.

Our present precarious condition results from our originative *yes-no*. We find it virtually impossible to face this signature sin. But we know ourselves now to be in this world, a *maybe* world. And there is *nothing maybe* about that.

Maybe the child did commit a particularly egregious originative sin, at least relative to many others. And *maybe not*. It is largely *maybe* for us. We are hardly in a position to make such a judgment about an individual, even in the midst of affirming the general lines of good and evil, justice and injustice, found in cosmic creation itself.

No one can be judged as better or worse than any other simply based on present physical, mental, or moral appearances.

On the one hand, those who live apparently saintly lives may abide hidden crevices of spiritual weakness, unsuspected by themselves as well as by others. On the other hand, those who manifest obnoxious features of attitude and behavior could possibly harbor, within their being, avenues of undetected access to grace and glory.

We can be sure that a particular force of *yes*-and-*no* was effected at the originative moment of someone's being. And yet we can be sure likewise that we do *not know*, in any case, how forceful it was relative to that of any other *maybe*-person. While entirely related to our cosmic existence now, our originative activity transpired in a protoconscious dimension of being that is different in kind from our present condition.

Although it is often misused, the well-known injunction of Jesus, "Judge not, lest you yourselves be judged," would seem to apply. To judge can mean to evaluate and assess or it can mean to commend or condemn. Obviously, the latter is meant.

We must evaluate ourselves and others under many circumstances. But we cannot be our own authority of ultimate commendation or condemnation, much less the judge of others. We cannot honestly give a definitive approval or dismissal of the being of ourselves or of others. We are in the muddle of "maybe." We cry out for infinite Mercy.

Many individuals might undergo most of their due suffering right here in this world. Many others might have to wait for an immensely long purgatory after death. Anyone judging the character of a particular person's originative sin on the basis of observed *temporal* affliction might be one who will suffer much more agony later in this life or in the world to come.

Normally, none of us can definitively say of individuals, who sinned when; much less, how badly. Nevertheless, we must try to discern our own condition of soul and try to help others do likewise, when we are called upon.

Besides, we do judge and we must judge about the meaning of life, who we are, and why we are here. We are even now living in both a *maybe* and a non-maybe world.

Not to judge about prime conditions for the destiny of all is to judge negatively concerning the import of our present participation in life. We must judge, as best we can, what is good and what is bad. "Thou shalt not do that which is unjust, nor judge unjustly. Respect not the person of the poor, nor honour the countenance of the mighty. But judge thy neighbour according to justice" (*Leviticus* 19:15). And God will be judging us eventually on how *sincerely* we made efforts to find and to live the truth.

Moreover, we must be open to God's way of relating to what is good and bad. The infinite power, infinite goodness, and infinite justice of God are present—both at the moment of creation *ex nihilo* and at this very moment in space and time. God allows an evil because it is due, granted the particular confluence of struggling human freedoms. God is the Creator of real freedom. So, it is good and just that divine Providence include the allowance of evil.

God cannot do any activity that is even slightly, yet truly unjust, nor for so-called good purposes. God is not a manipulator or a "utilitarian in the sky" arranging the greatest good for the greatest number of people. God "arranges" the best for each and all.

Christians, for instance, ought to believe that even the suffering of Christ was ultimately an act of justice. Not that Jesus was guilty, but that he freely received the commission of suffering unjustly for our sins—because we could never do it adequately for ourselves. By his infinitely loving response to us in our sin, his truly unjust suffering in space and time is eternally an act of infinitely perfect justice. "By his wounds, we are healed" (1 *Peter* 2:24).

Blessedly, God's infinite justice is not the same as our defectively finite justice. The two are radically different kinds of justice. By his suffering injustice, we are justified and sanctified—if we contritely receive it. The justice or justification then is not brought out of the injustice (of the sin), but out of the *yes* in our *maybe* and by the activity of God's unlimited love.

Christians can reassess the meaning of baptism. The sacrament can be understood as removing the stain of sin caused by Adam and Eve in the world of be-coming. But it could also be acknowledged, additionally, as forgiveness for, and releasing of, the partial lockout of being, caused by the baptized one's deformation of originative freedom. This sacramental release, hitherto known implicitly, would become known and lived out explicitly.

Many holy persons among us may be suffering in union with Jesus both on account of their own sins and willingly for the sake of the healing of many others. They are suffering justly.

Their suffering is just and due to them for their own originative transgression. But it is also just, if not due to them, because they are freely suffering injustice in union with the savior Christ, on behalf of extending divine salvation to other persons under purgation. Their suffering serves to aid in "the final choices" of those for whom they suffer. They are receiving on behalf of these other sinners the grace of final conversion—if the choosers themselves finally cooperate.

We are all equal in dignity as human persons. But we are not equal in the *exercise* of our personhood.

Nonetheless, our approach to our neighbor must ever be based on who he or she is *as this unique human person*, gifted by God with an originative dignity. The person's originally immaculate essence still reigns, despite his or her activities of past willfulness that obscure it.

Q. The starving homeless children, by the millions, must have sinned originatively worse than we did. We at least have homes. So, why do we not realize they would not be where they are if they had not sinned worse than we. Surely we do not *have* to feel any obligation to feed and clothe them, do we? I must have said more of a *yes* than they did in order to be positioned in such an advanced society. Shouldn't I concentrate on improving my state and the state of my children, since I and they still have a long way to go in order to attain "the abundant life."

R.   Your *attitude* seems to betray that you may well have said even *less yes* than the people who have directly exploited these starving children, as they pick through daily the local garbage dumps for items salvageable for cash and food.

There is absolutely no one-to-one correlation between the actual degree of culpability in each of us for our individual originative sins and our prosperity or poverty in the present life. Some who appear to "have it all" in this life and who jet set around the globe, or even many who are wealthy yet contribute vast sums to charity, are quite possibly worse sinners originatively than the homeless children or teen prostitutes or bag ladies or drunken brawlers. Eye-ball vision of prosperity and poverty does not produce effective discernment.

The main issue deals with *spiritual* wealth and poverty. Physical wealth and poverty—even emotional wealth and poverty—are real but minor factors in the full assessment of the results of originative sins as they manifest themselves in our present world.

To be in dire poverty, hunger, or torture in this life—at least, for many, though not necessarily for all—might be preparation for eternity far truer than comfortable conditions and even a religious education. This is said not to suggest that God desires us all to be in hunger physically or mentally or emotionally. We might spiritually thrive on the means of support that are provided in economically developed societies, in emotionally stable families, and in highly educated environments.

But, as Jesus proclaimed, "Blessed are the poor in spirit, for theirs is the kingdom of heaven." The key is in our poverty of "spirit": our simplicity, childlikeness, humility, readiness to receive and to do God's will, however pleasing or displeasing it might seem to our physical, emotional, and mental sensibilities.

The idea of being chiefly concerned with ourselves and with our own families has to be carefully known. We might start by realizing that we are not *primarily* members of domestic families, generated by a mother and father "biologically," as we say. We are primarily members of the human family on earth. We are in the care of *that* family. For example, every child who loses his or her parents shortly after—or anytime after—birth is resting in the family of society at large, in which there is a responsibility—a primary one—to care for those who are parent-deprived, homeless, malnourished, and the like.

The natural thing is for the newly orphaned to be cared for by next of kin. But sometimes that is not viable. And so, *if* it is *not*, our neighbor—who may be a 'stranger'—takes us in. Jesus made that clear in the parable of the Good Samaritan. He also spoke of his 'mother and brothers' as those who do his will—above all. Justice and charity come *ultimately* in and through the womb of society, as well as *specifically* through natural parenthood and kinship. We *are* our brother's "keeper" in the sense of being his care-giver when genuinely needed.

How Does God Suffer?

Q. But what if your whole thesis is wrong and there is another, even better explanation?

For instance, since you believe Jesus to be God, you think God suffered horribly and yet is infinitely innocent. Therefore, pain could not be evil in its origins or else God would not be so affected. It seems absurd to think of so much divine suffering in order to save us, when only "a little bit" of divine effort could have done so.

R.   There are no "little bits" to infinite Being. Infinite Being goes into everything God wills to do. God's infinite way of being and loving includes the receiving of the most horrendous evils. God receives all creaturely good and evil, but is not "done to" by anyone or anything.

God is not insecure, as are we who are inclined to flee from even the least of pains and troubles. God does not "react" to evil, but infinitely receives it just as it is, without approving of it in the slightest.

Our originative sin of failing to receive fully the totally good being we were given to be is right now blocking us from appreciating what receptivity really means and entails.

Actually, it is absurd to think that an infinitely loving God would not suffer the evil coming from created persons who were created by infinitely intimate love. Suffering evil, by receiving it innocently, does not mean approval or support of it. It means something like God saying this:

"I love you in the midst of your self-wrought torment and in spite of the evil you have created, such that your pain is the result. The very prospect or possibility of your genuine repentance and of your growing willingness to suffer works in accord with my own infinite willingness to suffer with you.

"Even if you would reject me totally, I will continue to receive, in my infinite way, the gift of being and freedom that I have given you—despite your own self-produced inability to appreciate this unconditional gift. I will love you with the same infinite love by which I gifted you to be and to be you."

Our own reticence and unwillingness to suffer our originatively self-imposed alienation—our being estranged from God, self, and others—amounts to an ontological and spiritual autism. We do not want to face the cause of our plight or to communicate about it. We do not want to be impressed by the quite painful source of our self-insulation.

We are all suffering in our moral and spiritual stupor. And so, Christians believe in meditating on the wounds of Christ, as the Person of God whose infinite love so identifies with us. This love reveals to our open eyes how personally hurtful to God we must have been originatively.

Indeed, only at the point of creation "out of nothing" could those we now call "innocent children" have so offended God. These little ones need to be especially afforded protection and care. They are truly innocent of any evil-doing in this world. But they are *not* innocent of *what brought them into* its conditions.

God does not suffer, of course, in the way that we suffer. God infinitely and perfectly receives what is. In God there is *no ability to suffer passively* and to be hurt as though something were taken away from God by our sin. God is infinite actuality of being. God has literally "nothing to lose."

But those of us who are Christians believe that in Jesus, who is the incarnate divine Person, God became united with human flesh, afflicted and afflictable as it is. While he did not suffer passively in his divine nature, Jesus suffered inconceivable misery, torture, and abandonment in the passivity of the human nature and condition that he assumed for our sake. As Paul the Apostle indicated, for our sake he was made sin, without being a sinner. (2 *Corinthians.* 5:21) In that way, through the Person who Jesus is, God knows the fullest depth of human suffering as no merely human creature ever could know it—or even as the whole of created persons together could know it.

The Main Idea

Q. What would you say is the main idea in your trilogy?

R. Underlying everything in the trilogy is God's infinity. I offer my understanding of unlimited Being, as I have come to believe in this Being through prayer and reflection.

An immediate corollary is the compelling realization that God created "out of nothing" only perfect (finite) persons. All are perfect, as gifted, in being and freedom. I have come to believe in what I call "the immaculate creation."

Many philosophers and theologians in the theistic traditions have slipped into thinking that *the infinite is the same as the perfect*. And they have *thereby* regarded *the finite as the imperfect*.

For instance, one common practice is to confuse, at least partly, logical and mathematical perfection with ontological and substantive perfection. But both mathematics and logic arise in our being and activity only because we are imperfect creatures. Both areas of knowing—critical for actions transpiring in an empirical world—are intrinsically imperfect, and not to be found in the "heavenly realms of glory." The perfections of form and proportion, involved in both mathematics and logic, remain helpful within our redemptively active reception of being. But they are useless and irrelevant to persons who have perfectly received themselves within the primal creation of beingful perfection.

God does not "do math," nor "think logically." God transcends thinking and reasoning, without "violating the rules" of math and logic. These quantitative and reflexive functions of thought are important endeavors of creatures who are in the *process* of being actually redeemed and potentially saved.

The obstacle is that our kind of being—fallen humanity and the physical world—is not *simply* finite. We are gravely *defective*, too. And we are, to say the least, disinclined to take this condition into account, especially when thinking about *be*-ing.

When they are following Aristotle, for instance, philosophers in both the Christian and the Islamic traditions tend to think that only God can be perfect. After all, they think, only God can be a pure act.

Without realizing it, they are deceived by the structural effects of originative evil that are inherent in—not originatively constitutive of—all fallen beings. They think that the profoundly defective way of being that is found in nature is "natural"—just the way it had to be.

Theologians, too, think that since the structure of beings in our ordinary experience includes primary matter or some kind of "essence-passivity," then that is "the way it is." The redeemable world of space and time is simplistically taken to be the created world.

So, theologians who are highly conditioned by the Aristotelian philosophical framework, even as they go far beyond it, think that fallen beings are created essentially as they are found—created by God, in both their fundamental actuality and their fundamental passivity. God is thought to create "out of nothing" the passive matter, as well as the forms. The "fall of Adam" is thought to be at worst a moral matter, and not ultimately an ontological act.

Hence, for any good Aristotelian, insofar as a being is constituted by prime matter, or by a principle of passivity, there is no hope for its absolute or total perfection. Christian theologians have come to regard the essence of even angelic persons as passive in relation to what they think of as the angelic "act of existence." They consider the presumed passivity as evidence of angelic creaturehood and thus of ontological imperfection, underlying all the spiritual and moral perfection of angels.

When conceiving basic principles of things, Aquinas, Averroes, Avicenna, and others did not make a radical correction in view of the inherent effects of originative evil. They failed thereby to realize that there can actually be finite beings that are perfect as finite and as be-ings—divine-like, without being divine. They seemed to think that to be finite is to be in a state of passive potency as the "capacity to be done to" by something else.

These quasi-Aristotelians claim that only God could be a pure act (actuality) of being or of essence, thus having no passive potency whatsoever. Even Thomas Aquinas confidently specifies how all the angels are a mix of actuality and potentiality in their being.

For this tradition, there is no such thing as a *finite pure* act. In all created beings, essence is portrayed as passive potency in relation to the act of be-ing.

But essence as a passive potency within being is not essence as God gifted us. That passive-potency kind of essence is the way we *received* our God-gifted essence at the moment of creation *ex nihilo*. Our less-than-fully receptive self "added" a passivity dimension to its essence by that ill-reception.

Because of my failure in signature freedom, what I am is not fully who I am. I am the kind of being that can be done to and that can be acted upon, rather than simply interacted with.

Such is the self-constituted part of my be-ing: I am the kind of be-ing that is *may-be*-ing, arrogantly giving "permission" to God to "work with me" or "work on me."

Following this way of thinking, it is virtually necessary, at least unconsciously, to blame God basically for the way we are now, in this precarious existence. While so thinking, of course, we know not what we do (or think).

Receptivity and a New Vision

Q. You agree with philosophers who say that passivity in finite beings signifies lack of fulfillment or, at least, imperfection. Where you disagree with them is their idea that being finite and fully receptive necessarily means having some passivity, as well as receptivity.

You regard receptivity without any passivity as an ontological dimension of pure act—whether infinite or finite. And you think that every direct creature of God is a finite, pure act of being. This idea is really where you obviously part company with other theists, including Christian thinkers. Do you think that some could be brought now to agree with you?

R. *Yes*, but only with better than usual understanding of receptivity. Crucial to the whole message of the trilogy is the realization that receptivity is quite proper to pure act. *Pure act necessarily entails receiving as well as giving*. I do think that Thomas Aquinas would agree, if he were to have the occasion to develop his metaphysical reflections further. In fact, some contemporary Christian theologians and philosophers, such as Hans Urs von Balthasar and, following him, David Schindler, Norris Clarke, and others, have written about receptivity—not passivity—in the Trinity.

But we have much more to do. Receptivity in each one of the divine Persons must be recognized. And the procession of persons within the Divine Being must include receptivity in God, the Father, who infinitely *receives himself* through knowing and loving himself infinitely in the eternal gifting to the Person of the Wisdom-Word. There is nothing at all passive or distancing in any true receptivity, including infinite receptivity.

The Judaic and Islamic traditions are also called to understand God as supremely receptive, even though they do not believe in the trinity of persons.

A whole new development of classical metaphysics is implied. I am planning to express this new meaning in a subsequent book.

But agreement—however desirable—is never the main issue. We can be complacently in agreement with others and be in error. Truth, as best each of us can know and understand it, is the most deeply desired outcome. And, in this pilgrim world, truth (not necessarily agreement) is the perpetual desire of those who love wisdom.

Q. If we *both are and do* the act of *be*-ing that God gives us, then, of course, we are responsible for receiving, or for refusing to receive, whatever good comes to us.

But how could you ever convince people that they themselves are personally responsible for the absolute origination of evil in their lives? How could they become convinced that they could just as well have been ecstatically happy with God right from the start, without the experience of any evil at all?

R. Many people are quite open-minded on the question of origins. They only have to see that the new hypothesis *develops*—and does not really threaten—the established pattern of explaining: reason working together with the awesome revelations of Scripture within the theological tradition. Then they will be able to take it seriously.

They will see that the new paradigm makes more sense by being less inadequate and by deepening the roots of their beliefs. They will begin to put it into practice as a way to enrich their understanding of God and of themselves.

Of course, there are many who will feel threatened simply because it amounts to something *new*. One can hardly blame them. In our supposedly "enlightened" age, we have had so much "new" that is worthless or misleading. But time itself will assist in providing perspective and expansive room for discussion.

Besides, the burden of proof might shift. For this to happen, we would have to realize at least two things: how burdened life-unto-death really is, and how, at the same time, Revelation requires faith in God as both transcendent and immanent.

God is wholly other than we are and yet cares infinitely for us, while being infinitely within us. God is infinitely other than we, yet infinitely "close to" us. Both perennial self-righteousness and the conceits of the "new age" can be seen as woefully inadequate.

People might come to realize that the former paradigm does not explain nearly as well as the new what we really are called to believe. Do we really believe that God is both infinitely good and infinitely powerful, but—at the same time—that we are personally and originally innocent of the origin of any evil, including our original inclinations toward sin?

That supposition requires much more explanation than the new one concerning our unconscious spiritual guilt and God's supremely compassionate Love. Those thinkers would carry the heavier burden who would still insist that we are *not at all* responsible personally for the origin of evil and for its inclination in our lives in this world.

We are persons who are obviously "cast out," as the *Book of Genesis* dramatically reveals. We were "cast out" not only morally, but also structurally and ontologically. We grow up, marry, and raise families, but all of it is done "unto death" in the very world in which it is happening.

Adam and Eve did not seem to have any children while in the Garden of Eden, though a plan was laid out for offspring under some conditions. Only as they were being sent away did the question arise about bearing offspring.

The Scriptural Revelation is not just telling of "history," but of mystery—the mystery of our *be*-ing, of who we are and who we are not. If we had originatively said *yes* there would clearly be no real "opportunity" for increasing and multiplying.

We only have to face honestly the truth that children, postnatal and prenatal, who cannot be said to have sinned in this present world, are nevertheless susceptible to evil, including death. From where else, other than themselves, comes their ultimate susceptibility to injustice?

Their vulnerability to injustice—their liability to aggression from others—ultimately cannot come from others, but from their denied self-woundedness. By conceiving, giving birth to, and educating children, parents afford these young ones the opportunity to awaken to their responsibilities as recovering persons. They enter the world in order to repent and to grow in knowledge and love of God.

The harm done to vulnerable children in this world comes mainly from others—often from parents. But the very possibility for such happening to them comes from what *they* have done to make it necessary that they themselves experience such a world as this. Blaming the infinitely loving and infinitely powerful God is not an option. It is blasphemy: material, if not formal.

Consequently, the task of showing that we are personally innocent victims in our origin would seem to weigh heavily upon those who hold the usual views and who would argue against the claims of this book.

A great part of the structure of our being and of our world says *maybe*. *Maybe* what we hear is true, *maybe* not. *Maybe* what we say is true is really true, *maybe* not. *Maybe* our love for others is sound, *maybe not*. *Maybe* tomorrow will be a better day, *maybe* not. *Maybe* we will be happy forever; *maybe* we will perish.

We created our own doubt-fullness of being. But we are still able to receive the grace of becoming certain that God infinitely loves us and that we are responsible for our self-destructive sin.

In Adam and Eve, we ate the "fruit" of the Maybe Tree, of the knowledge of good and evil. This "deed" reveals itself in all we experience, say, and do—and in all we can possibly foresee. We need desperately a Savior of our *be*-ing—not only a Savior of our spiritual life and of our moral direction in this world.

Christians believe that the Savior lives a life of resurrection among us—infinitely and incarnately. But that truth does not end the story. There remains our self-buried freedom to love our Savior perfectly, as well as our ability to reject forever unlimitedly perfect Love.

So, the question remains. Within the creating and saving heart of God, who will we be? A fully living *yes* person or a 'dead' *no* person? Will we experience or know a resurrection of our body and whole being—a union with the cosmos gloriously renewed—or will we be self-frustrated forever?

Q. You seem to offer a kind of theoretical choice. We can either accept the new hypothesis as a focus for belief on creation and sin or continue instead to adhere to the usual interpretations of theistic belief. But what is the practical difference?

R. There would seem to be many practical differences: in thinking and understanding, in our attitude and prayer. But, for purposes of practicality, the most critical difference is not in *what* the traditions believe and think on creation and sin, but in how *deeply* they understand these basic beliefs.

Traditional interpretations of our relationship with God seem to be fixed on the idea that all created persons are *dependent for their be-ing, essentially and forever*. These interpretations acknowledge a substantial freedom of the created person. Nevertheless, there seems to be hardly any awareness of the freedom to determine forever the intrinsic (ontological) relationship—the relationship *as received, not as gifted* between self and Creator. We *receive* our being *by our* be-ing.

Traditional theists seem to be muddled concerning the distinction between giving and receiving in creation: between the absolute giving by God and the absolute receiving by the created person, who is utterly other than the Giver and yet is not on "borrowed being." They fail to see the freedom of the created person in determining part of his or her *being—the critically receptive part*.

This originative freedom underlies our more readily observable moral and spiritual conditions of freedom and is the ultimate ground on which our everlasting destiny is finally decided and resolved. We know this protoconscious activity of the *be*-ing that we are *do*-ing. But we know it now largely preconsciously, *not* consciously.

The tradition has basically overlooked creation as an interpersonal act. By this infinite act of freedom, God creates, for each person, a unique, super-relational gift of be-ing and of being-who this person is. This gift of *be*-ing is an *act* that only the gift (the creature) can *do*.

The created person *is* this utterly self-determining gift, able to relate, as *be*-ing, to God and to all others in a way that is essentially *like* God. The created person ultimately relates either as essentially independent-*with* or as essentially independent-*of*. And, if the latter, the person thereby causes substantial dependence and misery of be-ing.

Traditional interpretations also miss the meaning of our pristine, originative independence-*with* God. They are not distinguishing well between causing effects "out of something" and causing effects "out of nothing." So, they fail to articulate God's *infinite* power to create all persons as beings who are independent *with* God. Instead, God is rather "locked into" our own narrow notions of causation—despite flourishes of rhetoric about "the infinite."

These traditional notions assume a common meaning for causality: that every effect has a cause upon which it depends for its "being or coming to be." Instead, they could begin to acknowledge that this is true only for causality that is created, limited, and also defective: causality that is indigenous to cosmic existence. Tragically, they are regarding God as subject to our own egocentric versions of causing and gift-giving. They are cosmolocked.

It is true that God causes us to *be*. But it is not true that we, the effects, who come "*from*" nothing at all, are dependent necessarily on God. Every effect has a cause—including the effects of primary creation. But the relationship of effect to cause in the creation *ex nihilo* is one of independence: 'independence-with' of the Creator in relation absolutely to the created, and either 'independence-with' or 'independence-from' with respect to the created in relation to the Creator. "Independence-with" has nothing at all to do with equality, superiority, or inferiority. But it has everything to do with the ability and willingness for a complete intimacy—of Gifter and gifted.

At the absolute, unconditional point of creational gifting, God invites a finite, perfect love-response from the gifted creature. In such a relationship, there is no kind of domination or of absolute and decisive control by the Creator. Simply, there is an infinite invitation to intimacy. The created person acts with complete independence. He or she is independent either *with* God or *not with* God. The creature thus responds neither infinitely nor dependently, but independently—as *this* person.

In causing us to be, the act of God is hardly like the act of any finite, defective cause. The effect of God's creating act is to gift unique persons with their *own* being, capable of fully intimate response to the Giver. The effect is perfect created persons who are truly like God—and *not* "like themselves." This effect is one of purely benign independence, capable of total intimacy with God, being-with-Being, immediately and forever.

If God's originative act of creation admitted even the slightest dependency of the effect on the cause, then total intimacy—pure and complete—would be *impossible*. Even the least passivity—which dependency essentially entails—would necessarily block perfect intimacy with the eternal One.

As it is, the usual interpretations of creation *ex nihilo* drag in the notions of passivity and dependency as integral to created persons. But that is because believers do not distinguish clearly between originative creation and redemptive creation. As a result, they are hung up, as we might say, on thinking that the very relationship of created persons to God is essentially one of dependency—whether these persons' responses to being created are fully positive or fully negative.

Whether it be of the greatest angels and saints or of Satan and his cohorts, the ontological relationship to God is thought to be one of absolute, unqualified, intrinsic dependency in being. For the *created* person, to be is to be *dependent*.

To the contrary, dependence comes *only* from and with sin. 'To be is to be dependent' could only be true for the sinner as sinner. This *supposed* ontological dependency can become, then, the basis for unconsciously blaming God.

The usual interpretations of creation treat both the creation-act of God (the *gifting*-act who *is* God) and the *gift*-act (who *is* the created person) as *facts*, not *acts*. But while every act is real, not every act is a fact—a *factum*, something that is made, produced, or passively effected. Because of this confusion of act and fact, we are inclined to assume that every act is a fact and hence is dependent on the *factor*, the maker or efficient cause. Dependency then is taken for granted.

But if that is so—if the essential relationship is one of dependency in being—then it is impossible for the created person to be, critically and ultimately, responsible for how such created being receives self. The dependency contaminates the receptivity.

If I am essentially dependent on God in my very being, I cannot do the *receiving* of being. I can only "be done to" by God. I cannot truly *be-with* God.

Yet, according to the usual perspective, the created person receives from God a perfectly dependent being and is obliged to affirm, in consequence, that very dependency of being.

This requested affirmation is to be done freely and thus apparently independently. Actually, it cannot be done freely to the extent that it is done dependently.

The clash of calls for both dependence and independence comes from our originative sin and requires careful attention.

If the created being is not itself independent with respect to God—if the finite person is essentially dependent on God for be-ing and not just for becoming—then this created being is unable to respond fully and freely (independently). Such a being could not even affirm the supposed originative "dependence" of being. An essentially dependent being cannot even begin—as this be-ing—to act freely (independently) either with God or against God. Prime interpersonal freedom is denied.

Merely moral or spiritual freedom is vacuous without ontological freedom. The freedom to be who one is and to do one's own be-ing (ontological freedom) can *be* without there being necessarily any moral or spiritual freedom. That is because, if one's originative response is fully *yes*, the reality of morality does not exist.

Moral freedom only exists because we have compromised our ontological freedom through our originative *maybe*. Moral freedom resulted alongside the good-and-evil world that was caused initially by our *may-be*-ing, our *yes-no* to being and to God.

Dependence on God would certainly mean that the created being would have to depend on God for everything, including the content of what to affirm about the gift of be-ing.

Such an essentially dependent person would be an ontological puppet. A puppet cannot freely affirm itself as a puppet, because it does not have the in-dependence to do so. It lacks the independence of being by which to receive and to respond actively to the gift of being. The puppet's "affirmation" would be simply or basically the doing of the puppeteer. The puppet would be puppeting its puppetry.

In other words, the creature would be acting according to its Maker, who would then not be a Creator—a Gifter of sheer being. And God would be interpreted—unconsciously at least—to be a pantheistic being, replete with functionalistic parts called creatures.

Finite persons are essentially not like puppets in any manner or form. Such persons are complete beings, with intellects and wills of their own. Not even God can exercise their intellects and wills—so absolute and unconditional is the *gift* of these powers to *them*.

This gift has to be absolute, or else we would not really be talking about persons or about intellects and wills—just about functional, if subtle, satellites. But the originator of satellites or minions is only a Maker, not a Creator.

God creates beings who "create" themselves. The first (supreme) act of any person's intellect and will is the act of receiving the being that he or she *is*—a receiving *done by that gifted being itself.* The being does the receiving, by way of intellect and will specifically. But the being itself is both giftedly perfect and giftedly free (to act as it will).

Immediately—by virtue of the exercise of these gifts—the being receives self well or poorly. As a result, we can say that while it is *giftedly perfect* and thereby perfectly free, the created being can be *receivedly* either perfect or imperfect; and it is thereby—through its own receptive activity—perfectly or imperfectly free.

The absurdity within the perennial concepts involves thinking that creation *ex nihilo* is something like normally observed causality. In our finest moments, however, we theoretically acknowledge the radical otherness of God's primal creation activity. But even then, our theoretical insight seems laden with the baggage of practical dependency in thought and in deed that has been caused ultimately by our originatively imperfect reception of being.

Despite ontological lethargy, we can, at least, begin to know that normal causality in this world is a bit like God's causality of finite being. Yet God's causality is not at all like "normal" causality. The likeness between divine and finite causality is, as it were, a one way street.

As with all attributes of God, we can say what the pristine creation act is *not*, more readily than we can say positively what it is. But we can know and say what it is, by analogy and faith. The insight of grace surpasses the grace of insight.

An immense practical difference is evident then between the new hypothesis and the older, long-standing form of conceiving creation and sin.

The older idea lets us be satisfied with depending on God to do things for us, in accordance with the needs of our redemption and salvation. But the new hypothesis impels us to admit both that we depend on God for salvation and that we once had full, independent, *untempted* responsibility for the whole of our being and we blew it. Hence, our cosmic predicament and grave dependency.

So, now all of our acts in this recuperative world include *both* personal dependence *and* personal independence. Acts of repentance and of adoration become especially important, requiring us to act *independently* dependent on God.

The infinite grace of God, who is being-with us, is ever-present. But only *we* can do the repenting, despite how much we might want to think that God can *make* us repent.

Always and everywhere, God gifts us unconditionally and also infinitely with the grace of repentance. God's gifting grace is present even in the dungeons of earth and in the depths of hell. But our receiving or rejecting that grace is an act that is truly our own, independently-*with* God or independently–*against* God.

We are not God's dependents in the ultimate sense, even as we do depend in the critically functional redemptive sense. There are acts that are completely ours and that God cannot in any way do—most auspiciously, our act of *be*-ing. God gives us this act: to be and to do. And we alone *do* it—for better or for worse in the covenant of the primal creation.

Saints know our relationship of essential independence-*with* God. They acknowledge it by a connaturality, even without exercising the terminology of "independence-with."

Saints are not *lackeys*. Often it seems we think saints are, or want to become, as it were, "holy marionettes of God." This unconscious likening of God to a puppet master in control of the puppets comes from our fixation on God's causality as like the causality exercised within our space-time world. Our complacency in this traditional way of interpreting our pivotal interpersonal relationship with God must be challenged.

Adoration of the one true God calls for worshippers who are true to the gifts of God that they *are*—not merely *have*. We *maybe*-saying worshippers are called to give our whole hearts and minds to God in gratitude for the grace of recovery upon which we totally depend.

But we are also called to give thanks for the grace of the *be*-ing that we were *gifted* to be. We were gifted to be independently-with ourselves, independently-with one another, and independently-with God.

As We Pray

Q.   Are you saying that by adopting this "new view" even our prayer lives could improve?

R.   *Yes.* There is an ancient formula, *Lex orandi, lex credendi*, that warrants our attention. This principle means that the way we go about praying indicates the way we believe or will come to believe. (We might state it briefly: As you pray, so shall you say.) This formula can be applied in each of the theistic traditions.

Even the simple wish or prayer like "God, help us" might be indicating mixed priorities. It is true that we need God's "help" in all things: sustaining grace. But it is much truer to say, "May we help

God." The only thing in question is our *cooperation* with divine grace. Are we going to help God save us and others or not?

God's love and mercy are infinitely unconditional, whether we pray or not. God, for instance, is always doing God's part, infinitely so. Our prayer and good will make the critical difference in whether we who have been redeemed are actually saved.

God can only save those who are *willing* to be saved. So, God really "needs" our "help" in order to effect the divine will: our salvation.

We cannot save ourselves at all. God does the actual saving. But we can and must provide the *crucial act* of receiving God's more-than-just-help: God's infinitely good and powerful rescue of our freely self-distorted beings.

Both God and we need our "help": our totally *sincere* goodwill. But we do not need from God merely help. When someone rescues you from certain drowning, you do not simply say, "Thanks for your help." You say, "Thank you for saving my life."

To pray, then, "God, help us," is good to do and to do often. But its meaning ought to grow. It can readily be self-misleading. Our egocentrism and misunderstanding of what life is all about serve to restrict our vision. And by our prayers, simple or complex, we can be programming ourselves unconsciously for ultimate failure. Our subconscious mind has the power ever to support or to subvert our intentions. We are being called to phrase our prayers as adequately as we can in order to pray effectively.

I have indicated earlier that theists need to be mindful of what they mean when they pray, such as saying, "Lord, have mercy" or "God bless you." By defective ways of *saying* in our praying, we tend to lock ourselves into ineffective ways of *believing*.

We can use words that hardly mean what we ought to intend to say. Or, by growing in awareness, we can mean by the same phrases ever deeper intent to be with God.

"Lord, have mercy," for instance, can be prayed as a confident way of receiving God's mercy "on the spot." Literally speaking, however, the same wording can amount to a supplication of distrust.

In some respects, the phrase appears to imply on God's part a lack of sufficient attention to suffering creatures. It overlooks what we certainly ought to believe, namely, that God's mercy is infinitely gifting to us and to *all* others, right now and at *all* times. In any case, there is no such thing as a lack of God's mercy anywhere.

We are the ones who are remiss. Not God. We fail to receive actively the unlimited mercy of God that is available, no matter what the conditions. We might then better pray, in attitude if not in words, "Lord, I receive your infinite love and mercy, for myself and for others who might not now be receiving you."

As long as we understand the often figurative, or even flowery, dimensions of what we say when we pray, we can hold to our beliefs in a celebrational way. There is nothing wrong with praying, "Lord, have mercy," while meaning something deeper than these words ordinarily signify.

But we might be taking words that signify anthropomorphically, and that have a distinctly human way of understanding, as though they were literally designating our meaning. We can fancy ourselves as directing God to give this or that person or oneself more mercy than has hitherto been gifted. Then we almost inevitably slip away from the heart of the truth in which we purport to believe.

Every prayer deserves careful attention. For instance, the "Our Father" is the powerfully instructive prayer that Jesus taught his disciples. This divine invocation is both worshipful (celebrational) and instructive (functional).

The "Lord's Prayer" is celebrated in the Gospels and in the hearts of Christians, as well as in other theists. It should be prayed with both celebrational and functional meanings in mind. The believer is called to exercise discernment as to which kind of meaning should be intended or emphasized by the different words and phrases.

The first words, "Our Father," call upon the Creator. These two words are profound. No one can say how long the supplicants might meditate in using them. For some, the word "father" might be taken rather figuratively. For others, "father" might mean something real and mystical. The differences and the range in meaning could be immense.

Further affirmations include, "Hallowed be thy name, thy kingdom come, thy will be done on earth as it is in heaven." These could be ways of saying "We acknowledge your infinite power and love, so that we and others might open our hearts more widely to your presence, and so that your name will be treated as holy and your rulership might enter ever more the hearts of all."

These expressions do not mean, for instance: "May you make your name holy and may you force your kingdom upon us or overwhelm our weak wills with your infinite power, such that your kingdom will spread."

We proceed to pray: "Give us this day our daily bread and forgive us our trespasses as we forgive those who trespass against us." These words might intend to affirm, "We receive at every moment, with profound gratitude, your daily sustenance for our lives and we receive your infinite willingness to forgive us for our offenses, even as we open ourselves and make real effort to forgive those who have offended us."

We then conclude: "And lead us not into temptation, but deliver us from evil." These words mean something to this effect: "By the grace of your infinite love and protection, may we not be led into temptation by the evil one or by our own lagging minds and hearts. We resolve to make our fullest effort to let your unlimited power into our every thought, word, and deed."

This concluding entreaty does not mean that "we are passive and ineffective in doing our best" and that "your infinite power can save us without our vital participation."

God is the One who saves us. But without our genuine consent, our salvation is impossible. Even for God. The critical issue is not whether God will save us, but whether or not we will cooperate with God's saving power.

We are called to intend to offer our weak and, in themselves, ineffective—but necessary—efforts to receive God's infinite power that effects our salvation. No matter how strong our wills, any passivity here militates against God's infinite love and mercy. God cannot shove us into heaven. God acts by infinite receiving, as well as by infinite giving and inviting.

Some of our prayers can be almost literally true. "Praise God!" is such a prayer. Similarly, for the expression, "May Allah be praised." The Hebrew expression, "Alleluia," likewise tends to "say it all."

We might mean something such as, "We praise you, Lord, and thank you with our whole hearts." And, in some contexts, we can mean, "Hey, friends, let's praise the infinitely loving Power and Grace now gifting us to *be*, and to be in *union*, forever."

In the formations of the word of prayer, the difference is striking between something like "Lord, have mercy" and "Praise God." Both kinds are needed. The devoutly functional "Lord, have mercy" complements the spontaneously celebrational words, "Praise God." Together they can represent our belief both in redemptive creation and in the originative creation out of nothing.

May all theist believers ever give praise to God…and increasingly receive God's unlimited mercy.

About the Author

Robert E. Joyce is professor emeritus of philosophy at St. John's University in Minnesota. He received a B.A. in philosophy from the University of St. Mary of the Lake, Mundelein, Illinois, 1957; an M.A. in philosophy from De Paul University, 1960; and a Ph.D. in philosophy from International College, 1978. The doctoral courses of study were completed at the University of Notre Dame, 1959-61. At Notre Dame, he served with a Teaching Fellowship, 1959-61, and was appointed instructor of philosophy, 1961-62. He has taught courses at De Paul University, Loyola University, and the College of St. Benedict. His principal teaching has been done at St. John's University, 1962-94. At St. John's, for several years he served as Director of the Tri-College Honors Program and for several years as Chair of the Philosophy Departments at St. John's and the College of St. Benedict.

Dr. Joyce is the author of various books and numerous articles in scholarly and popular publications. He published with Mary Rosera Joyce, his wife, the first pro-life paperback in the United States, *Let Us Be Born: The Inhumanity of Abortion* (Chicago: Franciscan Herald Press, 1970). In the same year, Mary and Robert published their unique introduction to the philosophy of man and woman, *New Dynamics in Sexual Love: A Revolutionary Approach to Marriage and Celibacy* (Collegeville, MN: St. John's University Press, 1970). Robert's doctoral dissertation was published in 1980 by University Press of America. *Human Sexual Ecology: A Philosophy and Ethics of Man and Woman* has been used in University courses and by several leaders in the natural family planning movement.

Works Cited

Armstrong, Karen. *The History of God.* New York: Ballantine Books, 1993.

Baars, Conrad. *Born Only Once: The Miracle of Affirmation.* Quincy, Ill.: Franciscan Press, 2001.

Bible. *The Holy Bible*, Douay Version.

Blumenthal, David. *Facing the Abusing God: A Theology of Protest.* Louisville, Ky.: Westminster John Knox, 1993.

Joyce, Robert E. *God Said, We Said: The Interpersonal Act of Creation.* St. Cloud, Minn.: LifeCom, 2010.

_____*God Says, We Say: The Interpersonal Act of Redemption.* St. Cloud, Minn.: LifeCom, 2010.

Kushner, Harold. *When Bad Things Happen to Good People.* New York: Avon, 1981.

Miles, Jack. *God: A Biography.* New York: Knopf, 1995.

Quran. *The Holy Quran*, paraphrased from multiple sources.

Terruwe, Anna. *The Abode of Love.* St. Meinrad, Ind.: Abbey Press, 1970.

Weinandy, Thomas G. *Does God Suffer?* Notre Dame, Ind.: University of Notre Dame Press, 2000.

Wiesel, Elie. *Night.* Westminster, Md.: Bantam Dell, 1982.

Yancey, Philip. *Where Is God When It Hurts?* Grand Rapids, Mich.: Zondervan, 1977.

Meeting the Challenge Posed by the Perennial *Conflation of Creations*

I am interested in gaining various responses to the new perspective that is briefly introduced in the present trilogy of books, including this one, *God Will Say, We Will Say: The Interpersonal Act of Salvation.* The first book of this set is entitled, *God Said, We Said: The Interpersonal Act of Creation.* The second book is *God Says, We Say: The Interpersonal Act of Redemption.* The series is called *When God Said Be, We Said Maybe: An Inside Story of the Creation, the Crash, and the Recovery of Being.*

God's acts of Creation, Redemption, and Salvation are momentously intertwined. So, each book deals with all three interpersonal acts of God, but emphasizes one of the three themes, respectively.

On behalf of this project, any observations, suggestions, or objections will be afforded careful attention in subsequent publications. Also, any suggested relevant material will be welcome.

I also encourage dialog by email.

Robert E. Joyce, Ph.D.
Professor Emeritus
St. John's University
Collegeville, Minnesota

Phone   320-252-9866
email   robertjoyce@charter.net
Website   www.Lifemeaning.com

Glossary

The new theistic view calls for an adventure in revisiting traditional terms. Faith and reason need an increase in depth-perspective on perennial truths.

Painters, for instance, once rendered their images in largely flat, 2-dimensional presentations. They seemed to be incapable of knowing how to present the third dimension successfully. Similarly, because of a cosmological crunch, traditional philosophy and theology tend to be 2-dimensional in representing the great truths. If possible, our effort immediately is to change *not the truths, but the perspective for the sake of better vision.*

The following definitions and delineations of the key terms might assist the reader's thinking about prospects for a better theistic view. These words and phrases are analogical, *not univocal.* They do not have one single, exclusive meaning. For brevity and practicality, however, only one or two main meanings are set down for each term.

Some of the following terms are not used in this particular book, but might serve to fill out the perspective for readers interested in philosophical and theological "details." The Glossary may be read in itself as a review.

Being and Becoming

Being (*ens*) can mean the totality of a given being: who or what it is. But, more specifically, be-ing (*esse*) is the actuality of being-at-all. Be-ing is the most important act of a whole being. All other acts and actualities, such as thinking, drinking, walking, talking, and so forth are "branches of the *act* of be-ing." Somewhat counter to the traditional theism, being is regarded, in this book, as what we *are* and *do.* Be-ing is the gift God gives us to be and to do. We *do* our being. God does *not.* Being is an *act*, not merely a *fact*.

We do not simply "have" being. We *are* the entire be-ing God gifted us uniquely to be and to do. No part of our being is of God or of anyone else.

We are fully and forever our own unique being, thanks to the infinitely powerful gifting of God.

Only persons are whole (complete) beings. Subpersonal beings (from molecules to monkeys) are part (incomplete) beings. They cannot receive themselves within themselves and so are not, and cannot be, fully what they are. (See *excidents*.)

To be is to be unique (to be *not the same* as anything else) and to be uniquely related (to *every other* being that is). For person-beings, to be is (also) to be-*with*.

Existence is a *way* of being, of standing outside of self and other things. *Ex-sistere* means to "stand out of." But God and all created persons who said fully *yes* to creation *ex nihilo* do not *exist*; they simply *are*. They have *no* passivity to "overcome" by striving to get out of or go beyond their condition of being.

All material beings, as we know them now, not only *are*, but *ex*-ist. Subpersonal beings exist by having "parts outside of parts," by being extended, material realities. Personal beings who, like us, have fallen and are defective, *ex*-ist also by reflective consciousness, whereby they "stand outside" themselves by being conscious of themselves, the better to direct themselves and make choices (the existentialist aspect).

Failure to distinguish meaningfully between being and existence (in any language equivalent) can be seen as a particularly instructive sign of our originative *repression* of our first act of *be*-ing and of the *ex*-istence that this act caused.

The pre-conceptive latency of our fallen being (ontological latency) is the coma-like, disordered manner of being from which we emerge at conception. It was caused immediately by the crash of saying *maybe* at the moment of creation *ex nihilo*.

This condition of our collapsed being, before *formal* existence (before conception), has *nothing* to do with reincarnation or even incarnation. There was *no* "taking on" of any kind. The perfect (finite) ontological structure with which we were gifted at creation *ex nihilo* was compromised by our imperfect response. Immediately, we became imperfect created persons by way of adding an *imperfect receiving* to our originative perfection or giftedness. We became, as it were, "bloated in our being." Our perfect, God-gifted essence remained, but our nature—the disposition to act according to essence—was self-distorted.

Maybe-sayers thus subsist prior to their ex-istence in space and time at conception. Our pre-conceptive latency results from the condition of our being, that followed the moment of imperfect response given to originative creation right up to the moment of *conception*. Our self-conflicted be-ing (including powers to know and love) was relatively dysfunctional until that event. We were not fallen angels, but simply fallen humans.

Energy is the natural capacity to work: to struggle, strain, move forward, exercise potencies to do and to be done to. It arises from the fractuation (fractured actuation) done by the maybe-saying of originatively sinning persons. Energy comes in many forms at various levels of redemptive causality. Without any originative sin, there would be no need or occasion for energy. Every reality would be itself a pure act or actuality—whether infinite or finite. No work to be done. Simply, the play of everlasting life.

Essence is *what* someone or something *is*. While one can focus on the essences of qualities and activities of entities, the prime signification relates to the *fundamental what*: *what* is a person, *what* is this thing or that thing as such. Fundamentally, what *kind* of person or thing is this as different from other kinds of reality?

But there are really two different—almost always confused—*kinds of essence*: common (e.g., human) and individual (e.g., *this* human). The confusion between, say, the humanness and Jamesness of James makes for much metaphysical mischief in giving an account of *being as being*. *What* James *is* as *this* unique human (his uniqueness of person) is *not* at all the same as his being a human kind of being.

Nature is the essence of someone or something as this essence is disposed to act. What kinds of *activity* can be expected from a particular entity? Granted the essence of a peach tree is to produce peaches—not apples, oranges, *etc.*—its nature is the inexorable disposition to do just that. The *way* the being expresses itself, or *can* express itself, in action is its nature. Nature is, so to say, how the essence can reveal itself in acting. In saying *maybe* to being and to God, the self acts *through* its essence, but *in* and *by* its nature.

Form (substantial form), traditionally conceived, is that principle in the essence of a person or thing *by which* the entity is *fundamentally* what it is. It is an intrinsic *part* of the essence. All things have substantial forms: one for each kind of thing.

This traditional meaning is considerably modified by the theses of the new view. In the new understanding, substantial form is the principle of the *person* (not of things), *by which* he or she is able to give self to self and to all others as a principle of essence. In the new view, it is called "givity":

the capacity specifically to *give in a receiving way*. It is the principle that is co-active with matter and is a *dimension* of the act of be-ing. To be is to be giftive (and to be receptive).

In the new vision, human *souls* are the substantial forms as they serve human persons in their recovering from defective exercise of "givity" at the moment of their originative creation. Souls as (*reparative*) substantial forms serve fallen humans in their struggle to attain the pristine, God-intended condition of gifting selves fully at the moment of creation.

Matter (prime matter), traditionally conceived, is that principle in the essence of the human person or of a thing *out of which* that entity is *fundamentally* what it is. Matter is an intrinsic *part* of the essence. All things in matter and motion, space and time, involve prime matter, from which every diverse kind of thing is developed. It remains the ultimately common feature of substances in the cosmos. None can exist without it. This traditional meaning has been, however, considerably modified—not negated—by the theses of this book.

Prime matter (reconceived in the super-light of Faith and of ontological reflection), first of all, is the principle of the human person (not of *any* thing) *by which* he or she is able to *receive self from within self* as a characteristic of essence. (Angels have *no* prime matter. Their kind of essence itself is pure receptivity to their be-ing.) (God's Being is pure infinite receptivity, as well as infinite givity.) This pure receptivity-power, co-constitutive of the essence, was gifted at the moment of creation *ex nihilo*.

In the new view, matter is a kind of receptivity: the capacity to *receive one's essence in a giving way*—and not at all "to be done to" or "to be determined." The prime matter and substantial form are totally correlative as the *roots* of all receiving and giving in the human person from the moment of originative creation.

Originative matter was purely **active receptivity**—the active power or potency to receive who and what we are. It was not—originatively—the passivity or passive receptivity delineated by Aristotle.

Pure originative receiving is actually just as active and real as giving. Originatively, there is *no* passivity.

With our bad originative response, prime matter as sheer receptivity within our essence had to begin functioning as prime matter that is passive, a capacity to "be done to" right within the essence and to function in common with the extrinsic energy of subpersonal creation. Out of this passive condition, human bodies were formed. Our bodies are prime matter as it serves human persons in attempting to attain the pristine condition of receptivity intended by God at the moment of creation.

Angelic persons, however, in their greater simplicity and likeness to God's infinite receptivity, *are* without anything of this co-principle within their essence. Originatively, angels are simple, sheer receptivities for the act of *be*-ing.

Soul and Body are terms we employ unconsciously, for the most part, to indicate the form and matter principles of human essence in their self-weakened condition. By these principles of becoming, we humans grope for salvation. Soul and body, however, are distinct from the originative **form** and **matter** that are purely active.

In the tradition, the soul is the principle of life in that which has life and is discerned in Aristotle's philosophy of nature. The body is the "stuff" of matter that the form specifically determines. The body is 'supinely' related to form as to its virtually sole principle of intelligibility. This manner of conceiving represents the unawareness in the tradition of an originative sin that has passivized *both* form *and* matter into the conditions of crash and hopeful recovery now recognized as soul and body.

The following terms—except purely active potency—apply strictly to existents in the cosmos, and not to angelic creatures.

Substance is, above all, quite like what Aristotle said it was in the first instance (primary substance): *this whole being...its* essence, with all its attributes and weaknesses, concretely and singly. More specifically, in accord with the common tradition, substance (second substance) is also that principle in the being of a person or thing by which the entity is or exists *in and through itself and not in and through any other*. Every created substance is its own principle of intrinsic being and activity (but not its own ultimate cause). It remains the source of natural stability in the midst of accident-modifications or changes. In space and time, substance relates to accidents as passive potency (*q.v.*), out of which qualities and acts develop.

Accidents are *not* the substance, but parts of the substance, through which the substance manifests itself. An accident, such as the color of a tree or the thought of a human, does not be or exist in and through itself, but only in and through another (a substance). The *act* of walking and even the *power* to walk, as instances, are accidents and cannot be or exist "on their own" or in and through themselves. There is no act of walking without a walker, nor act of thinking without a thinker. Yet the acts are *real*; they express or manifest the substance or the agent; they are never discounted —even if minor.

Excidents, according to the new theistic view, are the super-multiplicity of substances and their accidents in the cosmos that are not entitatively human. Excidents are everything in the whole of space and time, including every particle of organic and inorganic matter—and excluding human substances (persons) with all their accidents. At the base of all excidents lies the supremely low level of human (non-entitative) *fallen* (crashed) freedom that empowers the telic character of all matter and motion. All material things tend, however erratically, to an end or fulfillment of inherent purpose by virtue of their being entities created by God out of fallen human freedom (energy).

At the absolute moment of creation *ex nihilo*, excidents resulted from the ontological explosion caused by our immediate response. They are forms of the passive-reactivity (i.e., energy) emanating from the originative sin that was constituted by the first acts of innumerable humans who said *maybe* to their be-ing. These elements of discarded human freedom were separated from malreceptive, freedom-abusive sinning persons themselves. They are subpersonal (partial) beings (from molecules to monkeys) that were developed by God's infinitely loving activity of compassion on the *maybe*-sayers—God's creating *ex aliquo*.

Energy originally emanated from the partial rejection (the fractuality) of perfect personal beings as we were gifted to be. All energy is originatively human energy—frustrated human freedom—and is of two basic kinds: fragmental and *non*-fragmental. On the one hand, excidents are fragmental energy, "broken off" from the substance of the maybe-sayers in and by the *ontological* "big bang." On the other hand, the fallen human substances retained a kind of *non*-fragmental energy that is therapeutic and intrinsic to them. The result is our defective substances ex-isting with their accidents (including *bodily* life in the cosmos).

Active potency is the ability or capacity *to do* something or to perform a certain kind of activity. By creation *ex nihilo* we were gifted to be pure active potencies of be-ing—each person fully able both to receive and to give personal be-ing. After originative sin, fallen human being has the active (natural) capacity (whether functional or not) to reason and to love; a dog does not. A dog has the active potency to bark and wag its tail; a human does not. Pure active potency, however, is the kind of being we were gifted to be out of nothing with the angels. It was not mixed with any passive potency. We created the latter by our less-than-full response.

Passive potency is the ability or capacity to *be done to*, to be affected by or determined by someone else or something else. A tree has the capacity (passive potency) to be bent by the wind; a boulder does not. A boulder has the capacity (passive potency) to be rolled down a hill; a (living) tree does not.

Moreover, "prime matter" in the traditional sense is a sheerly passive receptivity—prime passive potency. In the new view, however, prime matter is originatively a supreme, *purely active, receptivity* of essence right within the essence—an active potency. God does not, and cannot, create directly out of nothing any passive potency.

As perfectly self-actuated, angels and saints in heaven are purely active potencies that co-act with God and the others, *without being acted upon* or determined in any way. There is *no* passive potency in beatitude.

Creation

Creation *ex nihilo* (out of nothing) is the originative beginning of all finite being. God infinitely loved persons into being. In this creation, only persons resulted—out of nothing, and not out of any preceding substance. The creation was immediate, non-durational, and immaculate. Each person was unique and perfect in every way, including the freedom (purely active potency) to say *yes fully*. There was *no* temptation or *ability to be tempted*. Simply, there was gifted an invitation to being-*with*-God and with all others 'ecstatically' forever.

This creation was perfectly *interpersonal* in divine intent and *solely* an act of God.

Creation *ex aliquo* (out of something) is the secondary or derivative act of creation: a creation of be-coming or of being coming back to itself from a crash and from its own ontological self-conflict. This remedial act of God began at the same moment as creation *ex nihilo* and as our response. God "works with and out of" the dire results of the originative crash of those persons who said *maybe* to the gift of being at the moment of the *ex nihilo* creation. Infinite love and power interacts with finite, free *resistance* that is both conscious and unconscious.

This redemptive opportunity for saving these "fallen human persons" is what is directly the subject of *Genesis* and other Scriptures. According to Christian teaching, this redemptive creation of becoming culminated in the death and resurrectional life of Jesus Christ. At least, it can be said that, for all three theistic traditions, only God can redeem and save us.

Originative creation is interpersonal, yet solely the act of God. But the act of salvation itself is more. It is an interpersonal action of finite freedom completely cooperating with infinite freedom.

Immaculate creation is another name for the interpersonal, immediate, durationless originative creation *ex nihilo* by which God gifted into being *perfect* persons with *perfect* freedom. Being pure and unique acts of personhood, these persons are able to *receive* their being *perfectly*. The result of God's act of creating was beings unstained by any passivity at all. All gifted persons (angelic and human) were purely (immaculately) who and what they were by the power of the infinitely loving heart of God and necessarily gave their interpersonal response (*yes*, *no*, or maybe). The act of angels was either *yes* or *no*. The act of humans was *yes*, *no*, or maybe.

Freedom and Sin

Freedom is the correlative capacity of intellect and will to let the person be present to, and unite with, the Being of God and to participate in the fundamental goods of human personhood. **Essence-freedom** is structured to *unite* directly with—*not* an *identity* with—the essence of God, if or when beatitude is attained.

Natural freedom is, then, the essential disposition to know and to love, to the fullest extent of one's capacity of *be*-ing.

Functional freedom is the actual ability to do the knowing and loving. Both natural and functional freedom are gifted in originative creation. But the defective response of the first act of our freedom maimed them both, functionally separating them from each other and also from the freedom of essence, the being as originatively gifted.

The alternatives of *yes*, *no*, or maybe were not set up "ahead of time." Our originative freedom was "*pre*-alternative." Before we broke out into the alternative conditions of being-and-becoming, we were, like God, free only to say *yes*. But being finite, we were *able* to say *no*. We were *not free* to say *no*; but we were able and did, *de facto*—severely damaging our freedom. Only with that defective response did there arise the passively based kind of freedom with its alternatives and choices.

Originative sin is our first *maybe* (less than a full *yes*), said to God and ourselves with perfect, *untempted* freedom, given at the non-durational, immediate moment of creation *ex nihilo*. The degree of *no* in that *maybe* is not the only cause, but it is the ultimate cause, of all evil in which we find ourselves involved.

This primal sin caused our very exposure to the evils done by others—including the forces of Satan—as well as evils done by ourselves. Without originative sin we would be completely blissful in *be*-ing. By this abuse of perfect freedom we are now in the cosmic world of space and time—"all spaced out" and "doing time."

Original sin in Eden is a subject for *reportorial* Revelation. It is known by Faith in Scripture and Tradition. *Originative* sin, however, is a subject for our *personal admission*. It was not at all one of our temporal decisions or events, and thereby it could not be readily "reported." But it can be admitted in the light of Revelation. This signature sin is surely received unconsciously by Faith in Scripture and Tradition; and it is discerned, at least somewhat, by the awareness of our being as be-ing—by beingfully (ontologically) received Faith.

Original sin is the first recorded historical sin. Adam and Eve committed this disobedience as they were tested through the serpent. God "predicted" it in saying that on the day you "eat of it (the forbidden fruit), you will die the death." This sin manifested to Adam and Eve their own weakness, already present in the Garden of Eden, as the result of their ontologically prior and repressed originative sin, committed along with all the rest of us. The original sin in Eden has initiated the execution of the punishment of originative sin for Adam and Eve and for all of us. It has included our generation in the world of space and time, that made it possible for us to wake up to our sinfulness and our need for a Savior.

Knowing

Knowing is, quintessentially, a personal activity by which we are related intentionally to the being and essence of everyone and everything. It is proper to all persons. Every person is knowing, *even if unconsciously*. Despite our present degree of consciousness, therefore, knowing is *also* vastly unconscious for us in the fallen world. The largely repressed origin of our unconscious knowing is our response in the moment of creation *ex nihilo*.

Starting from our present fixation on an implicit framework of space and time for everything, we think that conscious knowing in this world initiates the connection between knower and known, that is, between ourselves and the world we are knowing. But the connection or "intactness" is already there—having been buried by our initial ontological repression.

Knowing in the spatiotemporal world, then, is remedial. It is a knowing derivative of the primal knowing, done by our being as be-ing. It is the tip of the iceberg.

We cannot not know—however remotely and confusedly—all that is. To be is to know (finitely, for created persons) *all* that is—at least to some degree. God is known by everyone, whether consciously or unconsciously or partly both. So, too, is every being in creation, spiritual and temporal (past, present, and future). Unconscious, subconscious, and preconscious knowing are bases, out of which ordinary conscious knowing occurs.

Sensory knowing is also real, but peripheral, and not as such personal. By sensation alone (i.e. as in animals)—whether internal or external sense knowing—the essence of something can *never* be known. *Human* sense knowing, however, is essentially intellective.

We have been hardened perennially by the idea that there is nothing in the intellect that was not first, in some manner, in the senses. So, we are inclined to think that substantial knowing is a kind of "gap jumping." By the power of its "intentionality" (other-directedness) and by the light of an "agent intellect," the ordinary (potential) intellect is thought to initiate contact with the essences of people and things (called "objects" of knowledge) by 'jumping the gap' between knowing power and known realities.

Such a knowing, however, is to be found only in redemptive creation (*ex aliquo*). This knowing is itself founded on the gapless and super-dynamic radiation of knowledge coming from the nurturing originative knowing at the moment of creation *ex nihilo*. In that originative creation, we knew, and still know (protoconsciously), all that is, by our finite powers of intellect and will, now so sorely self-damaged. The common practice that identifies our knowing as solely within our earthly predicament reinforces our originative repression and keeps us "locked out" of the depths of our be-ing and of the much fuller meaning for who we are even at present.

The empirical and quasi-empirical dimensions of intellection, here and now, must be supported by the strictly non-empirical, but archetypally relevant, dimensions. Wisdom is a loving kind of knowing and a knowing kind of love.

Conscious is the manner of knowing that we all rightly desire now. As experienced in the spatiotemporal world, conscious knowing is necessarily narrow and focused. It precludes much. Yet, before we can come to know things consciously, we have to be knowing them unconsciously, perhaps also subconsciously, and definitely preconsciously. Above all, we know them *protoconsciously*. Conscious knowledge and awareness of someone or something can come about in various ways (such as an immediate intellection or intuition, instruction from another, recalling or memory, individual or collective probing and by our investigation, meditation, contemplation, and so forth).

Subconscious is the manner of knowing things that are just below the surface of ordinary consciousness. We are always knowing subconsciously particular things, many of which are semi-conscious, or at least partially conscious. Subconscious things often can be brought into consciousness. How to do ordinary tasks such as eating, washing dishes, playing tennis, playing the piano, and all manner of "automatic" activities constitute one major area of the subconscious.

Unconscious is the repressed manner of knowing persons, things, and meanings that are buried deeply away from conscious life. Much is rarely accessible to consciousness as formed in this world. But the whole of the unconscious plays a large part in influencing thought and behavior. It is meaningful to distinguish the emotional, that is, the psychic unconscious (recognized psychoanalytically) from the ontological unconscious, so prominent in this book.

We might even speak of the physical unconscious. It includes all human physiological and physical actions of which we are not overtly conscious. Together, the physical, psychic, and spiritual unconscious, including the "collective and archetypal unconscious," form the virtually horizonless ocean of potential meaning.

Some have represented the unconscious as featuring levels. Included are the subconscious, along with various kinds of deeply buried meaning.

From the ontological standpoint of this book, we know *protoconsciously* everything that is. Such knowledge was "smashed and packed down" by the sin forming our unconsciousness. Therefore, when we consciously know something in this world, especially new meanings, we do not simply come to know it "out of the blue." Rather, we come to know that we know it finitely, and yet with much inadequacy.

Preconscious (non-Freudian) is the immediate manner of knowing persons and activities that are *spiritually* unconscious. Persons and activities that are critical to our sheer being are known particularly in this way. The preconscious area of reality occurs prior to the development of ordinary consciousness. It is most directly beingful in its bearing upon us. It is the condition for the possibility of any and all transitions of knowledge. This ontological level of knowing includes the spiritually unconscious and is quite closely associated with the protoconscious, our originative act of freedom in creation *ex nihilo*.

Protoconscious is the pure manner of knowing by which we originatively received our be-ing from God. It is our originative knowing of God, self, and all others at the non-durational, first moment of creation. This is the *archetype* of what we now know and call our consciousness: ordinary consciousness that is partial, functional, and privileged as redemptive.

Repression is the unconscious denial that we know some event, actuality, emotion, feeling, or value even as we do know it unconsciously. This mechanism of human knowing is an attempt to protect the knower from impulses, images, concepts, memories, meanings, and values that would likely cause anxiety and various disturbances. Repression is never good, but often inevitable.

The supreme instance of such "protection" is our immediate denial to ourselves of what we failed to do at the moment of being created out of nothing. This prime repression keeps us from recognizing our originative sin, the ultimate cause of all evil in our lives. It virtually requires blaming Adam, Eve, the serpent, *and* God for originating our predicament.

Psychoanalytic repression—repression of unwanted emotional and mental content—is better known at present and to be taken seriously; but it does not even get near to the root of our spiritual denial of originative sin. The latter is the supreme reason for *all* repression and suppression.

Suppression is the virtually or actually *conscious* attempt to be unaware of, or not to attend to, the multiplicity of events, actualities, emotions, feelings, or values that flood our everyday lives. Generally, it is a good and necessary endeavor that is ongoing and allows us to concentrate on one thing at a time. Often it entails the explicitly deliberate attempt to block, however rapidly, awareness of something undesirable. This activity can be good or bad, depending on the issue at hand.

Suppression is a conscious activity, even if quick and minimally explicit. Repression, however, is always an unconscious activity.

Intellect

In the new view, intellect and will are co-dimensions of the *be*-ing that each created person is. They are the "know and love" powers of be-ing. To be, for a person, is to know and to will. A person cannot be without also knowing and willing protoconsciously—however well or poorly.

Intellect and will are more than simply faculties of reparative and recuperative action in the world of be-coming, as we first come to be aware of them. They are the created being as knowing and willing (loving or hating) originatively and forever.

Potential Intellect is the power to know by which we are in touch with, and called to become wedded to, the essence and being of everyone and everything good.

In our common earthly life, this power does the conceiving, judging, and reasoning. It operates in being determined ("stimulated") by the objects of knowledge. It is the ability to be-done-to by whatever it conceives. It is ecstatically fulfilled in heaven, and is an instrument of supreme self-torture in hell.

Agent intellect, in traditional thought from Aristotle onward, is a pure act of intelligibility-giving. It is characterized as a supreme light that renders what is potentially knowable by the potential intellect actually knowable. It is a supreme instrument of knowledge, without itself being a knowing power.

In the new view, however, agent intellect is the originative capacity to know (fully and directly) (a *purely active power to know*)—to be united with all persons, infinite and finite, in their being and essence. It is the only way knowing transpires in heaven.

Will

Potential Will is the power, in space and time, to love, by which we affirm, and are called to unite with, the essence and the being of everyone and everything good. The objects of the will determine or "act upon" it in the holistic processes such as loving, desiring, delighting, being repelled, and the like. Thus will functions in the redemptive creation as a critical means of coming to what God has prepared for those who would love forever.

Agent Will is the power to love, to say fully *yes* to God, self, and others immediately and forever—right from the originative beginning. From "moment one" in creation, we did not fully exercise it. This power is now almost totally repressed.

In classical philosophy, the missing elements are curious concerning the agent (active) intellect and the agent (active) will. The agent intellect is portrayed as not *knowing* anything. And the notion of an agent will is virtually non-existent. But one cannot reasonably conceive of intellect without a corresponding will, and vice versa. That idea has been axiomatic in terms of the traditional understanding of potential intellect and potential will. Such can be no less true for active intellect and active will.

It is interesting to realize that the classical tradition recognizes, from the thought of Aristotle, the reality of an agent (purely active) intellect. But it fails to acknowledge it as both a light and a purely receptive knowing power for executing a pure act of knowing.

Nowhere, however, do we find acknowledgement of the truly agent (purely active) will, by which we committed our personal originative sin, but could have instead related perfectly with God forever.

At the heart of all knowing and loving, **agent intellect** is our purely active power of emphatically receiving ourselves and others, even as **agent will** is our purely active power of emphatically gifting to ourselves and others. In hell, **agent will** represses itself so severely that one can blame all adversity on God. In heaven, **agent will** is our central loving power, uniting us with God in utter bliss forever.

By their originatively defective activity, **agent intellect** and **agent will** are found in this world to have been largely passivized (contaminated). Yet every passive condition of intellection and of volition requires, as its base, a purely active agency, as gifted by God at the core of one's being. Only by **agent will**, for instance, can we love God with our "whole mind and heart." The slightest passivity prevents wholeness of activity.

Loving

Loving is willing the truest and best for self and all others, despite the cost. Not wanting or wishing, but *willing*. Our loving comes in degrees of intensity. At any given time, however, we love everyone, including God, with the same intensity. Often confused with liking, loving has nothing essentially to do with pleasure and pain. Love of enemies and of friends is the call to all that they may live well the be-ing with which they were originatively gifted.

At any given moment, we love everyone with the same intensity, but we know and love some persons with much greater richness than others, based on our mutual experience, affection, and value sharing. If we were to consider whom we *love* least in this world: we can know that that is how *intensely* we love God, all others, and ourselves.

Affirmational love (see loving) is the central form of at least five kinds of love. Affirmation is the attitude of spontaneously delighting in another person and giving the other to himself or herself in an unqualified manner. The beloved feels loved and gifted as good unconditionally by the lover. Obviously, God is the supreme Gifter of being: gifting to another (the created person) his or her whole being, without any "strings" attached.

Traditionally, *storge, eros, philia,* and *agape* are often cited. In general, they are forms either of giving others to self (such as *eros*) or of giving self to others (such as *agape*).

None of these, however, expresses the central meaning of love found in the originative creation. And when created persons come to realize existentially how they have been gifted by God, they are much better able to "pass it on" in attitude and in deed to their companions in being. God's act of creating was an infinite affirmation: an infinite willing of each of us to *be*, to be this *unique* person, and to be-*with* God—literally *giving us to ourselves to be forever.*

Friendship is a relationship that is of genuine love (see above) in which the persons share some sense of equality and esteem, including affection, and an ever-increasing participation in common values. The depth of the friendship can be assessed by the degree to which the friends participate in the most fundamental, spiritual values of human life. We love our friends more richly than others, but not more intensely.

In brief, friendship is loving plus liking. It is opposite to "enemyship," that is, loving plus disliking.

Assorted Terms

Experience is the conscious participation in the world of space and time. It is essentially a felt being-done-to. It can be pleasant or unpleasant, happy or unhappy, by virtue of how one's consciousness is affected by the interaction with others and the movements of the self.

Experience is a bit like the wrapping or insulation on an electric wire. It can serve as a protection from what is really going on, what is going through the wire. Or it can be stripped away...by death. Experience is the conscious impact upon us of the world of passive potency.

But our activities or acts that the experience surrounds are independent of the "wrapping" or experience. We inveterately fail to identify the difference between acting and being acted upon while acting, even as we fail to identify the difference between being and existence. Ex-perience happens only in ex-istence and in our outsideness kind of agency. Every experience—including the mystical—"hides" an act or acting that is at least a little bit other than the experience itself, even as every existent—being that ex-ists—hides the act that is the be-ing of it all....However positive our experience is, it is basically passive (passive-reactive in the ontological sense).

There is *no* experience in heaven. No beatific *experience*. Just sheerly ecstatic, egoless participation in the Being of God and of one another, incomparably more joyful than any experience. The heart of acting and co-acting is passivity-free, existence-free, and experience-free. All is be-ing and lov-ing in consummate joy.

Experience provides opportunity for learning here in creation *ex aliquo*. But experience is *not* "the best teacher." It is not a *teacher* at all. The *one who* experiences teaches self or is taught *through* experience, not *by* it.

Perfection is a term that literally suggests the fulfillment of a process, a making (*per-ficere*, from *per-facere* to do or make through and through). Nevertheless, traditionally, it seems to be purged of any suggestion of process as when it is applied to God and angels. For the most part, it means flawless, without blemish or defect.

The scholastic philosophers and theologians made much of a distinction between what they called pure and mixed perfections. Pure perfections are those attributes such as intellect, knowledge, love, truth, and others that do not *necessarily* suggest any passivity or "limitation." Mixed perfections are those qualities that necessarily are a mix of actuality and passive potency, such as colors, sounds, bodies, and so forth.

In the new view, these perspectives on perfection are included, but a new and critical emphasis is placed on the difference between perfection (flawlessness) that is finite, including the immediate effects of the divine Creator's action, and perfection that is infinite (God).

Created goodness, for instance, is not fulfilled in *infinite* Goodness, but in its own kind of finite gifted perfection.

We are fulfilled *by* God—and by our *cooperative* selves. But God is not (pantheistically) our fullness. This fullness is finitely perfect, not infinitely perfect. Infinite goodness is the only *ultimate cause* of our complete fulfillment, but *not* the fulfillment of our perfection itself. The infinite cannot "fulfill" the finite. The finite is fulfilled in the perfect finite, *by* the cooperative activity of the infinite and the finite.

Conception (human) is our individual entry into the cosmos. Prior to conception we were redeemable, but we would have been almost entirely dysfunctional. Conception is *not* the beginning of the person's *being*, but the beginning of the *becoming* (positive growth and awareness)—the person's coming back, within God's redeeming action, to a condition of originatively-intended being. Conception really *happens to* the person and initiates formal participation in the challenging spatiotemporal dimension of redemptive activity.

Death is the exit of the redeemed person from the opportunities of the awakening, alerting life in the cosmos. It is entry into everlasting destiny, through divine judgment—into heaven, hell, or final purgation for heaven. What is left in space and time are the remains of that person's cosmic participation. The corpse is *not* the body *itself*, but "exhaust" from the person's dynamic thrust through space and time.

The internal or spiritual body by which the earthly participation was specifically effected *goes with* the whole person and is *not separated* from the soul. What happens to be separated is the person's empirical (placenta-like) *connectedness* with life in cosmic matter.

The soul and the ontological body are reparative dimensions of the originative form (givity) and matter (receptivity) of the person. They could *not really separate* from each other, without loss of *essential* ontological integrity. In hell, they are "impossibly united" as essential parts and are inexorably at war with each other forever. In heaven, they are "radiantly harmonious" with each other forever.

Grace is the infinitely affirming Being of God as gifting us with the union of love and of perfect friendship. The grace of creation—being brought to be "out of nothing" in an unlimitedly unconditional way—is the supreme gift that we failed to receive fully. The grace involved in redemption and in salvation is the same open union of love offered to us in myriad ways.

Temptable is the condition of human persons who said maybe to the gift of being originatively. God's creation *ex nihilo* could only be infinitely perfect, yielding finitely perfect effects. These created persons were *not temptable as gifted*, but as received. "God's best" needs no test. But they immediately rendered themselves imperfect. They were thereby in need of testing or revealing—to themselves and to others—how reliable they could be.

Adam and Eve and their historic children, with two notable exceptions, were to be tested by being tempted throughout their lives, however long or short these might be. Death might bring on some of the most dreadful temptations for many. Temptability itself indicates the need of salvation and provides a necessary sign of anyone who has committed an originative sin.

Reincarnation is impossible. The intrinsic integrity of body and soul as the remedial dimensions of the originative matter (receptivity) and form (givity) of human being make such theory absurd. The form and matter of the person are absolutely essential, correlative parts of the very essence of human personhood.

Reincarnation is an attempt to make intelligible the 'law of karma' that is supposed to need many bodies for mediation over lengthy periods of soul activity, picking up and discarding bodies. Personal identity is egregiously compromised. And body is demeaned, along with the soul.

Likewise, in the Western world, the traditional theory of hylomorphism (matter-and-form) has *not succeeded* in telling adequately of the integrity of human beings within their essence. If God's absolute act of creating perfect essences *ex nihilo* is adequately recognized, the soul cannot be separated from the body, in the way that classical theology has conceived it, any more than the form can be separate from the matter. The activity essential to persons receiving redemption—who are becoming, that is, being created *ex aliquo*—requires genuine self-identity at every point in the process, including especially the period between death and ultimate resurrection. The use of the theory of hylomorphism requires a deepening within the tradition from the way the theory is normally conceived.

Human Life and Sexuality Series

Along with others, this book by Mary Rosera Joyce:

The Future of Adam and Eve: Finding the Lost Gift

(LifeCom, 2009) 267 pages

Adam's Puritan-Playboy America; True Sexual Freedom; Friendship; Sexual Likeness to God; True Feminism; Sexuality and the Trinity; the Meaning of Personhood; the Origin of Evil; *et al.*

Two Creations Series

The following three books by Robert E. Joyce form a trilogy: *When God Said Be, We Said Maybe: An Inside Story of the Creation, the Crash, and the Recovery of Being*

God Said, We Said: The Interpersonal Act of Creation
(LifeCom 2010) 170 pages. First book in the trilogy. Glossary.

God Says, We Say: The Interpersonal Act of Redemption
(LifeCom 2010) 290 pages. Second book in the trilogy. Includes Qs and As. Glossary.

God Will Say, We Will Say: The Interpersonal Act of Salvation (LifeCom 2010) 256 pages. Third book in the trilogy. Qs and As. Glossary.

In addition to these books, there are others by R. E. Joyce:

Affirming Our Freedom in God:
The Untold Story of Creation
(LifeCom, 2001) 100 pages.

The Cry of Why, beneath the Holocaust; Are We Hiding Something? God Freely Creates Our Freedom to Create, *et al.*

Facing the Dark Side of Genesis:
A New Understanding of Ourselves
(LifeCom, 2008) 84 pages.

The Genesis Gap; Originative Sin; Theology of the Person's Being; Two Creations: Originative and Redemptive; Consequences for a Life of Faith, *et al.*

A Perfect Creation: The Light behind the Dark Side of Genesis
(LifeCom, 2008) 170 pages.

From Cosmess to Cosmos; The Missing Infinity of God; God's Intimate Act of Creation; The Meaning of Evil and Its Cause, *et al.*

All of the books above are available at Amazon.com, Barnesandnoble.com, and other outlets, as well as by order through any bookstore, or directly from *LifeCom.*

Booklets available through LifeCom

The Origin of Pain and Evil *(LifeCom 2008) 40 pages.*

The ultimate, uncaused cause of all pain and evil in our lives.

The Immaculate Conception: An Inside Story

LifeCom 2008) 20 pages.

Deepening the meaning of the origin of the Blessed Virgin Mary.

New Light within the Christian Worldview: Clarification on Creation and the Origin of Evil *(LifeCom 2011) 35 pages.*

Two essays: Why Do Bad Things Happen to Good People? and A Case for a Perfect Creation and an Originative Sin.

www.ingramcontent.com/pod-product-compliance
Lightning Source LLC
Chambersburg PA
CBHW031244090426
42742CB00007B/302